2ND EDITION

LOGISTICS and RETAIL MANAGEMENT

Insights into Current Practice and Trends from Leading Experts

EDITED BY

JOHN FERNIE & LEIGH SPARKS

The Chartered Institute of
Logistics and Transport (UK)

KOGAN
PAGE

London and Philadelphia

First published in Great Britain and the United States in 1998 by Kogan Page Limited
Second edition 2004
Reprinted 2005, 2007

120 Pentonville Road
London N1 9JN
United Kingdom
www.kogan-page.co.uk

525 South 4th Street #241
Philadelphia PA 19147
USA

© Individual contributors, 2004

ISBN-10   0 7494 4091 0
ISBN-13   978 0 7494 4091 6

British Library Cataloguing-in-Publication Data

A CIP record for this book is available from the British Library.

Library of Congress Cataloging-in-Publication Data

Logistics and retail management : insights into current practice and trends from leading experts / edited by John Fernie and Leigh Sparks.--2nd ed.
    p. cm.
Includes bibliographical references and index.
ISSBN 0-7494-4091-0
1. Business logistics. 2. Retail trade--Management. I. Fernie, John, 1948- II. Sparks, Leigh
HD38.5L614 2004
658.5--dc22
                                2004002540

Typeset by Saxon Graphics Ltd, Derby
Printed and bound in Great Britain by MPG Books Ltd, Bodmin, Cornwall

Contents

Contributors

Nobu Azuma is Assistant Professor (researcher) of Business Organization and Fashion Studies at the Institute of Marketing and Distribution Sciences (IMDS), Kobe, Japan. He is also engaged in a variety of research activities at the School of Management and Languages, Heriot-Watt University, Edinburgh, UK (part-time). His current research interests cover fashion, culture and consumption, industrial/commercial agglomeration, market orientation and supply chain management in the fashion industry. He emphasizes the importance of the 'soft variables' in management studies by employing an interdisciplinary research approach.

Martin Christopher is Professor of Marketing and Logistics at Cranfield School of Management. His work in the field of logistics and supply chain management has gained international recognition. He has published widely and his recent books include *Logistics and Supply Chain Management* and *Marketing Logistics*. Martin Christopher is also co-editor of the *International Journal of Logistics Management* and is a regular contributor to conferences and workshops around the world. At Cranfield, Martin chairs the Centre for Logistics and Supply Chain Management, the largest activity of its type in Europe. The work of the centre covers all aspects of transportation and logistics and offers both full-time and part-time Masters degree courses as well as extensive management development programmes. Research plays a key role in the work of the Centre and contributes to its international standing.

John Fernie is Professor of Retail Marketing and Head of School of Management and Languages at Heriot-Watt University, Scotland. He has written and contributed to numerous textbooks and papers on retail management, especially in the field of retail logistics and the internationalization of retail formats. He is editor of the *International Journal of Retail* *and Distribution Management*, published by Emerald, and received the prestigious award of Editor of the Year in 1997 in addition to Leading Editor awards in 1994, 1998 and 2000. He is on the editorial board of the *Journal of Product and Brand Management*, also published by Emerald. He is an active member of the Institute of Logistics and Transport and the Chartered Institute of Marketing in the UK as well as holding office in the American Collegiate Retail Association. In 2001 he became a member of the Logistics Directors Forum, a group of leading professionals in supply chain management and logistics in the UK.

Toshikazu Higashi is Associate Professor of Marketing at the University of Marketing and Distribution Sciences (UMDS), Kobe, Japan. Prior to joining UMDS, he completed Master's and Doctoral courses at the Graduate School of Commerce, Keio University, Tokyo, Japan. He specializes in general marketing studies. His ongoing research projects tackle the issues of strategic marketing and relationship marketing. He places a particular focus on the salience of entrepreneurship and 'intrepreneurship' in directing a firm's customer orientation strategies.

Dr Robert (Bob) Lowson is the Director of the Strategic Operations Management Centre at the University of East Anglia and a Senior Lecturer. As a current Leverhulme Trust Research Fellow, his research interests include operations strategies and operational management approaches that offer flexibility and responsiveness for retailers and manufacturers in fast-moving consumer goods sectors, and the role of the small and medium-sized enterprises in these supply systems. He has published widely on operations strategy and general management issues in a number of international journals, and was awarded the best paper in 2001 for his publication in the *International Journal of Logistics*. His latest book, *Strategic Operations Management: The new competitive advantage* has recently been published by Routledge. He works as a consultant in various sectors and has management and business experience that includes work for a number of international retailers and manufacturers.

Alan McKinnon is Professor and Director of the Logistics Research Centre in the School of Management and Languages at Heriot-Watt University, Edinburgh. Alan has been researching and teaching in the field of logistics for 25 years, has published widely on the subject, and been an adviser to several UK government departments and consultant to numerous public and private sector organizations on a variety of logistics and transport issues. In 2000–1 he was chair of the UK government's Retail Logistics Task Force. Alan is a fellow of the Institute of Logistics and Transport, founder member of its Logistics Research Network and recipient of its highest distinction, the Sir Robert Lawrence Award.

Dr Helen Peck is a Senior Research Fellow in Marketing and Logistics. She joined Cranfield in 1983 from a major UK retail bank, working initially with the School's Library and Information Services and Management Development Unit, before taking up a research post within the Marketing and Logistics Group. Her research interests are in supply chain management, particularly supply chain risk and vulnerability. Her published work includes papers and journal articles, joint editorship and authorship of several books, with contributions to many others. She is also an award-winning writer of management case studies, whose work is used extensively on marketing and logistics programmes at Cranfield and by other teaching institutions in Europe, North America and Australasia.

David Smith was Head of Primary Distribution at Tesco. After working in other sectors of high street retail distribution he joined Tesco in 1984 in the distribution division and worked in the fast-moving food consumer and temperature controlled distribution networks in both secondary and primary distribution. In 1993 he completed an MBA at Stirling University with a dissertation on 'Integrated supply chain management: the case of fresh produce in Tesco'. Since 1998 he has been an independent consultant in retail supply chain logistics. In 1998 he was seconded to the UK government's Department of the Environment, Transport and the Regions (DETR) best practice programme on freight distribution and logistics, and worked with several cross-industry working groups for road, rail and packaging. A Fellow of the Institute of Logistics and Transport, he has written articles and given lectures on logistics.

Leigh Sparks is Professor of Retail Studies at the Institute for Retail Studies, University of Stirling, Scotland, UK. Leigh has been previously the Head of the Department of Marketing, the Director of the Institute for Retail Studies and the Dean of the Faculty of Management (1995–2000). In 1989 Leigh was awarded a Winston Churchill Travelling Fellowship for a study of customer service in retailing in the United States and Canada, and from July 2000 to July 2001 he was a Visiting Professor at the College of Human Sciences at Florida State University, in Tallahassee, Florida. He is co-editor of the *International Review of Retail, Distribution and Consumer Research*, the leading academic journal on retailing in Europe. Leigh is also on the editorial boards of the *Journal of Marketing Management* and the *Journal of Marketing Channels*. He is a member of the Institute of Logistics and Transport and a founder member of the Academy of Marketing Research Committee. Leigh's research concentrates on structural and spatial change in retailing, including logistics and supply chain issues. This research has been disseminated widely through a number of books, many reports and over 100 academic and professional articles.

Beverly Wagner is a lecturer in the Department of Marketing, Stirling University. Since 1996, she has been involved in research into formation and implementation of partnering and business alliances in the drinks and packaging sector, and also in the microelectronics and oil and gas industries. Her research interests include customer–supplier relationships, inter-organizational cooperation, and logistics and supply chain management. She is a committee member of the Institute of Logistics and Transport and also of the Pharmaceutical Supply Chain Working Group (PSCWG).

Mark West, MBA, MILT, MIEX (GRAD), MIFP (GRAD), began his career in the third-party environment of customs brokerage, shipping and freight forwarding during the early 1980s. He was involved in providing innovative sourcing and physical distribution solutions to UK and European retailers for retail products emanating from the then Eastern Bloc group of countries and emerging tiger economies. Moving into department store retailing during the late 1980s, Mark successfully completed a Graduate Management Training Scheme before holding various senior management positions across the end-to-end supply chain of the business over a 15-year period. Before leaving the retailer in May 2002, Mark had served a two-year term as Distribution Director on the management board of the company. After completing an MBA at the Institute for Retail Studies, University of Stirling, Mark set up his own interim management consultancy, People Processes and Solutions Ltd (www.ppsmanagement.co.uk) which provides interim and strategic management consultancy tailored to extracting value from retail and FMCG supply chains through streamlining and change management. Clients include Aquascutum, Axxis International, Hamleys of London, HMV Media Group and the Salvation Army Trading Co Ltd.

Phil Whiteoak has worked in FMCG manufacturing businesses since 1969. Between 1991 and early 2001 he was Logistics Director for Mars in the UK and Ireland, and was also European Logistics Development Director, responsible for the development of networks, commercial practices and IT strategy. During this period he was extensively involved in the ECR Europe initiative and was co-chair of the Efficient Replenishment Project during 1995–6. His subsequent initiatives have included working within an internal new business development 'incubator' considering new business propositions, and particularly e-business opportunities; running the merger of Pedigree Masterfoods and Mars Confectionery to create a single business entity of Masterfoods in 2002; and working on a large internal business transformation programme.

Preface

As educators involved in the teaching of logistics and the supply chain, particularly in the context of retailing, we find it increasingly hard to get over to students how much things have changed in the retail supply chain, and also how many challenges remain. Many approaches and results are taken for granted, and it is assumed that supply chains have always been at the forefront of retail innovation and have always delivered the goods. Nothing of course could be further from the truth. For a long time, the supply of products into retail outlets was controlled by manufacturers and was very much a hit or miss affair. Consumers had to put up with the product they found (or did not find) on the shelves, and retailers and manufacturers operated in something of an efficiency vacuum. This situation has now been transformed. Retailers have recognized the need to have more involvement in supply chains and noted that benefits can be achieved in both service levels and cost reduction. Massive efforts have been made to reorganize and reprioritize activities in moving products from production to consumption. Notwithstanding the major strides made, some challenges remain.

In 1990 John Fernie edited *Retail Distribution Management* for Kogan Page. That volume, one of the first to look explicitly at distribution (as it then was) in retailing, combined retail academic and practitioner studies and viewpoints to provide a glimpse into what was a fast-changing situation. That groundbreaking volume pointed to a revolution in logistical support to retail stores over the 1980s in the UK. Through academic work and practical case examples the volume showed how retailers were gaining control of supply chains and reorganizing their own operations, and those of manufacturers, suppliers and distribution specialists, to transform the flow of goods and information in supply chains. In the process, new forms of working, using new technologies, were improving the quality of products moving through the system, both in physical terms and in terms of time appropriateness. Through the building of relationships with supply partners, efficiency and effectiveness were introduced into previously inefficient and ineffective supply systems. From a concentration on functional silos in physical distribution and materials management, the logistics concept and a focus on end-to-end supply chains was developed.

By 1998, John Fernie and Leigh Sparks were in a position to put together a second edited volume, again combining academic and practitioner viewpoints on changes in the retail supply chain. This volume showed that the 1990s had experienced further change, mainly focused on incremental improvements and relationship change, though in some circumstances major one-off efficiency gains were still possible. Through the adoption of further technological developments and the integration of the entire retail supply chain, costs were squeezed out of the system, yet at the same time service improvements were still possible.

The 1998 edited volume, by now entitled *Logistics and Retail Management*, has been a considerable success. In its comparatively short life it has been recommended reading in both academic and practitioner situations. It was no surprise therefore that the publishers, on seeing it go out of print, requested in 2002 a revised second edition. This raised an interesting problem. Although the book was only four years old, it was clear that many of the detailed situations described in the volume had been overtaken by events. We had concluded the 1998 volume by suggesting that 'exciting and interesting challenges' for retail logisticians and supply specialists were ahead. We could perhaps be forgiven for not realizing quite how interesting these changes were going to be, both in the supply chains themselves and in the very dimensions of retailing itself. From deepening relationships and control demanded by retailers, to the incredible developments in different forms of technology, there has been another transformation in many retail supply systems. Allied to changes in the retail sector itself, with global developments of supply and concentration, the supply of products has taken on new dimensions. This is not to say that the subject matter of retail logistics has been totally changed. Many of the issues remain the same from the late 1990s, but the way these are tackled, and the dimensions of the issues, have perhaps altered.

In agreeing a second revised edition therefore, we had to consider how much of the first edition should be kept. One approach would have been to simply update the introduction and add postscripts to some chapters. We felt this was inadequate, given the dynamic nature of retail logistics in the last decade. A hard look at the various chapters therefore was undertaken. The end result has been that only one chapter has remained unscathed and identical to the last edition. Some are lightly changed, as the issues remain broadly the same, but many are brand new and developed especially for this revised edition. This is not a light updating, but rather an extensive rethinking of how much retail supply systems have changed in such a short space of time.

Readers should be able to discern four main sections to the book. First, three chapters provide a context for the more detailed sectoral considerations that follow. Second and third, there are chapters on non-food (two) and food (three) logistics respectively. For a long time, food retail logistics were seen to be at the forefront of techniques and results, as exemplified perhaps by Tesco in the UK. In the late 1990s however, fashion retailers such as Zara have shown how supply chain reorganization in non-food sectors can produce dramatic results and competitive advantage. Finally there are three chapters covering aspects of technology adoption and implementation in the supply chain. If one thing has been learnt since Drucker's 1962 claim about distribution being the last cost frontier, it is that logistics is as much about information use as it is about product movement.

The opening chapter of the book ('Retail logistics: changes and challenges') has been written by John Fernie and Leigh Sparks. The aim of this chapter is to provide a context for the remainder of the volume. It begins by pointing to the way in which many people tend to forget that supplying products and services is not necessarily a straightforward task. Rather, it is the managed integration of a range of tasks, both within and increasingly beyond the boundaries of the company. The traditional functional silos of warehousing and transport have been removed by the need to integrate the logistics tasks and to develop a stronger sense of supply chain management. Through a close examination of the needs in different situations and the development of techniques such as Quick Response and Efficient Consumer Response, leading to ideas of lean and agile supply systems, effectiveness and efficiency have been attained in very different circumstances.

This is not to say that challenges do not exist, but rather to point to the great strides forward that have been taken. Retailers that have not critically examined their supply systems are now realizing that they need to catch up. So for example Coles Myer in Australia has announced a major supply chain reconsideration in order to meet its national and potentially global competitors. It argues that the steps it is taking are not new, but rather have become the standards required in major retailers. Coles Myer therefore needs to catch up. Other retailers are recognizing that they also need to look at every aspect of their supply systems. This is certainly the case when retailers get involved in e-commerce, where challenges to efficiency are fundamental, and throughout supply systems, when waste and environmental impact reductions are potential hazards for all retailers.

One of the biggest areas of change for retailers has been the development of pan-company relationships. It has been remarked that retailers now compete not on the basis of their activities alone, but on the basis of the effectiveness and efficiency of their whole supply chain. If problems are present in production and primary distribution then these will inevitably have an effect on the price, quality and availability of the products on the shelves for consumers. Relationships in the supply chain are therefore now fundamental. An analysis of these changing relationships forms the basis of the second chapter, prepared by John Fernie. In this chapter key themes in relationships, such as power and dependence, trust and commitment and co-operation and competition, are examined initially. Much of the emphasis on relationships in the supply chain, as noted in the introductory chapter, has focused on the concepts of Quick Response and Efficient Consumer Response. These are analysed in detail in this chapter, along with ideas of Collaborative Planning, Forecasting and Replenishment. Finally, the role of third-party logistics providers in helping retailers meet their strategic objectives is considered. As the retail logistics environment changes, so logistic service providers can capitalize on a range of opportunities.

One of these logistics environment changes occurs in the spatial component of supply. Globalization is an over-used term, but there can be no doubt that there has been a greater internationalization in retail supply, both in terms of the internationalization of the major retailers themselves, and in the sources of product supply. Chapter 3, by John Fernie, focuses therefore on 'The internationalization of the retail supply chain'. In this chapter he points initially to the major changes that have occurred in the sourcing of products in recent decades. In both food and non-food there has been an increasing internationalization of product supply, developed both through the potential of low cost supply, and simply because of the increasing international operations generally by major retailers. Internationalization is probably a better term than globalization in this area (as in some others) as it is clear that the distribution and supply practices ('culture') and infrastructure in different countries and parts of the world are substantially different. There is no global logistics approach that can be identified, though it is becoming increasingly clear that the growing internationalization of retailing is leading to the internationalization of logistics practices, both within retailers and through their supply partners. Perhaps the closest to a global approach can be found in some of the logistics services providers.

These first three chapters provide a context for the detailed studies that follow. Together they suggest that retail supply has been transformed in recent decades, not without problems in some cases. Chief among the issues being confronted by many retailers are the relationships throughout the supply chain and the increasing breadth in spatial terms of the sources of supply. The next five chapters provide illustrations of these issues in the non-food and food sectors.

Chapter 4 by Nobukaza J Azuma, John Fernie and Toshikazu Higashi is on 'Market orientation and supply chain management in the fashion industry'. The fashion industry has recently been changed by enhancements in time-based competition, and to a considerable extent, such techniques and time compression are becoming the de facto standard in the sector. The chapter therefore considers the market orientation of firms in the sector, with a particular focus on the supply chain and the possibilities of organizational learning. An integrated approach to market orientation and supply chain management has potential to provide competitive advantage, but in the fashion industry, such potential is mitigated by the short-term nature of fashion and by the ability of retailers to learn from the past and from competitors.

This broad examination of the fashion industry is complemented by a more detailed consideration of 'Fashion logistics and quick response' by Martin Christopher, Bob Lowson and Helen Peck. This chapter integrates three of the issues that have thus far formed the core of the book: issues of time, internationalization and quick response systems. Through a detailed examination of the fashion sector, they show how an agile or quick response supply chain is essential in order to compete effectively.

The case of Tesco has received considerable academic and practitioner attention over the last decades. Initially this was probably due to the very public transformation of the business that was being attempted. More recently this attention has been due to the success of this transformation and the growing realization that Tesco has been a pioneer in the supply chain and has developed a world-class logistics approach. To some extent this success was due to the particular circumstances in the UK, which allowed a conforming and standard retail offer to be serviced by a straightforward and regular supply system. Such circumstances no longer apply, as the market in the UK has been altered and Tesco itself has become a much more international retailer (and product sourcing has also become more international). Chapter 6 provides therefore a review of 'Logistics in Tesco: past, present and future'. David Smith and Leigh Sparks, who have been involved in studying Tesco logistics for a number of years, have written the chapter. Particular emphasis is placed on the need to change logistics and supply to reflect the changing nature of the retail operations. With the plans for the store component of the business well known, the chapter considers less well-known themes for logistics and supply in future years. One component of this is the way in which Tesco has been influenced by dimensions of lean supply.

While there are particular aspects of fashion logistics that require special consideration and handling, issues are probably more pointed in the food sector. Chapter 7 for example, also by David Smith and Leigh Sparks, is concerned with 'Temperature-controlled supply chains'. These chains are essential to the safe supply of food to consumers, not least because breakdowns in such systems can cause serious health hazards in the general population. At a time when food scares have become more common, retailers have therefore had to pay special attention to channels that need specially controlled handling systems. Smith and Sparks review the importance of temperature-controlled supply chains before outlining the issues that are confronting retailers in meeting legal and other standards, then examining the future concerns that are likely to arise.

The final chapter on aspects of the food sector is by Phil Whiteoak on 'Rethinking efficient replenishment in the grocery sector'. This is the one chapter that remains entirely unchanged from the previous edition. The chapter reviews the facts and myths of efficient replenishment, a key component of Efficient Consumer Response. Whiteoak's main plea is that supply chain integration should be viewed across the supply chain as well as along the supply chain. He argues that there are real opportunities for rationalizing and managing the transport and consolidation functions on an industry rather than a company basis. He concluded the chapter in the 1998 volume by questioning whether the industry was fit for the challenge. Nothing has really changed in the meantime to make this question any the less pertinent.

The final three chapters in the book take a somewhat different approach, by looking at aspects of technology use in logistics. While technology is implicit in many of the chapters that have gone before, here the focus is explicit.

The first of these chapters is by John Fernie and Alan McKinnon, who consider 'The development of e-tail logistics'. Non-store shopping is of course not new. Systems to deliver products to homes have been around for a long time. The late 1990s however saw massive hype around the development of e-commerce, and predictions that over time (though this varied enormously) a significant proportion of retail sales would migrate to the Internet. The collapse of the dot.com boom has brought such claims into stark reality. Nonetheless, successful Internet shopping does occur using a variety of models, and many retailers have essentially become multi-channel (albeit skewed) businesses. The future rate of growth will partly depend on the quality and efficiency of the supporting system of order fulfilment. Many e-tailers have developed effective logistical systems and built up consumer confidence in their supply and delivery operations. Challenges remain however, particularly in the grocery sector, where options for picking and the 'last mile' delivery remain to be resolved. The retailers themselves drive some of these choices, whereas other options may be constrained by consumer acceptance and desires from local government to manage the environmental issues of home delivery from multiple sources. This chapter reviews the development of e-tail logistics and considers the decisions that remain to be worked through.

Chapter 10, by Leigh Sparks and Beverly Wagner, considers two 'Transforming technologies: retail exchanges and RFID'. Since supply chains became the focus of attention some decades ago, many wild claims for various technologies have been made. Technology implementation has held out promise of supply chain transformation. These promises have not often materialized. In the late 1990s, B2B marketplaces became the rage, as they were seen as a 'killer application' of the Internet. In practice progress has been much slower than anticipated, and while some successes have been recorded, transformation seems to be too ambitious a term. Today RFID is seen as another technology that will transform the retail supply chain, but despite its overt promise, RFID may have many implementation problems to overcome. The chapter asks whether one issue in technology introduction is the problem of matching people, processes and technology at a time when the technology is both simultaneously unready and being hyped, and the ramifications of extensive implementation inside an organization are under-analysed. By focusing too much on technology and emphasizing the all-encompassing transformative properties, businesses may be missing opportunities for more specific benefits.

The final chapter in the book takes a broad view of technology introduction by considering 'Enterprise Resource Planning (ERP) systems: issues in implementation'. Written by Mark West and Leigh Sparks, it is essentially a case study of the implementation of an ERP. ERP systems became very fashionable in retail supply chains in the late 1990s, for a number of very good practical reasons, and also because of potential issues with the 'Millennium bug'. Such systems however, like many technology applications, are not simple replacements for previous practices. Rather, they make retailers reconsider how they undertake activities, and as such can confront 'sacred cows' in retail operations. In this case, the initial introduction of the ERP system was not successful, primarily because of the lack of balance in the emphasis between people, processes and technology. Technology introduction has to be balanced by examination of the necessary changes to business processes and the impact these have on managers and employees. Learning from the initial implementation, the case retailer has now produced a better balanced approach to ERP systems introduction. The second phase of introduction has been much more successful and accepted. The case shows how it is easy to make assumptions and sweeping statements about relationships and technology use, but that in practice, the issues of implementation of any change in retail logistics can be extensive and need careful management.

In any book on a topic as wide as retail logistics it is inevitable that some issues will be missed. We hope that those that we have included are of interest, and demonstrate the complexity and challenge of modern retail logistics. As before we have resisted the temptation to have a chapter focusing on future issues. Rather, we provide a brief afterword to focus attention on some of the issues we believe are important in our examination of changes and challenges in retail logistics. Product supply has been transformed in recent years. The only thing we can be reasonably sure of is that changes will continue to be made as retailers continue to search for the most appropriate systems to meet the changing consumer and operational demands. As before, the future remains challenging and exciting.

John Fernie and Leigh Sparks
Scotland, December 2003

1

Retail logistics: changes and challenges

John Fernie and Leigh Sparks

It is often taken for granted that products will be available to buy in the shops. The cornucopia of goods that is available in a hypermarket or a department store sometimes means that we forget how the products were supplied. We expect our lettuces to be fresh, the new Playstation to be available on launch day and our clothes to be in good condition and ready to wear. With the introduction of e-commerce we have come to demand complete availability and home delivery at times of our choosing.

Consumer beliefs and needs have altered. Our willingness to wait to be satisfied or served has reduced and we expect instant product availability and gratification. It should be obvious from this that the supply or logistics system that gets products from production through retailing to consumption has also needed to be transformed. Physical distribution and materials management have been replaced by logistics management and a subsequent concern for the whole supply chain (Figure 1.1).

This logistics transformation derives from cost and service requirements as well as consumer and retailer change (see Fernie, 1990; Fernie and Sparks, 1998). Elements of logistics are remarkably expensive, if not controlled effectively. Holding stock or inventory in warehouses just in case it is needed is a highly costly activity. The stock itself is expensive and might not sell or could become obsolete. Warehouses and distribution centres generally are expensive to build, operate and maintain. Vehicles to transport goods between warehouses and shops are expensive, in terms

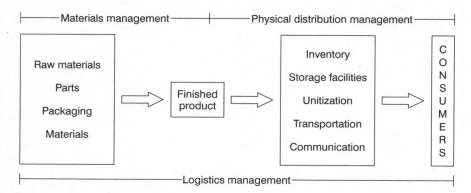

Figure 1.1 Logistics Management

of both capital and running costs. There is thus a cost imperative to making sure that logistics is carried out effectively and efficiently, through the most appropriate allocation of resources along the supply chain.

At the same time, there can be service benefits. By appropriate integration of demand and supply, mainly through the widespread use of information technology and systems, retailers can provide a better service to consumers by, for example, having fresher, higher quality produce arriving to meet consumer demand for such products. With the appropriate logistics, products should be of a better presentational quality, could possibly be cheaper, have a longer shelf life and there should be far fewer instances of stock outs. Reaction time to spurts in demand can be radically improved through the use of information transmission and dissemination technologies. If operating properly, a good logistics system can therefore both reduce costs and improve service, providing a competitive advantage for the retailer.

THE LOGISTICS TASK

Retailing and logistics are concerned with product availability. Many have described this as 'getting the right products to the right place at the right time'. Unfortunately however that description does not do justice to the amount of effort that has to go into a logistics supply system and the multitude of ways that supply systems can go wrong. The very simplicity of the statement suggests logistics is an easy process. As the boxed example shows, problems and mistakes can be all too apparent. The real management 'trick' is in making logistics look easy, day in and day out, whilst reacting to quite volatile consumer demand.

Carelessness at Mothercare Leaves Cupboard Bare

Sales at Mothercare dived by 6 per cent in three weeks after its move to a new hi-tech distribution centre caused problems. The childrenswear retailer admitted that staff shortcomings meant its heralded autumn/winter clothing range had languished at the new Northamptonshire warehouse, causing huge stock shortages in its stores.

Chief Executive Chris Martin, who was recruited to turn around the chain, admitted the setback was 'exceptionally frustrating' given that like-for-like sales until this period had been up about 10 per cent, and that the new range had been well received.

It was doubly frustrating, he said, as management of the Daventry warehouse was sub-contracted to a third party, Tibbett & Britten. 'Some of their staff just weren't doing their job', said a source.

Tibbett responded by placing a senior director at the building to sort out the problems and establish a proper flow of stock to the stores. Asked if he was considering legal action, Mr Martin said: 'This is a five-year relationship. We are working it through together.'

He added that a fifth less stock than usual had been in the shops but stressed that it was 'now coming through'. In a trading statement Mr Martin revealed that sales rose by 9.6 per cent for the 26 weeks to 28 September 2001, with like-for-like sales up by 7.6 per cent. Brokers at Charterhouse Securities cut their recommendation from hold to sell after the news, but Seymour Pierce retail analyst Richard Ratner said, 'If they sort the warehouse problems out in the next few weeks I won't be unduly concerned, particularly as the 2.1 percentage point improvement in margin was better than expected.' Mothercare planned to continue with the roll-out of its larger Mothercare World format after Christmas 2001.

Source: Helen Slingsby, *Guardian*, Tuesday 9 October 2001

For example, if the temperature rises and the sun comes out in an atypical Scottish summer, then demand for ice-cream, soft drinks and even salad items rises dramatically. How does a retailer make sure they remain in stock and satisfy this transient demand? Or we might think about Valentine's Day, when demand for certain products in the days before increases exponentially. If a retailer stocks Valentine's cards and demand does not materialize, then the retailer has stock that will not sell. There is little demand for Valentine's cards on 15 February. While over-stocks in this case will not perish, the cost of their storage and handling for the intervening year can be considerable.

The examples above demonstrate that retailers must be concerned with the flows of product and information both within the business and in the wider supply chain. In order to make products available retailers have to manage their logistics in terms of product movement and demand management. They need to know what is selling in the stores and both anticipate and react quickly to changes in this demand. At the same time they need to be able to move less demand-volatile products in an efficient and cost-effective manner.

The logistics management task is therefore initially concerned with managing the components of the 'logistics mix'. We can identify five components:

- **Storage facilities:** these might be warehouses or distribution centres or simply the stock rooms of retail stores. Retailers manage these facilities to enable them to keep stock in anticipation of or to react to, demand for products.
- **Inventory:** all retailers hold stock to some extent. The question for retailers is the amount of stock or inventory (finished products and/or component parts) that has to be held for each product, and the location of this stock to meet demand changes.
- **Transportation:** most products have to be transported in some way at some stage of their journey from production to consumption. Retailers therefore have to manage a transport operation that might involve different forms of transport, different sizes of containers and vehicles and the scheduling and availability of drivers and vehicles.
- **Unitization and packaging:** consumers generally buy products in small quantities. They sometimes make purchase decisions based on product presentation and packaging. Retailers are concerned to develop products that are easy to handle in logistics terms, do not cost too much to package or handle, yet retain their selling ability on the shelves.
- **Communications:** to get products to where retailers need them, it is necessary to have information, not only about demand and supply, but also about volumes, stock, prices and movements. Retailers have thus become increasingly concerned with being able to capture data at appropriate points in the system and to use that information to have a more efficient and effective logistics operation.

It should be clear that all of these elements are interlinked. In the past they were often managed as functional areas or 'silos', and while potentially optimal within each function, the business as a whole was sub-optimal in logistics terms. More recently the management approach has been to integrate these logistics tasks and reduce the functional barriers. So, if a retailer gets good sales data from the checkout system, this can be used in scheduling transport and deciding levels and locations of stock holding. If the level of inventory can be reduced, perhaps fewer warehouses are needed. If communications and transport can be linked effectively, a retailer can move from keeping stock in a warehouse to running a distribution centre which sorts products for immediate store delivery: that is, approaching a 'Just-In-Time' system. Internal integration has therefore been a major concern.

It should also be clear, however, that retailers are but one part of the supply system. Retailers are involved in the selling of goods and services to the consumer. For this they draw upon manufacturers to provide the necessary products. They may outsource certain functions such as transport and warehousing to specialist logistics services providers. Retailers therefore have a direct interest in the logistics systems of their suppliers and other intermediaries. If a retailer is effective, but its suppliers are not, errors and delays in supply from the manufacturer or logistics services provider will impact the retailer and the retailer's consumers, in terms of either higher prices or stock-outs (no products available on the store shelves). This was the essence of the problem in the Mothercare example (page 3). If a retailer can integrate effectively its logistics system with that of its suppliers, such problems may be minimized. Much more importantly, however, the entire supply chain can then be optimized and managed as a single entity. This brings potential advantages of cost reduction and service enhancement, not only for the retailer, but also for the supplier. It should also mean that products reach the stores more rapidly, thus better meeting sometimes transient customer demand. In some instances it may mean the production of products in merchandisable ready units, which flow through the distribution systems from production to the shop floor without the need for assembly or disassembly. Such developments clearly require supply chain co-operation and coordination.

We may be describing highly complex and advanced operations here. Retail suppliers are increasingly spread across the world. A retailer may have thousands of stores in a number of countries, with tens of thousands of individual product lines. They may make millions of individual sales per day. Utilizing data to ensure effective operation amongst retailers, manufacturers, suppliers, logistics services providers, head office, shops and distribution centres is not straightforward. There is thus always a tension between overall complexity and the desire for the simplest possible process.

Summarizing the discussion above, the logistics task therefore can be described as:

> The process of strategically managing the procurement, movement and storage of materials, parts and finished inventory (and the related information flows) through the organization and its marketing channels in such a way that current and future profitability are maximized through the cost effective fulfilment of orders.

(Christopher, 1998: 4)

Managing the logistics mix in an integrated retail supply chain, while aiming to balance cost and service requirements, is the essential element of logistics management (Figure 1.2). As retailers have begun to embrace this logistics approach and examine their wider supply chains, many have realized that to carry out logistics properly, there has to be a transformation of approach and operations (Sparks, 1998).

RETAIL LOGISTICS AND SUPPLY CHAIN TRANSFORMATION

Retailers were once effectively the passive recipients of products, allocated to stores by manufacturers in anticipation of demand. Today, retailers are the active designers and controllers of product supply in reaction to known customer demand. They control, organize and manage the supply chain from production to consumption. This is the essence of the retail logistics and supply chain transformation that has taken place.

Times have changed and retail logistics has changed also. Retailers are the channel captains and set the pace in logistics. Having extended their channel control and focused on efficiency and effectiveness, retailers are now attempting to engender a more co-operative and collaborative stance in many aspects of logistics. They are recognizing that there are still gains to be made on standards and efficiency, but that these are probably

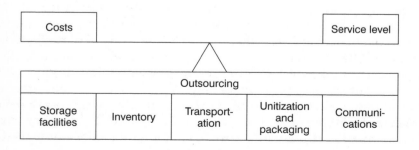

Figure 1.2 The Management Task in Logistics

only obtained as channel gains (that is, in association with manufacturers and logistics services providers) rather than at the single firm level.

In 1996 Alan McKinnon reviewed and summarized the key components of this retail logistics transformation. He identified six closely related and mutually reinforcing trends:

1 Increased control over secondary distribution

Retailers have increased their control over secondary distribution (warehouse to shop) by channelling an increasing proportion of their supplies through distribution centres (DCs). In some sectors such as food this process is now virtually complete. British retailers exert much tighter control over the supply chain than their counterparts in most other countries. Their logistical operations are heavily dependent on information technology (IT), particularly the large integrated stock replenishment systems that control the movement and storage of an enormous number of separate products.

2 Restructured logistical systems

Retailers have reduced inventory and generally improved efficiency through for example the development of 'composite distribution' (the distribution of mixed temperature items through the same distribution centre and on the same vehicle) and centralization in specialist warehouses of slower moving stock. In the case of mixed retail businesses common stock rooms have been developed, where stock is shared across a number of stores, with demand deciding to which store it is allocated.

3 Adoption of 'Quick Response' (QR)

The aim has been to cut inventory levels and improve the speed of product flow. This has involved reducing order lead-time and moving to a more frequent delivery of smaller consignments both internally (between DC and shop) and externally (between supplier and DC). This has greatly increased both the rate of stock-turn and the amount of product being 'cross-docked', rather than stored at DCs.

QR (Lowson, King and Hunter, 1999) was made possible by the development of EDI (Electronic Data Interchange) and EPOS (Electronic Point of Sale), the latter driving the 'Sales Based Ordering' (SBO) systems that most of the larger retailers have installed. In other words as an item is sold and scanned in a shop, this data is used to inform replenishment and reordering systems and thus react quickly to demand. Sharing such data with key suppliers further integrates production with the supply function. Major British retailers have been faster to adopt these technologies than their counterparts in other European countries, although they still have to diffuse to many small retail businesses.

4   Rationalization of primary distribution (factory to warehouse)

Partly as a result of QR pressures and partly as a result of intensifying competition, retailers have extended their control upstream of the DC (that is, from the DC to the manufacturer). In an effort to improve the utilization of their logistical assets, many have integrated their secondary and primary distribution operations and run them as a single 'network system'. This reduces waste and improves efficiency.

5   Increased return flow of packaged material and handling equipment for recycling/reuse

Retailers have become much more heavily involved in this 'reverse logistics' operation. This trend has been reinforced by the introduction of the EU packaging directive. Although the United Kingdom currently lags behind other European countries, particularly Germany, in this field, there remain opportunities to develop new forms of reusable container and new reverse logistics systems to manage their circulation.

6   Introduction of Supply Chain Management (SCM) and Efficient Consumer Response (ECR)

Having improved the efficiency of their own logistics operations, many retailers have begun to collaborate closely with suppliers to maximize the efficiency of the retail supply chain as a whole. SCM (and within this, ECR) provides a management framework within which retailers and suppliers can more effectively coordinate their activities. The underpinning technologies for SCM and ECR have been well established in the United Kingdom, so conditions have been ripe for such developments.

It is clear that many of these trends identified in McKinnon (1996) have been the focus for retailers in the intervening years. Issues such as primary distribution and factory gate pricing, consolidation centres and stockless depots and Collaborative Planning Forecasting and Replenishment (CPFR) have occupied much attention. The overall focus in retail logistics has been altered from an emphasis on the functional aspects of moving products to an integrative approach that attempts to develop end-to-end supply chains. This outcome is normally referred to as supply chain management.

SUPPLY CHAIN MANAGEMENT

The roots of supply chain management are often attributed to Peter Drucker and his seminal 1962 article. At this time he was discussing distribution as one of the key areas of business where major efficiency gains could be achieved and costs saved. Then, and through the next two decades, the supply chain was still viewed as a series of disparate functions. Once the functions began to be integrated and considered as a supply chain rather than separately, several key themes emerged:

- a shift from a push to a pull: that is, a demand-driven supply chain;
- customers gaining more power in the marketing channel;
- an enhanced role of information systems to gain better control of the supply chain;
- the elimination of unnecessary inventory in the supply chain;
- a focus upon core capabilities and increased outsourcing of non-core activities to specialists.

To achieve maximum effectiveness of supply chains, it became clear that integration, or 'the linking together of previously separated activities within a single system' (Slack et al, 1998: 303) was required. Companies have had therefore to review their internal organization to eliminate duplication and ensure that total costs can be reduced, rather than allow separate functions to control their costs in a sub-optimal manner. Similarly, supply chain integration can be achieved by establishing ongoing relationships with trading partners throughout the supply chain.

In industrial markets supply chain integration focused upon the changes promulgated by the processes involved in improving efficiencies in manufacturing. Total quality management, business process re-engineering and continuous improvement brought Japanese business thinking to western manufacturing operations. The implementation of these practices was popularized by Womack, Jones and Roos's (1990) book *The Machine that Changed the World*, which focused on supply systems and buyer–seller relationships in car manufacturing. In a retail context it is claimed that food retailers such as Tesco are increasingly embracing such lean principles for parts of their business (see Jones, 2002).

During the 1990s this focus on so-called 'lean production' was challenged in the United States and the UK, because of an over-reliance on efficiency measures ('lean') rather than innovative ('agile') responses. Table 1.1 shows how lean and agile supply chains differ. Agility as a concept was developed in the United States in response to the Japanese success in lean production. Agility plays to US strengths of entrepreneurship and information systems technology. An agile supply chain (Figure 1.3) is highly responsive to market demand. Harrison *et al* (1999) argue that the improvements in the use of information technology to capture 'real time' data mean less reliance on forecasts and create a virtual supply chain between trading partners. When information is shared, process integration takes place between partners who focus on their core competencies. The final link in the agile supply chain is the network where a confederation of partners structure, coordinate and manage relationships to meet customer needs (Aldridge and Harrison, 2000).

Both approaches of course have their proponents. There is however no reason why supply systems may not be a combination of both lean and agile approaches, with each used when most appropriate (the so-called 'leagile' approach: Naylor, Naim and Berry, 2002; Mason-Jones, Naylor and Towill, 2000). In either case, emphasis is placed on the demands of supply chain management.

It can be suggested that the key concepts within Supply Chain Management (SCM) include the value chain, resource-based theory (RBT) of the firm, transaction cost economics and network theory. The thrust of all these concepts is the obtaining of competitive advantage through managing the supply chain (within and beyond the single firm) more

Table 1.1 Alternative Supply Chain Processes

	Efficient/ function (lean)	Innovative/ responsive (agile)
Primary purpose	Supply predictable demand efficiently at lowest cost	Respond quickly to unpredictable demand in order to minimize stock-outs, forced mark-downs, and obsolete inventory
Manufacturing focus	Maintain high average utilization rate	Deploy excess buffer capacity
Inventory strategy	Generate high turns and minimize inventory	Deploy significant buffer stock of parts
Lead time focus	Shorten lead time as long as it doesn't increase cost	Invest aggressively in ways to reduce lead time
Approach to supplier selection	Select primarily for cost and quality	Select primarily for speed, flexibility and quality

Source: adapted from Harrison, Christopher and Van Hoek, 1999

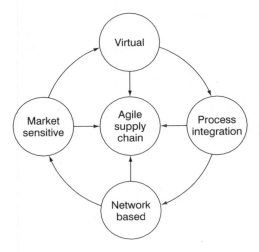

Figure 1.3 The Agile Supply Chain

effectively. They all explore possible benefits of a pan-firm orientation. Figure 1.4 is a supply chain model showing how value may be added to the product through manufacturing, branding, packaging, display at the store and so on. At the same time, at each stage cost is added in terms of production costs, branding costs and overall logistics costs. The aim for retailers (and their supply partners) is to manage this chain to create value for the customer at an acceptable cost. The managing of this so-called 'pipeline' has been a key challenge for logistics professionals, especially with the realization that the reduction of time not only reduced costs, but also gave competitive advantage.

According to Christopher (1997) there are three dimensions to time-based competition that must be managed effectively if an organization is going to be responsive to market changes. These are:

- time to market: the speed at bringing a business opportunity to market;
- time to serve: the speed at meeting a customer's order;
- time to react: the speed at adjusting output to volatile responses in demand.

Christopher (1997) uses these principles to develop strategies for strategic lead-time management. If the lead times of the integrated web of suppliers necessary to manufacture a product are understood, he argues that a 'pipeline map' can be drawn to represent each stage in the supply chain process from raw materials to customer.

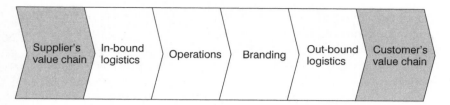

Figure 1.4 The Extended Value Chain

In these maps it is useful to differentiate between 'horizontal' and 'vertical' time. Horizontal time is time spent on processes such as manufacture, assembly, in-transit or order processing. Vertical time is the time when nothing is happening, no value is added but only cost and products/materials are standing as inventory.

It was in fashion markets that the notion of 'time-based competition' had most significance, in view of the short time window for changing styles. In addition, the prominent trend in the last 20 years has been to source products globally, often in low-cost Pacific Rim nations, which lengthened the physical supply chain pipeline. These factors combined to illustrate the trade-offs that have to be made in supply chain management, and suggested an imperative to develop closer working relationships with supply chain partners. The box below and Figure 1.5 detail these processes through the example of Zara.

Zara: Time-Based Competition in a Fashion Market

Zara is one of Spain's most successful and dynamic apparel companies, producing fashionable clothing to appeal to an international target market of 18–35-year-olds. Zara's rapid growth and ongoing success in such a fiercely competitive environment are based on the dual objectives of working without stocks and responding quickly to market needs. It does this as well as, or even more effectively than, its internationally acclaimed rivals such as Benetton or The Gap. Zara has developed one of the most effective quick-response systems in its industry.

The process of supplying goods to the stores begins with cross-functional teams working within Zara's design department at the company headquarters in La Coruna. The designs reflect the latest in international fashion trends, with inspiration gleaned through visits to fashion shows, competitors' stores, university campuses, pubs, cafes and clubs plus any other venues or events deemed to be relevant to the lifestyles of the target customers. The team's understanding of directional fashion trends is further guided by regular inflows of EPOS data and other information from all of the company's stores and sites around the world.

If a proposed design is accepted, commercial specialists proceed to negotiate with suppliers, agree purchase prices, analyse costs and margins, and fix a standard cross-currency price position for the garments. The size of the production run and launch dates are also determined at this point. A global sourcing policy, organized through the company's buying offices in the UK, China and the Netherlands, and using a broad supplier base, provides the widest possible selection of fashion fabrics, while reducing the risk of dependence on any source or supplier. Approximately 40 per cent of garments – those with the broadest and least transient appeal – are imported as finished goods from low-cost manufacturing centres in the Far East. The rest are produced by quick response in Spain, using Zara's own highly auto-mated factories and a network of smaller contractors.

Only those operations that enhance cost-efficiency through economies of scale are conducted in-house (such as dyeing, cutting, labelling and packaging). All other manufacturing activities, including the labour-intensive finishing stages, are completed by networks of more than 300 small exclusive subcontractors, each specializing in one particular part of the production process or garment type. The system is flexible enough to cope with sudden changes in demand, though production is always kept at a level slightly below expected sales, to keep stock moving. Zara has opted for under-supply, viewing it as a lesser evil than holding slow-moving or obsolete stock.

Finished goods are labelled, price-tagged and packed at the company's distribution centre in La Coruna. From there they travel by third-party contractors by road and/or air to their penultimate destinations. The shops themselves receive deliveries of new stock on a twice-weekly basis, according to shop-by-shop stock allocations calculated by the design department. The whole production cycle takes only two weeks. In an industry where lead times of many months are still the norm, Zara has reduced its lead-time to a level unmatched by any of its European or North American competitors.

The hub of the operation is the manufacturing and logistics centre near La Coruna. About 10,000 new items per year are turned out. New products are tested in particular stores before production runs are finalized, reducing failure rates to around 1 per cent, compared with the typical industry average of 10 per cent. The design, production and market cycle has been reduced to 22–30 days, in an industry where nine months has been the traditional lead time.

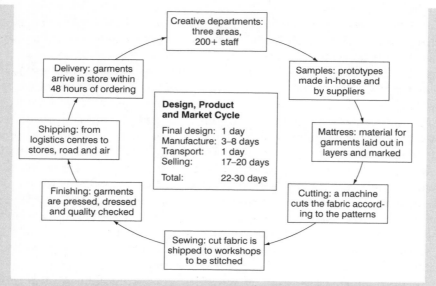

Figure 1.5 Zara's Design, Product and Market Cycle

Significant investment in information technology drives the supply chain. The five-storey, 500,000 sq m logistics centre contains over 200 kilometres of moving rails, and automated routing systems deliver electronically tagged garments to the appropriate loading bays for dispersal via third party subcontracted distributors. Products are ready for dispatch eight hours after arrival. It is claimed that distribution is 98.9 per cent accurate, with shrinkage levels less than 0.5 per cent.

Zara's pre-season inventory level (the production committed before the season begins) is 15–20 per cent compared with 40–60 per cent norms in the industry, with its in-season commitment, allowed by the fast response, flexible production process in the 40–50 per cent region. This approach allows a closer alignment of production to sales forecasts, reducing the need to clear unwanted stock. Store sales are recorded daily on hand-held computers and store orders are made at pre-determined times. This discipline, allied to pre-determined dispatch times at the logistics centre, provides control and reduces costs.

Sources: Christopher, 1998: 155–57; Burt, Dawson and Larke,2003; *Retail Week* 21 Nov 2003: 16–17.

Another catalyst for many of the initiatives in lead-time reduction came from work undertaken by Kurt Salmon Associates (KSA) in the United States in the mid-1980s. KSA was commissioned by US garment suppliers to investigate how they could compete with Far East suppliers.

The results were revealing in that the supply chains were long (one and a quarter years from loom to store), badly coordinated and inefficient (Christopher and Peck, 1998). The concept of quick response was therefore initiated to reduce lead times and improve coordination across the apparel supply chain. In Europe, quick response principles have been applied across the clothing retail sector. Supply base rationalization has been a feature of the last decade, as companies have dramatically reduced the number of suppliers and have worked much more closely with the remaining suppliers to ensure more responsiveness to the marketplace.

Complex webs of relationships have been formed in many supply chains. This has led Christopher to claim that as an outcome of supply chain management 'there is a strong case for arguing that individual companies no longer compete with other stand alone companies, but rather, that supply chain now competes against supply chain' (1997: 22).

In many supply chains, tiers of suppliers have been created to manufacture specific component parts. Other supplier associations have been formed to coordinate supply chain activities. In these businesses the trend has often been to buy rather than make, and to outsource non-core activities. Benetton, which has been hailed as the archetypal example of a network organization, is however bucking this trend by increasing vertical integration and ownership of assets in the supply chain (Camuffo, Romano and Vinelli, 2001). While it is retaining its network structure, it is refining the network from product design through to distribution to its stores. While Benetton previously customized around 20 per cent of its ranges to satisfy national markets, it has reduced this to around 5 to 10 per cent in order to communicate one image of Benetton in global markets. The streamlining of its brands and in-store testing have allowed it to respond quicker to changing market trends.

Benetton is renowned for its relationship with small and medium-sized enterprises (SMEs) in north-eastern Italy. These SMEs supplied the labour-intensive phases of production (tailoring, finishing, ironing) while the company kept 'in house' the capital-intensive parts of the operation (weaving, cutting and dyeing). In the last decade it has established a high-tech production pole at Castrette, near its headquarters, to cope with increased volumes. The Castrette model has been recreated in foreign production poles in Spain, Portugal, Tunisia, Hungary, Croatia, South Korea, Egypt and India, with a SME network which focuses on specific products and skills in the area. Control also has been increased both upstream and downstream of production. The company now controls 85 per cent of its textile and thread suppliers to ensure speedy quality control and reduce lead times to workshops.

THE GROCERY RETAIL SUPPLY CHAIN IN THE UK

This development of supply chain management and the consequent implementation of relationship initiatives have been identified as the fourth and final stage of the evolution of grocery logistics in the UK (Fernie, Pfab and Marchant, 2000). This relationship stage relates to a more collaborative approach to supply chain management after decades of confrontation. The UK is often mooted to have the most efficient grocery supply chain in the world, and this is a key contributor to the profit margins of its grocery retailers.

This logistical transformation of UK retailing has occurred in a short period of time (Sparks, 1998). In the first stage of evolution (pre-1980) the dominant method of distribution to stores was by manufacturers that stored products at their factories or field warehouses for multiple drops to numerous small shops. As the retail multiple gained in prominence (especially after the abolition of resale price maintenance in 1964), retailers invested in regional distribution centres to consolidate deliveries from suppliers for onward delivery to stores. This was the first step change in the supply of fast-moving consumer goods (FMCGs) in that buying and distribution became a headquarters function in retailing, and the logistical infrastructure created a market for third-party logistics service providers.

To all intents and purposes, this marked the removal of suppliers from controlling the supply chain. This period of centralization throughout the 1980s enabled retailers to reduce lead times, minimize inventory and give greater product availability to customers in their stores. The 1990s witnessed a consolidation of this process. In many cases inventory had only been moved from store to RDC. By implementing JIT principles, retailers began to focus on their primary distribution networks (from supplier to RDC), demanding more frequent deliveries of smaller quantities. Clearly this created a problem for many suppliers in that they could not deliver full vehicle loads of product. To ensure that vehicle utilization could be maximized, consolidation centres have been created upstream of the RDC, and retailers have established supplier collection programmes to pick up products from suppliers' factories on return trips from stores.

In the early years of this century, retail networks continue to be upgraded as ECR initiatives are enacted and grocery retailers accommodate the increase in non-food products through their distribution centres. Furthermore, the greater sharing of information, especially through Internet exchanges, has fostered Collaborative Planning, Forecasting and Replenishment (CPFR) initiatives to reduce supply chain response times.

It should be stressed that UK grocery retail logistics is relatively unique. Retailers not only control the supply chain but also have taken over marketing responsibilities that were once the sole domain of the manufacturer, such as product development, branding, advertising and distribution. The high level of retail brand penetration has enabled them to build up store loyalty and diversify into other businesses such as banking. Control of channels is a way of life for such companies.

In other countries a more fragmented store offering is apparent, and different store choice attributes are evident. For example, price and promotions are key drivers of consumer choice in the United States, Germany and France when compared with the UK. This means the consumer buys in bulk and the retailer 'forward buys' promotional stock that needs to be housed in distribution centres. Of course, in these markets land and property costs are relatively low compared with the UK, so that the savings in buying costs can outweigh the additional logistics costs. When Safeway in the UK adopted a high/low promotional strategy in order to compete with Asda (Wal-Mart), this led to significant disruption and changes in the operation of its RDC network.

FUTURE CHALLENGES

While members of the supply chain have sought ways to foster collaboration, the rise of e-commerce has posed another set of challenges for retailers. The rise and subsequent fall of many dot.com companies led to a high degree of speculation as to the reconfiguration of the business to consumer (B2C) channel. Ultimately, e-fulfilment, especially the 'last mile' problem of delivering goods to the final customer, holds the key to success in this channel. The business to business (B2B) channel, however, has more to offer members of the supply chain because of the number and complexity of transactions and the greater adoption of Internet technology by businesses compared with consumers.

There have been numerous B2B exchange marketplaces created since the late 1990s, with most of these exchanges being created in highly concentrated global market sectors with a 'streamlined' number of buyers and sellers, for example in the automobile, chemical and steel industries. The more proactive retailers developed B2B Internet exchanges as an extension of the EDI platforms created a decade earlier. This has enabled companies such as Tesco, Sainsbury and Wal-Mart to establish their own private exchanges with suppliers to share data on sales, product forecasting, promotion tracking and production planning. There are major benefits to be derived from pooling EDI efforts into a smaller number of B2B platforms. For example it is easier to standardize processes for communication, reduce development costs and give members access to a larger customer base.

In 2000 several Internet trading exchanges were created, promising a revolution in product procurement. The two major exchanges, GlobalNet Xchange (GNX) and World Wide Retail Exchange (WWRE), have made some progress. Although the Global Commerce Initiative established draft standards for global Internet trading, many issues need to be resolved to ensure the seamless flow of data across the supply chain. The complexity of dealing with thousands of stock-keeping units (SKUs) has meant that retailers have had to be selective in the projects that can be routed through their private exchanges compared with these global exchanges. To date the focus of the GNX exchange has been on special promotions, perishables and own-label products: for example, 600 out of potential 2,000 suppliers of Sainsbury's retail brand products are on GNX.

In the business to consumer (B2C) channel, the rise and fall of Internet retailers has brought a touch of realism to the evolving market potential of online shopping. In Europe, grocery retailers are powerful 'bricks and mortar' companies and the approach to Internet retailing has been reactive rather than proactive. Most Internet operations have been small, and few pure players have entered the market to challenge the conventional supermarket chains. Tesco is one of the few success stories in e-grocery, having adopted an unconventional model (see box below).

Tesco.com: Delivering Home Shopping

Tesco.com has become the world's largest Internet grocery system in a very short time. Unlike many of its competitors, it has opted for an in-store picking and home delivery operation, rather than starting with a dedicated distribution centre system. This choice came about for three reasons:

- Warehouse-based picking and delivery was not believed to be economic due to low penetration levels and drive times for vehicles being high.
- Customers confirmed that they did not want a reduced offer online as this destroyed the point of shopping at Tesco for them.
- Outside of London, the penetration rates possible did not make a warehouse a valid option, even if other costs (such as picking) were solved.

Since introduction there has been a very rapid roll-out to effectively cover the UK through the network of stores. Each store involved has dedicated local delivery vehicles. The system in operation has thrown up a few surprises:

- Fresh food has been a big seller online, whereas people had initially expected big, bulky replenishment items to be the most popular.
- People plan their online order better than their in-store trip (aided by the Clubcard and Internet item recall availability), so a higher proportion of spend is made with Tesco.
- The non-food item offer can be more extensive online than in-store so sales in this area can be expanded.
- Knowledge is gained from the online shopping process of what items customers wanted to buy, that were not actually in stock. This helps enhance the supply system.

Source: adapted from Jones, 2001

Why have 'pure players' failed in this channel? Laseter *et al* (2000) identify four key challenges:

- limited online potential;
- high cost of delivery;
- selection–variety trade-offs;
- existing entrenched competition.

Ring and Tigert (2001) came to similar conclusions when comparing the Internet offering with the conventional 'bricks and mortar' experience. They looked at what consumers would trade away from a store in terms of the place, product, service and value for money by shopping online. They also detailed the 'killer costs' of the pure play Internet grocers, notably the picking and delivery costs. The gist of the argument presented by these critics is that the standard Internet model is flawed.

The two main fulfilment models are illustrated in Figures 1.6 and 1.7. The store-based model makes use of existing distribution assets, as products pass through regional distribution centres (RDCs) to stores where orders are assembled for delivery to online customers (Figure 1.6). The advantages of the store model are the low initial investment required and the speed of rolling out the service to a wide geographical market. Customers also receive the same products online as available in stores. The problem here, however, is that 'out of stocks' and substitutions of products are more prevalent as online shoppers compete with in store counterparts for products.

The dedicated order picking model (Figure 1.7) utilizes e-fulfilment centres to pick and deliver orders to customers. The advantage of this system is that it is dedicated purely to e-commerce customers so stock-outs should be low and delivery frequencies should be higher. These

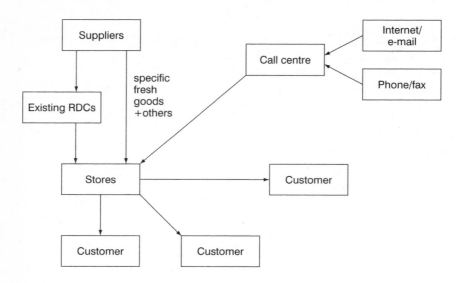

Figure 1.6 Logistics Model for Store-Based Picking of E-Commerce Orders

picking centres, however, have less of a product range and they need to be working at capacity to justify investment costs.

Ultimately the picking centre model will possibly be the long-term solution to online grocery fulfilment. The problem is that the economics of order fulfilment and delivery are so poor in the short run that companies are abandoning this approach or going bankrupt (Webvan). In the UK Asda has closed two picking centres in London, and Sainsbury is developing a hybrid model. So why has the so-called least efficient fulfilment model proven successful? The answer is simple. You need to create market demand before you invest in costly infrastructure.

E-commerce is here to stay, and B2B and B2C channels will increase in importance once established standards for data transfer across the supply chain are realized. Already, the information revolution has been the catalyst for improving supply chain efficiency and for fostering stronger relationships between supply chain partners. Private Internet exchanges developed by leading retailers, such as Wal-Mart with its Retail Link network, have enabled them to respond quickly to consumer choice at store level. Indeed, much of the focus of this chapter has been on how competitive advantage can be achieved through companies co-operating and thus responding flexibly and quickly to market needs; hence the acronyms of JIT for lean supply chains and QR and ECR for agile supply chains.

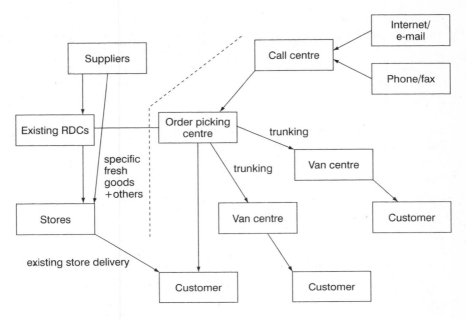

Figure 1.7   Logistics Model for the E-fulfilment Centre Route

Regardless of sector or industry, supply chain integration can only be achieved through greater collaboration and coordination of functions across supply chains. This means partnerships, alliances and networks that are created within and between organizations. Traditional functions can no longer be viewed in isolation or 'silos' independent from the workings of other parts of their own and other businesses. Cross-functional teamwork and inter-organizational co-operation will therefore hold the key to future developments in supply chain management.

In terms of future challenges it is worthwhile also to mention one other aspect of supply chains. One of the implicit reasons behind aspects of data communication in supply chains and the use of these data in such systems as are outlined above, is to reduce the demands for unnecessary product packaging and movement. It has long been recognized that costs, performance and services can be enhanced by appropriate movement of data and product. In essence this is a resource reduction strategy. More overtly, there has been increasing concern with the environmental impact of logistics, and companies have become increasingly concerned to ensure that their activities are appropriate. Through better use of data to understand activities, aspects of supply can be minimized. In addition, supply chains can be enhanced to ensure that resources are reused or recycled in the system, and that reverse channels of logistics can reclaim valuable resources from packaging and product. Much more needs be done in this regard, but this issue will be one of the challenges for the future.

It could be argued for example that many of the logistics efficiencies described above have been generated by operating systems that are insufficiently environmentally aware. Logistics can have a major adverse impact upon the environment. While improvements in vehicle design, engine efficiency, reusable handling systems and building standards have reduced the impacts, the distances products now have to travel have accentuated the problems. Environmental issues are thus one issue of future concern.

It has to be recognized that terminology in this area has been the subject of some confusion. A good starting point however is:

> Reverse logistics is a process whereby companies can become more environmentally efficient through the recycling, reuse and reducing the amount of materials used. Viewed narrowly, it can be thought of as the reverse distribution of materials among channel members. A more holistic view of reverse logistics includes the reduction of materials in the forward system in such a way that fewer materials flow back, reuse of materials is possible, and recycling is facilitated.

> (Carter and Ellram, 1998: 82)

In a retail context it is relatively straightforward to think of elements that fit these definitions. Many retailers operate a recycling policy for consumers to use and for aspects of their stores' waste. In some countries there may be legal or fiscal encouragement. Some recycling may be internalized in the company. Other material is sold on for external recycling purposes.

In the grocery industry, the use of plastic trays and boxes to carry and distribute fresh product has become standard. Many DCs contain specialist centres for cleaning and reusing such equipment. This is an example of a reverse logistics system in that a channel has had to be created in order to move the containers back down the chain. In reality, the vehicles delivering to store often back-haul containers to distribution centres or to manufacturers.

One of the key drivers for change is government. In March 1997 the Packaging Waste regulations came into force (see Fernie and Hart, 2001). These are the UK government's implementation of the requirements to meet the EU Directive on Packaging and Packaging Waste. The aim is to recover at least 50 per cent of the annual packaging waste created in the UK. The main obligations on retailers are to:

- register with the authorities or join a registered collective scheme;
- provide data on packaging handled, recovered and recycled;
- recover and recycle certain percentages of packaging waste;
- provide a Certificate of Compliance.

The amount a business has to recover and recycle depends on its position in the channel. Retailers can meet their obligations by either individually complying (primarily large companies) or joining a collective scheme (14 approved compliance programmes are registered nationally). Members of a collective scheme do not have to meet individual obligations, as the scheme assumes this responsibility on behalf of its members. Such regulations are not likely to disappear and are probably going to become more stringent in the future.

CONCLUSIONS

This consideration of the changes and challenges in retail logistics allows us to summarize the key issues in retail logistics and supply chains.

First, it should be clear by now that the modern logistics and supply systems are heavily dependent on the use of information technology. Logistics now is as much about information movement as it is about product movement. Anyone who believes that retail logistics is all about boxes and lorries needs to rethink. Of course it remains true that products have to be distributed. Vehicles and boxes are still involved. But increasingly it is the control of data and information that remains the key to a successful logistics system.

Second, the discussion above should have indicated that modern retail logistics is no longer a separate or functionally based activity. Within a company, warehousing and transport can not exist as separate operations. Instead logistics is all about integration, not only within a company, but also increasingly outside the business with suppliers, logistics service providers and customers. Partnership is a strong component of modern retail logistics, and an ability to work with other individuals and other companies is fundamental to success.

Third, it should have become apparent that the 'reach' of retail logistics has expanded enormously. Companies used to manage local suppliers and products to and from local warehouses. Nowadays, retailers are much more global in their outlook. Products are sourced from around the world and so the interactions and movements involved in logistics are now equally international.

Finally however, we must not forget that logistics is about the movement of product, and much work is undertaken on improving the mechanics of this task. For example, a modern supermarket contains good examples of packaging and standardization, the best of which make handling easier. Vehicle fleets may be equipped with GPS (Global Positioning Satellite) systems and advanced tachograph and communications equipment, allowing real-time driver and vehicle performance monitoring. Such detailed analysis remains a key component of supply chain integration.

With the pressure on to enhance service and reduce costs in supply chains, together with their enhanced complexity, there can be little doubt that retailers will be subjected to considerable logistical challenges in the years to come.

REFERENCES

Aldridge, D and Harrison, A (2000) Implementing agile methods in retail supply chains: a scenario for the future, *International Journal of Agile Manufacturing*, **3** (2), pp 37–44

Burt, S L, Dawson, J A and Larke, R (2003) Inditex-Zara: re-writing the rules in apparel retailing. Paper presented at the Second SARD Workshop, UMDS, Kobe, April 2003

Camuffo, A, Romano, P and Vinelli, A (2001) Back to the future: Benetton transforms its global network, *MIT Sloan Management Review*, **43** (1), Fall, pp 46–52

Carter, C R and Ellram, L M (1998) Reverse logistics: a review of the literature and framework for future investigation, *Journal of Business Logistics*, **19** (1), pp 85–102

Christopher, M (1997) *Marketing Logistics*, Butterworth-Heinemann, Oxford

Christopher, M (1998) *Logistics and Supply Chain Management*, FT/Prentice Hall, London

Christopher, M and Peck, H (1998) Fashion Logistics, chapter 6 in *Logistics and Retail Management*, ed J Fernie and L Sparks, Kogan Page, London

Department of Trade and Industry (DTI) (2001) @ *Your Home: New markets for customer service and delivery*, Retail Logistics Task Force, Foresight, London

Drucker, P (1962) The economy's dark continent, *Fortune*, April, pp 265–70

Fernie, J (1990) *Retail Distribution Management*, Kogan Page, London

Fernie, J and Hart, C (2001) UK packaging waste legislation: implications for food retailers, *British Food Journal*, **103** (3), pp 187–97

Fernie, J, Pfab, F and Marchant, C (2000) Retail grocery logistics in the UK, *International Journal of Logistics Management*, **11** (2), pp 83–90

Fernie, J and Sparks, L (1998) *Logistics and Retail Management*, Kogan Page, London

Foresight Retail Logistics Task Force (2000) @ Your Service: Future models of retail logistics, DTI, London

Harrison, A, and van Hoek, R (2002) *Logistics Management and Strategy*, Financial Times/Prentice Hall, Harlow

Harrison, A, Christopher, M and van Hoek, R (1999) *Creating the Agile Supply Chain*, Institute of Logistics and Transport, Corby

Jones, D T (2001) Tesco.com: delivering home shopping, *ECR Journal*, **1** (1), pp 37–43

Jones, D T (2002) Rethinking the grocery supply chain, in *State of the Art in Food*, ed J-W Grievink, L Josten and C Valk, Elsevier, Rotterdam [Online] www.leanuk.org/articles.htm (accessed 30 Oct 2003)

Laseter, T, Houston, P, Ching, A, Byrne, S, Turner, M and Devendran, A (2000) The last mile to nowhere, *Strategy and Business* 20, September, pp 40–48

Lowson, B, King, R and Hunter, A (1999) *Quick Response: Managing the supply chain to meet consumer demand*, Wiley, Chichester

Mason-Jones, R, Naylor, B and Towill, D R (2000) Lean, agile or leagile? Matching your supply chain to the marketplace, *International Journal of Production Research*, **38** (17), pp 4061–70

McKinnon, A C (1996) The development of retail logistics in the UK: a position paper, *Technology Foresight: Retail and Distribution Panel*, Heriot-Watt University, Edinburgh

Naylor, J B, Naim, M M and Berry, D (1997) Leagility: integrating the lean and agile manufacturing paradigm in the total supply chain, *International Journal of Production Economics*, **62**, pp 107–18

Retail Week (2003) At the heart of a retail giant, *Retail Week*, Nov 21, pp 16–18

Ring, L J and Tigert, D J (2001) Viewpoint: the decline and fall of Internet grocery retailers, *International Journal of Retail and Distribution Management*, **29** (6), pp 266–73

Slack, N, Chambers, S, Harland, S C, Harrison, A and Johnson, R (1988) *Operations Management*, 2nd edn, Pitman, London

Sparks, L (1998) The retail logistics transformation, Chapter 1 (pp 1–22) of *Logistics and Retail Management*, ed J Fernie and L Sparks, Kogan Page, London

Womack, J P, Jones, D and Roos, D (1990) *The Machine that Changed the World: The story of lean production*, Harper-Collins, New York

2

Relationships in the supply chain

John Fernie

INTRODUCTION

Relationship marketing (RM), Customer Relationship Marketing (CRM), e-CRM for online businesses and Collaborative Planning, Forecasting and Replenishment (CPFR) are only some of the acronyms to appear in the academic literature in the last 10 to 15 years. This represents a major paradigm shift in marketing and logistics away from a traditional transactional view of exchange between buyers and sellers to a more proactive, collaborative relationship approach. The purpose of this chapter is to discuss the conceptual framework of supply chain relationships and their applications to retailing through Quick Response (QR) and Efficient Consumer Response (ECR) initiatives. Finally, the role of logistical service providers in supply chain relationships will be reviewed.

CHANGING BUYER–SELLER RELATIONSHIPS

The origins of the relationship approach to understanding buyer–seller interaction at different parts of the supply chain goes back several decades, when the conventional marketing mix paradigm began to be challenged. The growth of the service sector, the move from mass marketing to micro marketing to mass customization, with the associated database infrastructure, allowed companies to target customers more effectively. While consumer marketing embraced a relationship approach to improve customer retention, these trends were particularly prominent in industrial markets where the Industrial Marketing and Purchasing Group (IMP) initiated much of the business to business research in this area.

In parallel with these developments was a growing literature in logistics and supply chain management embodying similar paradigms and constructs. The fourth P of the marketing mix, Place, was traditionally centred on the wholesale and retail trade and how suppliers would channel their products to market. By the 1980s two key factors would begin to elevate logistics to greater prominence in the literature: the rise in power of the multiple retailers, thereby changing power relationships, and the need to eliminate inventory and non-value added activities in getting products to market. Thus, to compete with Japanese manufacturing, European and US companies embraced Just-In-Time (JIT) techniques, reduced their supply base and worked more closely with the remaining suppliers. So throughout the 1990s debates emerged on the lean compared with the agile supply chain, the latter more relevant to the fast-moving consumer goods (FMCG) market.

Interestingly, with a few exceptions such as Martin Christopher, the academic literature on relationships tends to be published in discrete camps as evidenced by readers on marketing (Hart, 2003) and logistics (Waters, 2003) which exhibit similar constructs when discussing relationships but very rarely cross-reference between 'marketing' and 'supply chain' literatures. Nevertheless, key themes are common – power and dependence, trust and commitment, co-operation and co-opetition, which will be discussed in turn.

Power and Dependence

'Power in the supply chain can be defined operationally as the ability of one entity in the chain to control the decision of another entity' (Daparin and Hogarth-Scott, 2003: 259). It is generally agreed that the power base has shifted over time from supplier to retailer. When French and Raven (1959) produced their seminal work, the suppliers controlled the supply chain. The five power bases that they identified – reward power, coercive power, referent power, legitimate power and expert power – would lead to dependency of the retailer on the supplier, especially with regard to expert power in that the supplier had the marketing/logistics expertise in the channel. Clearly this has changed in 45 years in that retailers can delist (coercive), reward, joint promote (referent) and dictate terms (legitimate) to suppliers because of their dominant market position (expert power).

The nature of such relationships between manufacturers and retailers was discussed by Kumar (1996) in a study of 400 relationships. He categorized them into different levels of dependence (Figure 2.1). The 'win–win' quadrant is the top right category where there is a high level of interdependence between parties. The 'hostage' and 'drunk with power' categories could lead to a breakdown in the relationship.

Trust and Commitment

According to Kumar (1996) trust is the antithesis of power, and it is trust that leads to co-operation. However, trust can easily be heralded as 'the glue that holds a relationship' (O'Malley, 2003: 130), but it is difficult to measure because this involves social networks which are inherently fluid in a retail buying context. At an organizational level trust, and therefore commitment, can be related to the relationship lifecycle. Many UK private label suppliers have grown with the retailers which they supplied, especially in the area of chilled fresh food where the category was developed by the retailer in partnership with these companies. This does not guarantee stability as evidenced by Marks and Spencer's breakdown in relationship with some UK clothing suppliers when it decided to source products offshore and thereby sever links which had been fostered for generations. Similarly, the introduction of factory gate pricing by grocery

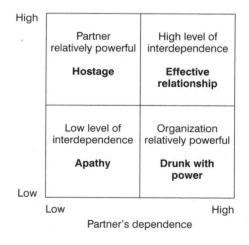

Figure 2.1   Effects of Interdependence

retailers is viewed by many suppliers in the UK as opportunistic behaviour which impacts upon trust in the relationship.

Co-operation and co-opetition

Much of the literature from ECR conferences and trade bodies implies greater collaboration between supply chain partners. This is discussed in more depth in the next section. In the academic literature, most attention has been focused upon collaborative advantage rather than competitive advantage (Christopher and Peck, 2003) and co-opetition (Brandenburger and Nalebüff, 1996) rather than competition. The thrust of this argument is that in sectors such as the FMCG industry where demand is stable, it is more appropriate for companies to 'grow the cake' in specific categories by boosting demand and compete on conventional marketing criteria. Similarly, companies have reviewed their logistics operations and are now willing to collaborate with competitors on 'invisible' shared resources but not on promotion or 'visible' marketing efforts. This mirrors the well established approach by Japanese manufacturing companies which co-operate on R&D but compete on the branded consumer goods in the marketplace.

The creation of value added partnerships within industrial sectors is based on the tenets of resource-based theory, transaction cost analysis and network theory. In essence, the key decisions that have to be taken by companies within the supply chain relate to their core competencies, the allocation of resources and the network of organizations with which they interact. The best examples of such a division of labour is in the clothing 'fast fashion' sector which is discussed in much length elsewhere in the book. Benetton is the classical example of the network organization, with its international poles throughout the world. Here Benetton keeps the capital-intensive parts of the operation 'in house', contracting out to small and medium sized enterprises (SMEs) the labour-intensive phase of production (tailoring, knitting, ironing). Likewise, Zara has developed its production pole at La Coruna with its integrated network of SMEs in Galicia and N. Portugal.

In other parts of the retail sector, the rosy picture of collaboration and co-operation is less evident from published empirical research. The previous edition of this volume cited work by Hogarth-Scott and Parkinson (1993) and Ogbonna and Wilkinson (1996) in the food sector of a more adversarial approach than the 'partnership' dialogue promulgated at the time. In the basic clothing sector similar trends were evident (Fernie, 1998) and the downward pressure in prices with the intense competition in the UK clothing market has done little to redress the emphasis on tough price negotiations. Indeed, Philip Green's takeovers of BHS and Arcadia have been marked by his public pronouncements on the renegotiating of supplier contracts.

The Competition Commission (2000) investigation of the nature of competition in the UK supermarket sector was generally supportive of the status quo except for the need for a supplier code of practice to eliminate the worst excesses of retailer power on suppliers. Anecdotal evidence would appear to suggest that prices were being driven down to unacceptable levels, plus retailers required other 'contributions' for slotting allowances and other discounts for volume purchases. In a more recent study of buyer–seller relationships in the UK and Australian markets, Daparin and Hogarth-Scott (2003) challenge many of the conventional views on co-operation, trust and power. They claim that much of the literature argues that power is a negative construct and is invariably viewed as a distinctive independent construct divorced from the construct of co-operation. From their research, they would maintain that co-operation occurs as a result of compliant behaviour brought about by the application of power.

Using the results from their survey, Daparin and Hogarth-Scott (2003) discuss dependence and power in relation to retail concentration and supplier dependency. Therefore, where retail concentration is high and there is low retailer dependence on the supplier, retailers will be more likely to use coercive power. Where concentration levels are high but dependence on suppliers is also high, retailers are more likely to use expert power, probably through the use of category management. The use of such expert power leads to co-operative behaviour which in turns leads to greater trust within the relationship. This model is illustrated in Figure 2.2, which shows that the use of coercive/reward power can lead to capitulation in the relationship even if trust is broken within the context of category management and the referent/expert power in the right hand quadrant disintegrates into coercive power.

QUICK RESPONSE

The term Quick Response (QR) was coined in the United States in 1985 (Fernie, 1994; Hines, 2001) when Kurt Salmon Associates (KSA) recognized deficiencies in the fashion supply chain. According to KSA, only 11 weeks out of the 66-week lead time in the pipeline are spent on the actual processes (value adding time / horizontal time), and the rest (non-value adding time/vertical time) are wasted in the form of work in progress (WIP) and finished inventories at various stages of the complex system (KSA, 1997; Christopher, 1997, 1998; Christopher and Peck, 1998). The

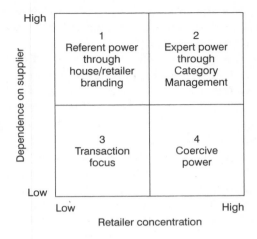

Figure 2.2   Power Strategies of Retailers

resultant losses arising from this were estimated at US $25 billion, due to stocking too large an inventory of unwanted items and too small of the fast movers.

In response to this situation, the American textiles, apparel and retail industries formed the VICS (Voluntary Interindustry Commerce Standards Association) in 1986 as their joint effort to streamline the supply chain and make a significant contribution in getting the in-vogue style at the right time in the right place (Fernie, 1994,1998) with increased variety (Giunipero *et al*, 2001; Lowson, 1998; Lowson, King and Hunter, 1999) and inexpensive prices. This is done by applying an industry standard in information technologies (such as bar-codes, EDI, shipping container marking and roll ID) and contractual procedures (Lowson *et al*, 1999; Ko, Kincade and Brown, 2000; Giunipero *et al*, 2001) among the supply chain members. Not only is QR an IT-driven systematic approach (Forza and Vinelli, 1996, 1997, 2000; Hunter, 1990; Riddle *et al*, 1999) to achieve supply chain efficiency from raw materials to retail stores, it is also a win–win partnership in which each member of the supply chain shares the risks and the benefits of the partnership on an equal basis to realize the philosophy of 'the whole is stronger than the parts'.

QR, in principle, requires the traditional buyer–supplier relationship, which is too often motivated by opportunism, to transform into a more collaborative partnership. In this QR partnership, the objectives of the vendor are to develop the customer's business. The benefit to the vendor is the likelihood that it will be treated as a preferred supplier. At the same time, the costs of serving that customer should be lower as a result of a greater sharing of information, integrated logistics systems and so on

(Christopher, 1997; Christopher and Juttner, 2000). Thus, partnership among the supply chain members is a prerequisite of QR programmes.

QR's ultimate goal, nonetheless, is to give customers the savings that are gained through the initiative (Giunipero *et al*, 2001). The last, and perhaps one of the most important tenets of the original proposition of the QR concept is that QR is a survival strategy of the domestic manufacturing sector in the advanced economies against competition from low-cost imports (Finnie, 1992; MITI, 1993, 1995, 1999; METI, 2002). In the case of the United States, the QR initiative was expected to make a considerable contribution to the Pride with the USA campaign, which promoted the excellence of US-made products to American consumers, who had already been familiar with inexpensive imported casual clothing.

With the basic fashion category, relatively steady demand is a feature of the market, therefore the US-born QR concept places much focus on the relationship between retailers and apparel manufacturers. The eventual benefits for both parties are detailed in Table 2.1. Giunipero *et al* (2001) summarize the hierarchical process of QR adaptation as an integral part of QR as business process re-engineering (BPR) (Table 2.2). This model, most appropriate for the apparel–retail linkage in basic clothing, has become a role model for QR programmes in other advanced economies.

Having achieved many of the QR goals, VICS has implemented a CPFR (Collaborative Planning, Forecasting and Replenishment) programme, to synchronize market fluctuations and the supply chain in a more real-time fashion. Through establishing firm contracts among supply chain members and allowing them to share key information, CPFR makes the forecasting, production and replenishment cycle ever closer to the actual demands in the marketplace (VICS, 1998). While the American practices have played a leading role in the QR and SCM initiatives in the apparel industry, much of the success is in the basic fashion segment, where the manufacturing phase is normally the first to be transferred offshore. In this sense, the philosophy of QR as the survival strategy of fashion manufacturing in the industrial economies has not been realized.

Table 2.1　Retailer and Supplier QR Benefits

Retailer QR benefits	Supplier QR benefits
Reduced costs	Reduced costs
Reduced inventories	Predictable production cycles
Faster merchandise flow	Frequency of orders
Customer satisfaction	Closer ties to retailers
Increased sales	Ability to monitor sales
Competitive advantage	Competitive advantage

Source: Quick Response Services (1995)

Table 2.2 Technological and Organizational QR Development Stages

STAGE 1	(Introduction of basic QR technologies) SKU level scanning JAN (standard) bar-code Use of EDI Use of standard EDI
STAGE 2	(Internal process re-engineering via technological and organizational improvement) Electronic communication for replenishment Use of cross-docking Small amounts of inventory in the system Small lot size order processing ARP (automatic replenishment programme) JIT (Just-In-Time) delivery SCM (shipping container marking) ASN (Advanced Shipping Notice)
STAGE 3	(Realization of a collaborative supply chain and win–win relationship) Real-time sales datasharing Stock-out data sharing QR team meets with partnerships MRP (Material Resource Planning)

Sources: Giunipero *et al*, 2001; KSA, 1997

QR in Japan

While the US apparel industry competes largely on a cost basis in the basic fashion segment, Japanese firms have forged their success on bridge fashion with flexible specialization (Piore and Sabel, 1984) in a subcontracting network of process specialists in the industrial districts (Sanchi) led by the 'apparel firms' with design and marketing expertise. The US fashion industry essentially produces for the international market that is mostly controlled by the largest retailers, which are the real promoters and the first to profit from QR (Scarso, 1997; Taplin and Ordovensky, 1995). Thus, the Japanese fashion industry shows clear contrasts to its US and most of the European counterparts, where large retailers control the supply chain (Azuma, 2001).

Harsh competition from offshore and stagnant domestic consumption in the past decade has come to highlight the costly structure and the lack of partnership in the Japanese fashion supply chain (MITI, 1993, 1999; METI, 2002). This led to the formation of QRPA (Quick Response Promotion Association; now FISPA-Fashion Industry SCM Promotion Association) in 1994, as a joint endeavour of the Japanese T–A–R (textiles, apparel and retailing) industries to regain competitiveness of the overall domestic industry in order to effectively and efficiently serve ever-changing customers needs.

Ten years has passed since the introduction of the first QR initiative in the Japanese fashion industry. A series of programmes has been implemented in an orderly manner, from the retail–textiles and textiles–apparel, to apparel–sewing interfaces (Figure 2.3). FBA (Fashion Business Architecture) is an application of CPFR to the interface of the Japanese department stores and apparel firms. With an increasing adaptation of the industry standard platforms, such as EDI (JAIC: Japan Apparel Industry Council format), JAN (Japan article number) code, and ASN (Advanced Shipping Notice), department stores and apparel firms have achieved some of the expected QR benefits by eliminating the labour-intensive and costly processes of ticketing and inspections in a smooth flow of information. Elsewhere in the supply chain, however, there are fewer QR initiatives, apart from some positive results at a textiles–apparel (T–A) collaboration programme in men's heavy garments manufacturing, and a fibre sourcing network at the highly concentrated sector upstream of the supply chain.

Thus, QR initiatives have not necessarily worked out throughout the domestic apparel manufacturing sector. Unless the ongoing partnership programme in the mid-stream of the supply chain is accomplished, the Japanese QR in the long run is likely to be limited to retailing and apparel firms, providing that offshore sourcing locations are becoming less important. Nevertheless, Apparel–Sewing (A–S) Net, one of the current initiatives linking the apparel firms with their sewing subcontractors, is designed to be applied for sourcing in China.

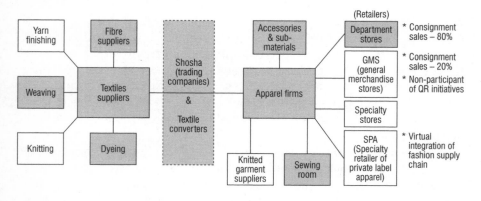

HIGHLIGHTED: (Partial) participation in the industry-wide QR initiatives

Figure 2.3 The Structure of the Japanese Fashion Industry

EFFICIENT CONSUMER RESPONSE

Efficient Consumer Response (ECR) emerged in the United States partly through the joint initiatives between Wal-Mart and Procter and Gamble and the increased competition in the traditional grocery industry in the early 1990s due to recession and competition from new retail formats. Once again, Kurt Salmon was commissioned to analyse the supply chain of a US industrial sector. Similar trends were evident to those in its earlier work in the apparel sector: excessive inventories, long uncoordinated supply chains and an estimated potential savings of US $30 billion, 10.8 per cent of sales turnover (see Table 2.3).

ECR programmes commenced in Europe in 1993, a European Executive Board was created in 1994 and a series of projects and pilot studies were commissioned. For example, the Coopers and Lybrand survey of the grocery value chain estimated potential savings of 5.7 per cent of sales turnover (Coopers and Lybrand, 1996). Since then ECR has been adopted by around 50 countries in all the continents of the world. The European ECR initiative defines ECR as a 'global movement in the grocery industry

Table 2.3   Comparison of Scope and Savings from Supply Chain Studies

Supply chain study	Scope of study	Estimated savings
Kurt Salmon Associates (1993)	US dry grocery sector	1. 10.8% of sales turnover (2.3% financial, 8.5% cost). 2. Total supply chain US $30 billion, warehouse supplier dry sector US $10 billion. 3. Supply chain cut by 41% from 104 days to 61 days.
Coca-Cola Supply Chain Collaboration (1994)	1. 127 European companies. 2. Focused on cost reduction from end of manufacturers line. 3. Small proportion of category management.	1. 2.3–3.4% percentage points of sales turnover (60% to retailers, 40% to manufacturer)
ECR Europe (1996 ongoing)	1. 15 value chain analysis studies (10 European manufacturers, 5 retailers). 2. 15 product categories. 3. 7 distribution channels.	1. 5.7% percentage points of sales turnover (4.8% operating costs, 0.9% inventory cost). 2. Total supply chain saving of US $21 billion. 3. UK savings £2 billion

Source: Fiddis, 1997

focusing on the total supply chain – suppliers, manufacturers, wholesalers and retailers, working closer together to fulfil the changing demands of the grocery consumer better, faster and at least cost' (Fiddis, 1997: 40).

Despite the apparent emphasis on the consumer, many of the early studies focused mainly on the supply side of ECR. Initially reports sought efficiencies in replenishment and the standardization of material handling equipment to eliminate unnecessary handling through the supply chain. The Coopers and Lybrand report in 1996 and subsequent re-prioritizing towards demand management, especially category management (see McGrath, 1997) have led to a more holistic view of the total supply chain being taken. Indeed, the greater cost savings attributed to the Coopers' study compared with that of Coca-Cola can be attributed to a more narrow perspective of the value chain in the Coca-Cola survey (Table 2.3).

The main focus areas addressed under ECR are Category Management, product replenishment and enabling technologies. As can been seen from Figure 2.4, these are broken down into 14 further areas where improvements can be made to enhance efficiency. After the exceptional success of ECR Europe's annual conferences in the late 1990s/early 2000s, a series of initiatives was promulgated which encouraged much greater international collaboration. ECR movements began to share best practice principles, most notably the bringing together of the different versions of the US, Europe, Latin America and Asia scorecards to form a Global Scorecard. The Scorecard was used to assess the performance of trading relationships. These relationships were measured under four categories – demand management, supply management, enablers and integrators (Figure 2.5). Comparing Figures 2.4 and 2.5 shows how ECR has developed in recent years to accommodate changes in the market environment. It is not surprising that the Global Commerce Initiative (GCI) has been the instigator of the Global Scorecard in that one of its key objectives is to advocate the promulgation of common data and communications standards, including those pertaining to global Web exchanges.

Retailers are becoming more sophisticated in their approach to demand and supply management, and there has been considerable progress in moving from a traditional organizational structure, the 'bow tie', to a multi-functional team structure (Figure 2.6) as relationships changed between retailers and their suppliers (Table 2.4). ECR conferences are replete with examples of how category performance has been improved through enhancing the consumer experience 'in store' by remerchandising traditional layouts. Such approaches are not only being adopted by major companies but also the small to medium sized retailers. Each year the Scottish Grocers Federation conference highlights the success of category planning between major snack and soft drink manufacturers

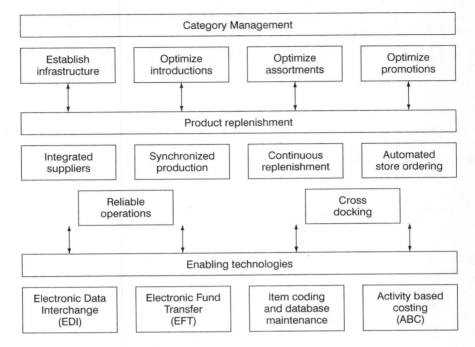

Figure 2.4 ECR Improvement Concepts

and their convenience store customers. After all, these businesses have limited store space and depend heavily on impulse purchases.

Although logisticians would prefer a consistent flow of product through the supply chain, tactical promotions remain a feature in many retailers' marketing strategies. Research by Hoch and Pomerantz (2002) on 19 food product categories in 106 supermarket chains in the United States shows that price sensitivity and promotional responsiveness are much greater with high frequency 'staple' purchases. Compared with more specialist niche products, however, where greater variety and range built store traffic, staple products benefited from range reduction – a strategy which has been adopted by multinational FMCG manufacturers.

In order to integrate this demand-side planning with continuous replenishment, collaborative planning is necessary (see Figure 2.6). The main catalyst to fostering integration has been the VICS initiative on Collaborative Planning, Forecasting and Replenishment (CPFR), previously alluded to in the Quick Response section. VICS, a non-profit organization, drew its membership primarily from US non-food retailers and their suppliers until the late 1990s when the grocery sector embraced the CPFR model. For example, Wal-Mart and Warner-Lambert are usually

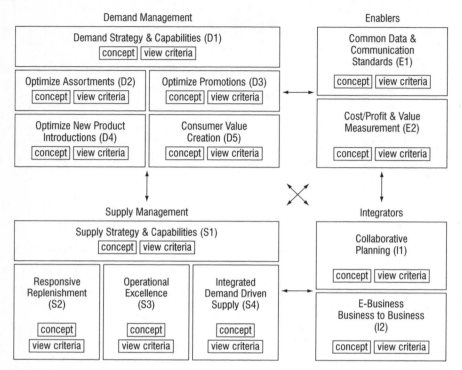

Figure 2.5   ECR Concepts

cited as key partners in sales forecast collaboration in the early to mid-1990s. The shift into grocery is hardly surprising in view of Wal-Mart's move into food through its supercentres in the United States and its overseas acquisitions of grocery businesses such as Asda in the UK.

By the late 1990s, VICS had produced a nine-step generic model bringing together elements of ECR initiatives – the development of collaborative arrangements, joint business plans, shared sales forecasts, continuous replenishment from orders generated. GCI has been the key player in globalizing this US initiative through collaboration between VICS, ECR Europe, other ECR country associations and global exchange groups. The CPFR sub-committees now have international co-chairs as the globalization of CPFR had grown to 62 members in 2002.

Although the tenets of CPFR have been established, the implementation of the model remains patchy and like ECR initiatives will tend to focus on 'quick wins' where measurable profit enhancement or cost savings can be achieved. Most pilot schemes have involved a handful of partners dealing with specific categories. Companies come from a variety of technical platforms and 'cultures' of collaboration. Indeed, the likes of

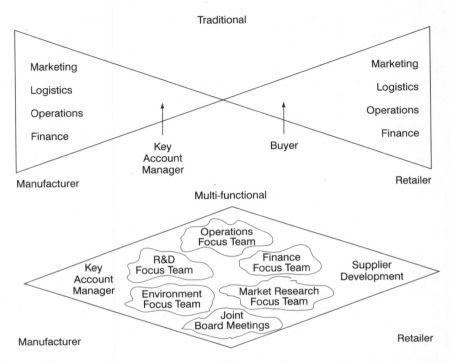

Figure 2.6 Transformation of the Interface Between Manufacturer and Retailer

Table 2.4 Changing Relationships between Manufacturers and their Suppliers

Current relationship	Target relationship
• Adversarial relationship	• Collaborative relationships
• Price	• Total Cost Management
• Many suppliers	• Few 'alliance' suppliers
• Functional silos	• Cross-functional
• Short-term buying	• Long-term buying
• High levels of Just-In-Case inventory	• Compressed cycle times and Improved demand visibility
• Expediting due to problems	• Anticipating due to continuous improvement
• Historical problems	• 'Real-time' information (EDI)
• Short shipments	• Reliability focus
• Inefficient use of capacity	• Run strategy and synchronization

Source: Coopers and Lybrand, 1996

Wal-Mart, Tesco and Sainsbury with their own intranet exchanges could actually impede more universal adoption of common standards!

Overall, however, to implement CPFR it is a prerequisite that a close working relationship has been fostered between trading partners in order to invest the necessary human resources to develop joint plans to generate real-time forecasts. In our discussion earlier on promotional activity, it was clear that demand is more volatile with price promotions, in addition to seasonal and event planning. CPFR would generate greater benefits in these heavily promoted channels where over-stocks or out-of-stocks are more evident than in high volume, staple, frequently purchased items where demand is more predictable.

THE ROLE OF LOGISTICS SERVICE PROVIDERS (LSPS)

Third-party logistics providers are 'the missing piece in the ECR puzzle' (Rozemund, quoted in Mitchell, 1997: 60). So much has been written on relationships throughout the supply chain, especially manufacturer–retailer relationships, but the actual physical process of getting the products to the stores has been largely ignored. Yet the decision on whether to outsource or not is very similar to the 'make or buy' decision in operations management. Although we will focus our attention on logistics outsourcing here, ECR draws a range of third-party activities into the equation. As companies move to become virtual organizations and concentrate upon their core competencies, relationships will be formed with IT providers, banks, advertising agencies and security companies in addition to logistics service firms.

The theoretical work on outsourcing is based on the seminal work of Williamson (1979, 1990) on transaction cost analysis, which has been further developed by Reve (1990) to a contractual theory of the firm, and applied by Cox (1996) and Aertsen (1993) to Supply Chain Management. In essence, these authors have revised Williamson's ideas on high asset specificity and 'sunk costs' to the notion of 'core competencies' within the firm. Therefore, a company with core skills in logistics would have high asset specificity and would have internal contracts within the firm. Complementary skills of medium asset specificity skills would be outsourced on an 'arms' length' contract basis.

Conceptual research tends to establish the context within which the outsourcing decision is taken. Much of this work emphasized that long-term relationships or alliances are being formed between purchasers and suppliers of logistical services (Bowerson, 1990; Gardner and Cooper,

1994; McKinnon, 2003). Empirical work on the use of logistics service providers and their relationship with purchasing companies has tended to be biased towards surveys of US manufacturing companies with regard to the provision of both domestic and international outsourcing services (Gentry, 1996; Sink, Langley and Gibson, 1996; McGinnis, Kochunny and Ackerman, 1995; Lieb and Randall, 1996). Throughout the latter half of the 1990s and the early years of the millennium, Langley, Allen and Tyndal (2002) have undertaken annual reviews of third-party logistics in the United States involving a range of industrial sectors, including the retail sector. In 2002 the geographical scope of the survey was widened to include Western Europe and Asia.

UK research has been driven largely by surveys by consultants or contractors, for example, CDC (1988) and Applied Distribution (1990), with the period surveys of PE International (1990, 1993, 1996) being the most comprehensive. Academic surveys have been limited to Fernie's exploratory work in the buying and marketing of distribution services in the retail market (Fernie, 1989, 1990) and two separate surveys on the role of dedicated distribution centres in the logistics network (Cooper and Johnston, 1990; Milburn and Murray, 1993).

These empirical surveys have shown that the contract logistics market has grown and the providers of these services have increased in status and professionalism. Logistics is no longer solely associated with trucking but also with warehousing, inventory control, systems and planning. However, the market is volatile and many of the reasons cited for contracting out such as cost, customer service and management expertise are also used to justify retention of the logistical service 'in house'. There is an impression that companies enter some form of partnership but in many cases lip service is being paid to the idea.

In a survey of British retailers by the author in the mid-1990s it was shown that outsourcing was of marginal significance to many British retailers, which have a tendency to retain logistics services 'in house' (Fernie, 1999). Indeed, retail management was much more positive about the factors for continuing to do so than for contracting out such services. Clearly retailers not only wished to maintain control over the logistics functions but felt that their staff could provide customer service at a lower cost. As with other industrial sectors, transport was the most likely logistics activity to be contracted out. Despite the growth of the third-party market in the 1980s and 1990s, at that time a degree of saturation appeared to have been reached in that few companies expected to increased their proportion of contracting out in the future.

This has been borne out by the annual retail logistics surveys by the IGD, which has indicated a levelling off in expenditure in outsourcing of transport and warehousing by supermarket chains. Nevertheless, since the Fernie (1999) survey, trends in retail logistics have changed the nature of third-party support to focus more upon the primary network rather than the traditional RDC to store business. Retailers, seeking to reduce inventory at RDCs, have incorporated primary consolidation centres in their logistics network to increase vehicle fill and increase frequency of deliveries. The notion of 'dedicated distribution' is less relevant now than when RDCs were initially rolled out in the 1980s and 1990s. Vehicles no longer return empty to RDCs after delivering to stores but either pick up loads from suppliers or return packaging waste for recycling. Finally, factory gate pricing will take these initiatives a step further through the coordination of vehicle planning to minimize vehicle movements throughout the primary and secondary network.

All of these changes will offer opportunities to LSPs, although there will be winners and losers in this new contractual environment with a rationalization of transport provision. Similar trends are evident in the clothing sector, which has come under intense price competition. In the early 2000s, the demerger of Arcadia led to outsourcing the logistics support to stores; more recently Matalan outsourced its logistics operation in 2003 and in order to save £20 million from its UK operation, Marks and Spencer continues to outsource but has rationalized its LSPs from five to two. It is currently reviewing its overseas logistics operation where savings of £100 million are expected to be achieved.

The outsourcing decision is a complex one, related to the size and historical evolution of the network. Companies with a long history of in-house logistics have 'sunk costs' within the organizations, equating with Williamson's (1990) view on asset specificity. The contract relationship will be intra-organizational, that is between the retail and logistics departments in a company. Retail businesses with large, complex networks, however, have invariably developed relationships with logistics providers as they have moved into new geographical markets or new retail sectors. This has necessitated the use of complementary skills of medium asset specificity and the development of a range of contractual relationships of an inter-organizational nature (Cox, 1996).

This research showed that the transport function was most commonly outsourced, primarily because the core competencies required are of a residual nature with low asset specificity. Contracts are generally shorter and the relationship is more 'arms' length' in nature, or what Cox (1996) classified as an adversarial leverage type of relationship.

The role of the outsourcing decision has to be seen within the context of a retailer's corporate strategy at discrete moments in a company's history. Acquisitions or demergers, expansion or withdrawal from markets can all influence logistical decisions. No two companies are the same, and invariably a third-party provider is utilized to solve a particular logistical problem pertaining to a retailer's investment strategy. This 'horses for courses' argument tends to support the work undertaken in the United States by Sink, Langley and Gibson (1996).

CONCLUSIONS

This chapter has illustrated the considerable research that has taken place into relationships through the supply chain. A background to the theoretical constructs underpinning buyer–seller relationships was given, drawing on research from the marketing and logistics literature.

The concepts of power and dependence, trust and commitment, co-operation and co-opetition were critically reviewed in the context of the retail sector. Much of the research on retailer–manufacturer relationships has focused on the concept of Quick Response and Efficient Consumer Response. The development of QR from its US origins to applications in the clothing sector in Japan was discussed to illustrate that QR has less relevance in the 'fast fashion' Japanese market. ECR, by contrast, has been embraced in numerous markets throughout the world. The harmonization of the VICS model of collaborative planning forecasting and replenishment (CPFR) with ECR Europe initiatives bodes well for future collaborative initiatives in the grocery supply chain.

Finally, the role of third-party logistics providers to instigate these strategic objectives was discussed. As the retail logistics environment changes – greater internationalization, integration of primary and secondary networks and reverse logistics – LSPs can capitalize on these marketing opportunities.

REFERENCES

Aertsen, F (1993) Contracting out the physical distribution function: a trade-off between asset specificity and performance measurement', *International Journal of Physical Distribution and Logistics Management*, **23** (1), pp 26–28

Applied Distribution (1991) *Third Party Contract Distribution*, Applied Distribution Ltd, Maidstone

Azuma, N (2001) The reality of Quick Response (QR) in the Japanese fashion sector and the strategy ahead for the domestic SME apparel manufacturers, pp 11–20 in *Logistics Research Network 2001 Conference Proceedings*, Heriot-Watt University, Edinburgh

Bowerson, P J (1990) The strategic benefits of logistics alliances, *Harvard Business Review*, **68** (4), pp 36–45

Brandenburger, A and Nalebüff, B (1996) *Co-opetition*, Doubleday, New York

Christopher, M (1997) *Marketing Logistics*, Butterworth Heinemann, Oxford

Christopher, M (1998) *Logistics and Supply Chain Management*, 2nd edn, Financial Times, London

Christopher, M and Juttner, U (2000) Achieving supply chain excellence: the role of relationship management, *International Journal of Logistics: Research and Application*, **3** (1), pp 5–23

Christopher, M and Peck, H (1998) Fashion logistics, in *Logistics and Retail Management*, ed J Fernie and L Sparks, Kogan Page, London

Christopher, M and Peck, H (2003) *Marketing Logistics*, Butterworth-Heinemann, Oxford

Competition Commission (2000) *Supermarkets: A report on the supply of groceries from multiple stores in the United Kingdom*, Competition Commission, London

Cooper, J and Johnston, M (1990) Dedicated contract distribution: an assessment of the UK market place, *International Journal of Physical Distribution and Logistics Management*, **20** (1), pp 25–31

Coopers and Lybrand (1996) *European Value Chain Analysis Study: Final report*, ECR Europe, Utrecht

Corporate Development Consultants (CDC) (1988) *The UK Market for Contract Distribution*, CDC, London

Cox, A (1996) Relationship competence and strategic procurement management: towards an entrepreneurial and contractual theory of the firm, *European Journal of Purchasing and Supply Management*, **2** (1), pp 57–70

Daparin, G P and Hogarth-Scott, S (2003) Are co-operation and trust being confused with power? An analysis of food retailing in Australia and the UK, *International Journal of Retail and Distribution Marketing*, **31** (5), pp 256–67

Daugherty, P J, Stank, T P and Rogers, D S (1996) Third-party logistics service providers: purchasers' perceptions, *International Journal of Purchasing and Materials Management*, **32** (2), pp 7–16

Fernie, J (1989) Contract distribution in multiple retailing, *International Journal of Physical Distribution and Materials Management*, **20** (1), pp 1–35

Fernie, J (1990) Third party or own account – trends in retail distribution, chapter 5 in *Retail Distribution Management*, Kogan Page, London

Fernie, J (1994) Quick response: an international perspective, *International Journal of Physical Distribution and Logistics Management*, **24** (6), pp 38–46

Fernie, J (1998) Relationships in the supply chain, in *Logistics and Retail Management*, ed J Fernie and L Sparks, Kogan Page, London

Fernie, J (1999) Outsourcing distribution in UK retailing, *Journal of Business Logistics*, **21** (2), pp 83–95

Fiddis, C (1997) *Manufacturer–Retailer Relationships in the Food and Drink Industry: Strategies and tactics in the battle for power*, FT Retail and Consumer Publishing, Pearson Professional, London

Finnie, T A (1992) Textiles and apparel in the USA: restructuring for the 1990s, Special Report no 2632, Economist Intelligence Unit, London

Forza, C and Vinelli, A (1996) An analytical scheme for the change of the apparel design process towards quick response, *International Journal of Clothing Science and Technology*, **8** (4), pp 28–43

Forza, C and Vinelli, A (1997) Quick Response in the textile-apparel industry and the support of information technologies, *Integrated Manufacturing Systems*, **8** (3), pp 125–36

Forza, C and Vinelli, A (2000) Time compression in production and distribution within the textile–apparel chain, *Integrated Manufacturing Systems*, **11** (2), pp 138–46

French, J R P and Raven, B H (1959) The basis of social power, in *Studies in Social Power*, ed P Cartwright, pp 150–67, Institute for Social Research, University of Michigan, Ann Arbor, Michigan

Gardner, J and Cooper, M (1994) Partnerships: a natural evolution in logistics, *Journal of Business Logistics*, **13** (2), pp 121–44

Gentry, J J (1996) Carrier involvement in buyer–seller supplier strategic partnerships, *International Journal of Physical Distribution and Logistics Management*, **26** (3), pp 14–25

Giunipero, L C, Fiorito, S S, Pearcy, D H and Dandeo, L (2001) The impact of vendor incentives on Quick Response, *International Review of Retail, Distribution and Consumer Research*, **11** (4), pp 359–76

Hart, S (2003) *Marketing Changes*, Thomson Learning, London

Hines, T (2001) From analogue to digital supply chain: implications for fashion marketing, in *Fashion Marketing, Contemporary Issues*, ed P Hines and M Bruce, Butterworth Heinemann, Oxford

Hoch, S J and Pomerantz, J J (2002) How effective is category management?, *ECR Journal*, **2** (1), pp 26–32

Hogarth-Scott, S and Parkinson, S T (1993) Retailer–supplier relationships in the food channel – a supplier perspective, *International Journal of Retail and Distribution Management*, **21** (8), pp 12–19

Hunter, A (1990) *Quick Response in Apparel Manufacturing: A survey of the American scene*, Textile Institute, Manchester

Ko, E, Kincade, D and Brown, J R (2000) Impact of business type upon the adoption of quick response technologies: the apparel industry experience, *International Journal of Operations and Production Management*, **20** (9), pp 1,093–111

Kumar, N (1996) The power of trust in manufacturer–retailer relationships, *Harvard Business Review*, **74** (6), pp 92–106

Kurt Salmon Associates (KSA) (1997) *Quick Response: Meeting customer needs*, KSA, Atlanta, GA

Langley, C J, Allen, G R and Tyndal, G R (2002) *Third-Party Logistics Study*, Georgia Institute of Technology, Atlanta, Georgia

Lieb, R and Randall, M (1996) A comparison of third party logistics services by large American manufacturers, 1991, 1994 and 1995, *Journal of Business Logistics*, **17** (1), pp 303–20

Lowson, B (1998) *Quick Response for Small and Medium-Sized Enterprises: A feasibility study*, Textile Institute, Manchester

Lowson, B, King, R and Hunter, A (1999) *Quick Response: Managing supply chain to meet consumer demand* , Wiley, New York

McGinnis, M A, Kochunny, C M and Ackerman, K B (1995) Third party logistics choice, *International Journal of Logistics Management*, **6** (2), pp 93–102

McGrath, M (1997) *A Guide to Category Management*, IGD, Letchmore Heath

McKinnon, A C (2003) Outsourcing the logistics function, in *Global Logistics and Distribution Planning*, ed D Waters, Kogan Page, London

METI (2002) *Seni Sangyo no Genjo to Seisaku Taiou* (*The Current Status of the Japanese Textile Industry and the Political Responses*), METI (Japanese Ministry of Economy, Trade, and Industry; formerly MITI), Tokyo

Milburn, J and Murray, W (1993) Saturation in the market for dedicated contract distribution, *Logistics Focus*, **1** (5), pp 6–9

Mitchell, A (1997) *Efficient Consumer Response: A new paradigm for the European FMCG sector*, FT Retail and Consumer Publishing, Pearson Professional, London

MITI (1993) *Seni Vision* (*Textile Vision*), MITI (Japanese Ministry of International Trades and Industries), Tokyo

MITI (1995) *Sekai Seni Sangyo Jijo* (*MITI World Textile Report*), MITI, Tokyo

MITI (1999) *Seni Vision* (*Textile Vision*), MITI, Tokyo

Ogbonna, E and Wilkinson, B (1996) Inter-organisational power relations in the UK grocery industry: contradictions and developments, *International Review of Retail, Distribution and Consumer Research*, **6** (4), pp 395–414

O'Malley, L (2003) Relationship marketing, in *Marketing Changes*, ed S Hart, pp 125–45, Thomson, London

PE International (1990) *Contract Distribution in the UK: What the customers really think*, PE International, Egham

PE International (1993) *Contracting-out or Selling out?*, PE International, Egham

PE International (1996) *The Changing Role of Third Party Logistics: Can the customer ever be satisfied?*, PE International, Egham

Piore, M J and Sabel, C F (1984) *The Second Industrial Divide: Possibilities for prosperity*, Basic Books, New York

Quick Response Services (1995) *Quick Response Services for Retailers and Manufacturers*, Quick Response Services, Richmond, CA

Reve, T (1990) The firm as a means of internal and external contracts, in *The Firm as a Nexus of Treaties*, ed M Aoki *et al*, pp 136–88, Sage, London

Riddle, E J, Bradbard, D A, Thomas, J B, and Kincade, D H (1999) The role of electronic data interchange in Quick Response, *Journal of Fashion Marketing and Management*, **3** (2), pp 133–46

Scarso, E (1997) Beyond fashion: emerging strategies in the Italian clothing industry, *Journal of Fashion Marketing and Management*, **1** (4), pp 359–71

Sink, H L, Langley, C J and Gibson, B J (1996) Buyer observations of the US third-party logistics market, *International Journal of Physical Distribution and Logistics Management*, **26** (3), pp 38–46

Taplin, I M and Ordovensky, J F (1995) Changes in buyer–supplier relationships and labor market structure: evidence from the United States, *Journal of Clothing Technology and Management*, **12**, pp 1–18

VICS (1998) *Collaborative Planning, Forecasting, and Replenishment Voluntary Guidelines*, VICS (Voluntary Interindustry Commerce Standards Association), Lawrenceville, NJ

Waters, D (ed) (2003) *Global Logistics and Distribution Planning*, Kogan Page, London

Williamson, O E (1979) Transaction-cost economics: the governance of contractual relations, *Journal of Law and Economics*, **22**, pp 232–61

Williamson, O E (1990) The firm as a nexus of treaties: an introduction, in *The Firm as a Nexus of Treaties*, ed M Aoki *et al*, Sage, London

3

The internationalization of the retail supply chain

John Fernie

The internationalization of retailing has attracted considerable academic attention in recent years. Although the retail industry is generally considered to be more 'culturally grounded' and therefore its foreign to total assets is lower than in manufacturing sectors, the last decade has witnessed a major restructuring of the retail marketplace. The meteoric rise of Wal-Mart to become the largest corporation in the world, with sales of around US $250 billion in 2003, has reshaped global competition in the food and general merchandise sectors. As Wal-Mart competes in Asia, Latin America and Europe with other mega groups (Wrigley, 2002; Fernie and Arnold, 2002), some retailers have scaled down or divested their international operations in order to compete more effectively in their domestic markets (Burt *et al*, 2002; Alexander and Quinn, 2002).

Despite all of the hype about international retailing, little has been written about the supply chain implications of the internationalization process. Sparks (1995) acknowledges that there are three main threads to understanding retail internationalization:

- international sourcing;
- international retail operations;
- internationalization of management ideas.

Of these, most researchers have concentrated upon retail operations, but by that they mean store, not logistics operations. Nevertheless, with the internationalization of key logistics concepts such as Quick Response (QR) and Efficient Consumer Response (ECR), it quickly became apparent that countries were at very different stages of the adoption process of these concepts. Distribution cultures vary within and between countries; hence companies seeking to expand into new markets need to be cognisant of the macro-environmental factors they will face in these markets. This chapter seeks to explore how retail logistics has evolved in different market environments, and how companies are transferring world-class logistics practices from market to market. Prior to discussing these issues, however, it is appropriate to comment upon international sourcing.

INTERNATIONAL SOURCING

Although the current debate on global strategies of retailers takes the form of entry to new geographical markets, most retailers are already familiar with the internationalization process through their sourcing policies. In much the same way as manufacturers have sought offshore production to reduce the costs of the manufactured product, retailers have looked beyond their domestic markets to source products of acceptable quality at competitive prices. It has been the apparel sector that has led in international sourcing policies, with US, Japanese and European companies targeting low-cost labour areas in the Far East, north Africa, eastern Europe and Latin America for finished and semi-finished product. The lengthening of the supply chain clearly has given logistics managers of these companies a set of challenges in terms of the cost trade-offs with regard to better buying terms but increased distribution costs. The US company, The Limited, revolutionized the fashion retail market in the United States through its global procurement strategy which is under-pinned by state of the art technology from computer-aided design to Electronic Data Interchange (EDI) links with suppliers. Those suppliers in south-east Asia have their goods consolidated in Hong Kong, from where chartered jumbo jets fly direct to their Columbus, Ohio distribution centre for onward distribution to their stores. This enabled the company to turn its inventory twice as quickly as the average for a US speciality store.

It was shown in the previous chapter that Quick Response (QR) initiatives were initially introduced to give domestic suppliers an opportunity to compete with low-cost offshore suppliers. The enormous labour cost advantages that many of these countries have over their 'developed' counterparts, however, have meant that offshore QR has been implemented, for example fashion retailers in Japan sourcing from the Dongdaemun Market in Seoul, Korea (Azuma, 2002).

In the UK the problem of making buying decisions too far in advance from Far East suppliers has been partially solved by using a combination of manufacturers from different sourcing locations. Thus basic lines from the Far East can be ordered three months in advance, seasonal lines are augmented by eastern European and north African suppliers in three weeks, and shorter runs of remakes are manufactured by British companies (Birtwhistle, Siddiqui and Fiorito, 2003).

It is not only the textile markets that have witnessed an increased globalization of sourcing: similar trends are evident in the grocery sector. As consumers acquire more cosmopolitan tastes and grocery retailers have developed their product ranges over the last 10 to 15 years, it is inevitable that many products cannot be sourced from the domestic market. Nonetheless grocery retailers in the UK invariably source some products from other parts of the EU outside the UK, not because of geographical or climatic reasons but because of the ability of non-UK suppliers to provide products in the volume, quality, variety and price to meet the demands of buyers.

The internationalization of sourcing has been facilitated by the liberalization of markets in the EU in the 1990s. This has been replicated in North America with the North American Free Trade Agreement (NAFTA) and the overall policies of the UN's World Trade Organization for liberalizing trade on a global scale. In the EU, for example, a natural consequence of the harmonization of markets in Europe has been for more manufacturing companies to treat the EU as one, rather than a host of individual national markets. Thus the removal of trade barriers, the deregulation of transport, especially road transport, and the acceptance of uniform standards in information systems, have all promoted the re-engineering of manufacturers' supply chains.

With the advent of factory gate pricing (FGP) by UK major grocery retailers, it is likely that the costs of product and transportation will be driven down as retailers exert more control further back down the supply chain. This is not to say that FGP is not being applied in the non-food sector. It is only that the non-food supply chain is longer and more complex than in the food sector. Thus both sectors are moving to the point of origin and therefore sourcing 'ex-works'. In non-food, however, 80 per cent of product is sourced from a non-UK supplier base, 90 per cent is moved by sea and therefore product lead times are longer, with a larger margin of error in matching demand with supply than in the more 'local' food market (Jones, 2003).

In essence, the principles of logistics are the same. In food we have moved from direct deliveries from UK manufacturers' factories to stores to FGP and the efficient transportation of product from factory through consolidation centre or retail distribution centre (RDC) to store. In non-food, the change has been from delivery directly paid to FOB, where the vendor was still responsible for shipping from country of origin, to ex-works where the retailer controls the whole supply chain.

This approach is exemplified by Toys'R'Us's relationship with Exel, the logistics service provider. Since 1996 Exel has been developing an end-to-end value-based solution to Toys'R'Us sourcing and logistics in China. Exel deals with 800 suppliers across south China, collecting goods and consolidating them at its Yantian distribution facility. Labelling and packing is carried out there prior to maximizing container fill for onward distribution to customers' distribution centres (DCs) (Jones, 2003). Complementing this physical flow is product visibility through the use of Log Net, which allows the transmission of orders and a tracking facility to monitor shipments throughout the supply chain cycle.

While it is accepted that a degree of internationalization is inevitable as trade barriers are removed, the international development of a retailer's store network poses another set of problems pertaining to sourcing decisions. In the same way as Japanese automobile companies have reconfigured their supply chain by creating a new network of suppliers in Europe and North America, retailers going global have to decide whether to source from traditional suppliers or seek new suppliers. Much will depend on the nature of the entry strategy. If entry is through organic growth, it may be possible to supply from the existing network; if a joint venture or an acquisition occurs, the retailer has to decide whether to retain or change the supply base that it inherited. If we take the case of J Sainsbury, nearer home it entered the Northern Ireland market with an organic growth strategy, reassuring representatives of the Province that it will generate considerable business for Northern Irish suppliers. In the United States, its gradual takeover of the Shaws and Giant chains has led to a radical transformation of its supplier base (Wrigley, 1997a, 1997 b).

In a similar way, Tesco's acquisition of ABF in Ireland led to a transformation of a distribution culture which was akin to the situation in Britain in the mid-1980s. Hence, it can be argued that foreign competition or even the threat of competition has produced changes in supply chain practices. Indeed, the advent of ECR and Quick Response can be attributed to traditional players in the US apparel and grocery sectors facing competition from new formats. Most of the success stories pertaining to the internationalization of the retail supply chain tend to relate to companies that have exerted strong control over their supply chain activities. This means the development of strong relationships with suppliers, the implementation of integrated technology systems and the willingness to be flexible in a changing market place. Zara, the Spanish fashion retailer, is renowned for its quick response to street fashion. With over 1,000 designers and a cost-effective production process it can take new products to stores within two to three weeks. This high product churn, 'live fashion' is fuelled by an integrated supply chain operated from its production hub at La Coruna and its networks of SMEs in Galicia and Northern Portugal.

It is also no coincidence that some companies such as Benetton have narrow product assortments. It should be noted that The Limited, although it is not an international firm in terms of store development, derived its name from its narrow range of high fashion sportswear. This streamlines and simplifies the logistical network. The success of Benetton can be attributed to all the factors listed above. The company has always been at the forefront of technological efficiency, from garment design, production and automated warehouses to the invoicing and transmission of orders by EDI. 'Benetton's long-term investment in logistics efficiency has been repaid with the fastest cycle times in the industry, no excess work in progress, little residual stock to be liquidated at the end of the season, and near perfect customer service' (Christopher, 1997: 127–28).

More recently Benetton is beginning to transform its business by retaining its network structure but changing the nature of the network. Unlike most of its competitors, it is increasing vertical integration within the business (Camuffo, Romano and Vinelli, 2001). As volumes have increased, Benetton set up a production pole at Castrette near its head-quarters. This large complex is responsible for producing around 120 million items per year. To take advantage of lower labour costs, Benetton has located foreign production poles, based on the Castrette model, in Spain, Portugal, Hungary, Croatia, Tunisia, Korea, Egypt and India. These foreign production centres focus on one type of product utilizing the skills of the region, so T-shirts are made in Spain, jackets in Eastern Europe.

In order to reduce time throughout the supply chain, Benetton has increased upstream vertical integration by consolidating its textile and thread supplies so that 85 per cent is controlled by the company. This means that Benetton can speed up the flow of materials from raw material suppliers through its production poles to ultimate distribution from Italy to its global retail network.

The retail network and the product on offer have also experienced changes. Benetton had offered a standard range in most markets but allowed for 20 per cent of its range to be customized for country markets. Now, to communicate a single global image, Benetton is only allowing 5–10 per cent of differentiation in each collection. Furthermore, it has streamlined its brand range to focus on the United Colors of Benetton and Sisley brands.

The company is also changing its store network to enable it to compete more effectively with its international competitors. It is enlarging its existing stores, where possible, to accommodate its full range of these key brands. Where this is not possible, it will focus on a specific segment or product. Finally, it is opening more than 100 megastores worldwide to sell the full range, focusing on garments with a high styling content. These stores are owned and managed solely by Benetton to ensure that the company can maintain control downstream and be able to respond quickly to market changes.

By contrast another vertically integrated company with a strong international brand name, Laura Ashley, has shown how a disastrous logistics operation can lead to the near demise of a company. In the early 1990s, the company began to incur losses, primarily because it could not deliver to its stores in time to meet a season's collection. It developed a series of uncoordinated management information systems which meant that orders invariably were not met despite its five major warehouses with over 55,000 lines of inventory (of which 15,000 were current stock). In addition, relationships with clothing suppliers, freight forwarders and transport companies were piecemeal and transactional in nature (Peck and Christopher, 1994).

In 1992 Laura Ashley contracted out its entire logistics operation to Federal Express with a view to upgrading its systems and utilizing Federal Express's global network to minimize stock levels. Although Laura Ashley's logistics performance improved markedly in the following years, it terminated the contract in 1996, less than halfway through the 10-year deal. Laura Ashley's continuing poor financial results in the late 1990s are perhaps a reflection on its having lost customer confidence in the 1990s. While logistics can give companies competitive advantage, in this case non-availability of product in stores and catalogues lost Laura Ashley goodwill and market share in what was becoming an increasingly competitive clothing market.

DIFFERENCES IN DISTRIBUTION CULTURE IN INTERNATIONAL MARKETS

It was shown in the last chapter how ECR principles have been adopted at different stages by different companies in international markets; also, in the previous section it was noted that new entrants to a market can change the distribution culture of that market. Differences in such markets are more likely to exist in the context of fast-moving consumer goods, especially groceries, because of the greater variations in tastes that occurs in not only national but regional markets. The catalyst for much of the interest in these international comparisons was the revealing statistic from the Kurt Salmon report in 1993 that it took 104 days for dry grocery products to pass through the US supply chain from the suppliers' picking line to the checkout. With the advent of ECR, it was hoped to reduce this time to 61 days, a figure that was still behind the lead times encountered in Europe, especially in the UK where inventory in the supply chain averages around 25 days (see the GEA, 1994 report for further details).

Mitchell (1997: 14) explains the differences between the United States and Europe in terms of trading conditions. For example, he states that:

- The US grocery retail trade is fragmented, not concentrated as in parts of Europe.
- US private label development is primitive compared with many European countries.
- The balance of power in the manufacturer–retailer relationship is very different in the United States compared with Europe.
- The trade structure is different in that wholesalers play a more important role in the United States.
- Trade practices such as forward buying are more deeply rooted in the United States than Europe.
- Trade promotional deals and the use of coupons in consumer promotions are unique to the United States.
- Legislation, especially anti-trust legislation, can inhibit supply chain collaboration.

Fernie (1994, 1995) cites the following factors to explain these variations in supply chain networks:

- the extent of retail power;
- the penetration of store brands in the market;
- the degree of supply chain control;
- types of trading format;
- geographical spread of stores;
- relative logistics costs;
- level of IT development;
- relative sophistication of the distribution industry.

These eight factors can be classified into those of a relationship nature (the first three) and operational factors. Clearly there has been a significant shift in the balance of power between manufacturer and retailer during the last 20 to 30 years as retailers increasingly take over responsibility for aspects of the value-added chain, namely product development, branding, packaging and marketing. As merger activity continues in Europe, retailers have grown in economic power to dominate their international branded manufacturer suppliers. While there are different levels of retail concentration at the country level, the trend is for increased concentration even in the southern European nations, which are experiencing an influx of French, German and Dutch retailers.

By contrast, Ohbora, Parsons and Riesenbeck (1992) maintain that this power struggle is more evenly poised in the United States, where the grocery market is more regional in character, enabling manufacturers to wield their power in the marketplace. This, however, is changing as Wal-Mart develops its supercenters and acted as a catalyst for the 'consolidation wave' throughout the 1990s and early 21st century (Wrigley, 2001). Nevertheless, the immense size of the United States has meant that there has never been a true national grocery retailer.

Commensurate with the growth of these powerful retailers has been the development of distributor labels. This is particularly relevant in Britain, where supermarket chains have followed the Marks and Spencer strategy of strong value-added brands that can compete with manufacturers' brands. British retailers dominate the list of top 25 own-label retailers in Europe. In the United States, own-label products did account for 15 per cent of sales in US supermarkets in the 1990s (Fiddis, 1997). This will change, however, with the drive by Wal-Mart to link its supercenter format and own-label strategy, in addition to the expansion by European retailers such as Ahold and J Sainsbury which have high own-label penetration in their domestic markets.

The net result of this shift to retail power and own-label development is that manufacturers have been either abdicating or losing their responsibility for controlling the supply chain. In the UK the transition from a supplier-driven system to one of retail control is complete compared with some parts of Europe and the United States.

Of the operational factors identified by Fernie (1994), the nature of trading format has been a key driver in shaping the type of logistics support to stores. For example, in the UK the predominant trading format has been the superstore in both food and specialist household products and appliances. This has led to the development of large regional distribution centres (RDCs) for the centralization of stock from suppliers. In the grocery sector, supermarket operations have introduced composite warehousing and trucking, whereby products of various temperature ranges can be stored in one warehouse and transported in one vehicle. This has been possible because of the scale of the logistics operation, namely large RDCs supplying large superstores. Further upstream primary consolidation centres have been created to minimize inventory held between factory and store. The implementation of factory gate pricing further reinforces the trend to retail supply chain control.

The size and spread of stores will therefore determine the form of logistical support to retail outlets. Geography also is an important consideration in terms of the physical distances products have to be moved in countries such as the UK, the Netherlands and Belgium compared with the United States and to a lesser extent, France and

Spain. Centralization of distribution into RDCs was more appropriate to urbanized environments where stores could be replenished regularly. By contrast, in France and Spain some hypermarket operators have few widely dispersed stores, often making it more cost-effective to hold stock in store rather than at an RDC.

The question of a trade-off of costs within the logistics mix is therefore appropriate at a country level. Labour costs permeate most aspects of the logistics mix – transport, warehousing, inventory and administration costs. Not surprisingly dependence on automation and mechanization increases as labour costs rise (the Scandinavian countries have been in the vanguard of innovation here because of high labour costs). Similarly, it can be argued that UK retailers, especially grocery retailers, have been innovators in ECR principles because of high inventory costs, the result of high interest rates in the 1970s and 1980s. This also is true of land and property costs. In Japan, the United Kingdom and the Benelux countries the high cost of retail property acts as an incentive to maximize sales space and minimize the carrying of stock in store. In France and the United States the relatively lower land costs lead to the development of rudimentary warehousing to house forward buy and promotional stock.

In order to achieve cost savings throughout the retail supply chain, it will be necessary for collaboration between parties to implement the ECR principles discussed in the previous chapter. The 'enabling technologies' identified by Coopers and Lybrand (1996) are available, but their implementation is patchy both within and between organizations. For example, McLaughlin, Perosio and Park (1997) in their study of US retail logistics comment that 40 per cent of order fulfilment problems are a result of miscommunications between retail buyers and their own distribution centre personnel. In Europe, Walker (1994) showed that EDI usage was much greater in the UK than other European countries, notably Italy where the cost of telecommunications, a lack of management commitment and an insufficient critical mass of participants left the Italians at the beginning of the adoption curve. Since then ECR initiatives on both sides of the Atlantic have led to greater use of enabling technologies, including Web-based technologies, to enhance collaboration between supply chain partners.

As mentioned in the previous chapter, one area of collaboration that is often overlooked is that between retailer and professional logistics contractors. The provision of third-party services to retailers varies markedly by country according to the regulatory environment, the competitiveness of the sector and other distribution cultural factors. For example, in the UK the deregulation of transport markets occurred in 1968, and many of the companies that provide dedicated distribution of RDCs today were the same companies that acted on behalf of suppliers when they controlled the supply chain 20 years ago. Retailers contracted out because of the opportunity cost of opening stores rather than RDCs, the cost was 'off balance sheet' and there was a cluster of well established professional companies available to offer the service. The situation is different in other geographical markets. In the United States, in particular, third-party logistics is much less developed and warehousing is primarily run by the retailer, while transportation is invariably contracted out to local haulers. Deregulation of transport markets happened relatively late in the United States, leading to more competitive pricing. Similarly the progressive deregulation of EU markets is breaking down some nationally protected markets. Nevertheless, most European retailers, like their US counterparts, tend only to contract out the transport function. Compared with the UK, the economics of outsourcing is less attractive. Indeed, in some markets a strong balance sheet and the investment in distribution assets is viewed more positively than in the UK.

THE INTERNATIONALIZATION OF LOGISTICS PRACTICES

The transfer of 'know how', originally proposed by Kacker (1988) in reference to trading formats and concepts, can be applied to logistics practices. Indeed, we have shown already that Tesco and Sainsbury's acquisition strategy has led to a transformation of the logistics culture in their host markets. Alternatively, companies can pursue an organic growth strategy by building up a retail presence in target markets before rolling out an RDC support function. For example, Marks and Spencer's European retail strategy initially was supported from distribution centres in southern Britain. As French and Spanish markets were developed, warehouses were built to support the stores in Paris and Madrid. Another dimension to the internationalization of retail logistics is the internationalization of logistics service providers, many of which were commissioned to operate sites on the basis of their relationship with retailers in the UK. In the Marks and Spencer example, Exel was the contractor operating the DCs in France and Spain.

The expansion of the retail giants with their 'big box' formats into new geographical markets is leading to internationalization of logistics practice. The approach to knowledge transfer is largely dependent on the different models of globalized retail operations utilized by these mega groups. Wrigley (2002) classified these retailers into two groups, one following the 'aggressively industrial' model, the other the 'intelligently federal' model (Table 3.1).

Table 3.1 Alternative Corporate Models of Globalized Retail Operation

'Aggressively industrial'	versus	'Intelligently federal'
Low format adaptation		Multiple/flexible formats
Lack of partnerships/alliances in emerging markets		Parnerships/alliances in emerging markets
Focus on economies of scale in purchasing, marketing, logistics		Focus on back-end integration, accessing economies of skills as much as scale, and best practice knowledge transfer
Centralized bureaucracy, export of key management and corporate culture from core		Absorb, utilize/transfer, best local management acquired
The global 'category killer' model		The umbrella organization/ corporate parent model

Source: Wrigley, 2002

In the former model, to which Wal-Mart and to a lesser extent Tesco can be classified, the focus is on economies of scale in purchasing and strong implementation of the corporate culture and management practices. Hence Tesco's implementation of centralized distribution in Ireland, the incorporation of a chilled 'composite' facility and the use of best practice ECR principles developed in the UK to Ireland. Wal-Mart, however, is the best example of the aggressively industrial model. In Europe, for example, it has integrated buying across the acquired chains in Germany and the UK. In Germany, supply chain systems were upgraded in stores and two new depots were developed as the logistics network was transformed from a direct store to a centralized distribution model. Tibbett and Britten, the UK logistics service provider, was entrusted with the task of improving efficiency in distribution operations, having previously worked with Wal-Mart in the aftermath of its Woolco acquisition in Canada.

In the UK, Wal-Mart's impact on Asda's logistics has been mainly in enhancing IT infrastructure and reconfiguring its distribution network to supply the increase in non-food lines. By 2005, 20 supercentres will have been opened with 50 per cent of their space devoted to non-food (general merchandise, clothing, electricals, and so on). Furthermore, existing stores will release more space for such lines with the release of space because of enhanced IT systems. Wal-Mart has revolutionized Asda's EPOS and stock data systems in Project Breakthrough which commenced in 2000 and was rolled out to stores, depots and finally Asda House by late 2002.

The incorporation of Wal-Mart's Retail Link system has allowed greater coordination of information from till to supplier, reducing costs and enhancing product availability (IGD, 2003).

Ahold, by contrast, adheres to the intelligently federal model. It has transformed logistics practices through its relationships in retail alliances (see below) and through synergies developed with its web of subsidiaries. In the United States, for example, it has retained the local store names post-acquisition and adopted best practice across subsidiaries. Furthermore, it shares distribution facilities for its own label and non-grocery lines.

Another method of transferring know-how is through retail alliances. Throughout Europe, a large number of alliances exist, most of which are buying groups (Robinson and Clarke-Hill, 1995). However, some of these alliances have been promoting a cross-fertilization of logistics ideas and practices. In the case of the European Retail Alliance, Safeway in the UK has partnered with Ahold of the Netherlands and Casino in France. In 1994 a 'composite' distribution centre was an UK phenomenon; now, composites have been developed by Safeway's European partners. These logistics practices have not only been applied in France and the Netherlands but in the parent companies' subsidiaries in the United States, Portugal and Czechoslovakia. John Harvey, Chairman of Tibbett and Britten, comments that 'in the space of three years they caught up seven' (1997: 6).

Not surprisingly, the exploitation of UK retail logistics expertise has enabled distribution contractors to penetrate foreign retail markets, not only in support of British retail companies' entry strategies but also for other international retailers. In 1997 Harvey argued that the success of his company and other UK logistics specialists could be derived from the success of the FMCG sector but like UK retailers, the success for the future lies with global opportunities. By the early 2000s he could report that over one-third of Tibbett and Britten's sales were in North America, where major structural changes were taking place in the grocery market.

REFERENCES

Alexander, N and Quinn, B (2002) International retail divestment, *International Journal of Retail and Distribution Management*, **30** (2), pp 112–25

Azuma, N (2002) Pronto moda Tokyo-style – emergence of collection-free street fashion in Tokyo and the Seoul-Tokyo fashion connection, *International Journal of Retailing and Distribution Management*, **30** (2), pp 137–44

Birtwhistle, G, Siddiqui N and Fiorito, S S (2003) Quick response: perceptions of UK fashion retailers, *International Journal of Retail and Distribution Management*, **31** (2), pp 118–28

Burt, S, Mellahi, K, Jackson, T P and Sparks, L (2002) Retail internationalisation and retail failure: issues from the case of Marks & Spencer, *International Review of Retail, Distribution and Consumer Research*, **12** (2), pp 191–219

Camuffo, A, Romano, P and Vinelli, A (2001) Back to the future: Benetton transforms its global network, *MIT Sloan Management Review*, **43** (1), Fall, pp 46–52

Christopher, M (1997) *Marketing Logistics*, Butterworth-Heinemann, Oxford

Coopers and Lybrand (1996) *European Value Chain Analysis Study: Final report*, ECR Europe, Utrecht

Fernie, J (1994) Quick Response: an international perspective, *International Journal of Physical Distribution and Logistics Management*, **24** (6), pp 38–46

Fernie, J (1995) International comparisons of supply chain management in grocery retailing, *Service Industries Journal*, **15** (4), pp 134–47

Fernie, J and Arnold, S J (2002) Wal-Mart in Europe: prospects for Germany, the UK and France, *International Journal of Retail and Distribution Management*, **30** (2), pp 93–102

Fiddis, C (1997) *Manufacturer–Retailer Relationships in the Food and Drink Industry: Strategies and tactics in the battle for power*; FT Retail and Consumer Publishing, Pearson Professional, London

GEA Consultia (1994) *Supplier–Retailer Collaboration in Supply Chain Management*, Coca-Cola Retailing Research Group Europe, London

Harvey, J (1997) International contract logistics, *Logistics Focus*, April, pp 2–6

Institute of Grocery Distribution (IGD) (2003) *Account Watch Asda*, IGD, Letchmore Heath

Jones, M (2003) An international perspective, paper presented at the IGD Conference, Factory Gate, Open Book and Beyond, London

Kacker, M (1988) International flows of retail know-how: bridging the technology gap in distribution, *Journal of Retailing*, **64** (1), pp 41–67

McLaughlin, E W, Perosio, D J and Park, J L (1997) *Retail Logistics and Merchandising: Requirements in the year 2000*, Cornell University, Ithaca, NY

Mitchell, A (1997) *Efficient Consumer Response: A new paradigm for the European FMCG sector*, FT Retail and Consumer Publishing, Pearson Professional, London

Ohbora, T, Parsons, A and Riesenbeck, H (1992) Alternative routes to global marketing, *McKinsey Quarterly*, 3, p 52–74

Peck, H and Christopher, M (1994) Laura Ashley: the logistics challenge, in *Cases in Retail Management*, ed P McGoldrick, pp 310–23, Pitman, London

Robinson and Clarke-Hill, C M (1995) International alliances in European retailing, in *International Retailing: Trade and Strategies*, ed P J McGoldrick and G Davies, Pitman, London

Sparks, L (1995) Reciprocal retail internationalisation: the Southend Corporation, Ito-Yokado and 7-Eleven Convenience Stores, *Service Industries Journal*, **15** (4), pp 57–96

Walker, M (1994) Supplier–retailer collaboration in European grocery distribution, paper presented at an IGD Conference on Profitable Collaboration in Supply Chain Management, London

Wrigley, N (1997a) British food retail capital in the USA – Part 1: Sainsbury and the Shaw's experience, *International Journal of Retail and Distribution Management*, **25** (1), pp 7–21

Wrigley, N (1997b) British food retail capital in the USA – Part 2: Giant prospects, *International Journal of Retail and Distribution Management*, **25** (2), pp 48–58

Wrigley, N (2001) The consolidation wave in US food retailing: a European perspective, *Agribusiness*, **17**, pp 489–513

Wrigley, N (2002) The landscape of pan-European food retail consolidation, *International Journal of Retail and Distribution Management*, **30** (2), pp 81–91

4

Market orientation and supply chain management in the fashion industry

Nobukaza J Azuma, John Fernie and Toshikazu Higashi

INTRODUCTION

The apparel industry has always been at the mercy of whims of styles and fickle customers who want the latest designs while they are still in fashion (Abernathy *et al*, 1999), along with uncontrollable parameters such as weather and economic conditions. The fashion market today is marked by ever-changing characteristics of consumers, competition and technologies. On the one hand, sophisticated consumers call for a relentless changeover of choices in products, brands, and even retail trading formats. A global spread of corporate activities in the textile and fashion industry, on the other hand, has accelerated the competition among fashion businesses at all levels. In addition to this, continuous improvement in the related technologies has created less room for a technology-driven differentiation and thus become a major barrier for a fashion firm to accomplish sustainable competitive advantage vis-à-vis its rivals (Tamura, 2003; Porter, 1985).

During the last few years, many apparel firms have forged their success by reshaping their supply chain and serving their customers in an increasingly timely manner. Quick Response (QR) within Supply Chain Management (SCM) has gained much attention as a key managerial philosophy (Fernie, 1994, 1998) to realize a firm's market-oriented strategy. In this an organization seeks to understand and anticipate customers' expressed and latent needs and develop superior solutions to these (Slater and Narver, 1999). The fashion industry is characterized by a high level of competitive intensity and market turbulence. It consists of notoriously labour-intensive multi-faceted processes with relative technological simplicity (Dickerson, 1995; Dicken, 1998). A successful implementation of a market orientation approach will, in theory, have a considerable impact upon improving a firm's business performance (Jaworski and Kohli, 1993; Kohli and Jaworski, 1990) as well as augmenting its customer value.

Despite such a logical fit between the QR/SCM concept and the market orientation approach, it is indeed a challenge for a fashion firm to achieve a sustainable competitive advantage within the limited scope of innovation that is dictated by the fashion process (in which the trend is directed long before the start of each season at various stages, such as colour, fibre, yarn, fabric, print, silhouette, styling details, and trims – Jackson, 2001). This systematic process considerably increases the competitive intensity in the marketplace, together with a short-term competitive horizon (Tamura, 1996) that is peculiar to fashion. The condition for a fashion firm to differentiate itself from competition, therefore, is to create a subtle yet a communicable value to customers in a seemingly homogenized and yet fast-moving environment. The economy of speed (Minami, 2003) can no longer be the single driver of a firm's competitive advantage, as time compression in the supply chain is increasingly becoming a de facto standard in the fashion industry.

This chapter investigates the factors that encompass fashion firms' competitive strategies in such a dynamic yet institutionally constrained homogenized system. First, this chapter reviews the theories behind the concept of market orientation, including an extended view of marketing logistics (Christopher, 1997, 1998) and Supply Chain Management. It is followed by a discussion on the role of imitation and innovation as part of the organizational learning process and hence the competitive strategy in the fashion industry. The concluding part proposes a research agenda for future studies on the basis of the conceptual framework that is presented in this study.

MARKET ORIENTATION APPROACH AND SUPPLY CHAIN MANAGEMENT: A FOCAL POINT

Competitive advantage is at the heart of a fashion firm's performance in a volatile business environment (Lewis and Hawkesley, 1990), characterized by fragmented markets with dynamic consumers, rapid technological changes and growing non-price competition (Weerawardena, 2003; Tamura, 2003). Market orientation is an approach in which a business seeks to understand and anticipate customers' expressed and latent needs, and develop superior solutions to these (Day, 1994; Kohli and Jaworski, 1990; Slater and Narver, 1995, 1999) in order to remain proactive as well as responsive to the changing nature of the marketplace.

Market orientation (Figure 4.1) is the organization-wide generation of market intelligence pertaining to current and future customer needs, dissemination of the intelligence across departments, and organization-wide coordination (Tamura, 2003; Ogawa, 2000a, 2000b) and responsiveness to it (Kohli and Jaworski, 1990) in an efficient and effectual manner. Tamura (2003), building upon a series of conceptual frameworks of market-oriented strategy (Narver and Slater, 1990; Day, 1994; Kohli and Jaworski, 1990; Deshpande, Farley and Webster, 1993; Deshpande, 1999; Jaworski and Kohli, 1993), proposes an operationalization model of market orientation.

Much of the earlier literature (Narver and Slater, 1990; Day, 1994; Kohli and Jaworski, 1990; Deshpande, 1999; Jaworski and Kohli, 1993) is centred around the market orientation approach within the scope of a single firm's internal organization mainly in the manufacturing sector. Kohli and Jaworski (1990) extrapolate the role of the supply-side and demand-side moderators and the environmental factors (such as market turbulence, competitive intensity and technological turbulence) (Jaworski and Kohli,

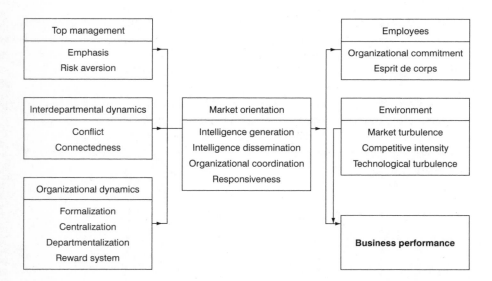

Figure 4.1 Antecedents and Consequences of Market Orientation

1993) as the external medium between a firm's market orientation and its business performance. The former stands for the nature of the competition among suppliers and the technology employed within a firm's value-adding behavioural system, and the latter represents the characteristics of demands in the industry, such as customer preferences and value consciousness.

While such references to the roles of external factors imply the potential benefit of incorporating marketing logistics (Christopher, 1997, 1998; Christopher and Peck, 1998; Christopher and Juttner, 2000) into the market orientation approach, it is Elg (2003) who explicitly emphasizes the impacts of market orientation at an inter- as well as an intra-organizational level by defining it as a joint process by retailers, suppliers, and other supply chain members (Figure 4.2). This proposition is inspired by Siguaw, Simpson and Baker's (1998, 1999) studies on the influence of a firm's market orientation programme over other supply chain players in the network. Looking at the boundary between retailers and suppliers, Elg (2003) demonstrates the latent benefit that lies in this integrated market orientation approach.

Dissemination and exchange of data about consumers among the members in a retail system (retailer's supply chain) is likely to encourage each player in the network to better understand and anticipate customer needs and expectations. This also contributes to minimizing the 'bullwhip effect' by synchronizing the flow of information and inventories in the supply chain. Joint investment in sharing a common platform in delivering quick and effective market responses facilitates the supply chain players with opportunities to develop an interdependent (De Toni and

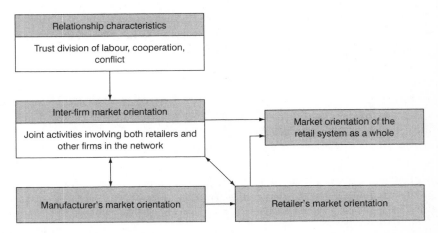

Figure 4.2 A Framework for Analysing a Retailer's Market Orientation

Nassimbeni, 1995) long-term partnership. A trust that is created through a transaction-specific investment (Yahagi, 1994; Yahagi, Ogawa and Yoshida, 1993) is recognized as a critical factor to maintain an efficient and effectual inter-organizational virtual integration (Fiorito, Guinipero and Oh, 1999) in a long-term perspective.

In addition to these official settings in supply chain relationships, Elg (2003) singles out the salience of informal occasions where representatives of different members of a distribution network may meet and exchange information (Stern,El-Ansary and Coughalan, 1996) and insights. This viewpoint shares much in common with the notion of 'shared space and atmosphere' (Ba) that is introduced by Itami (1999) in the context of the product innovation process at a Japanese automotive company. It has often been applied to explain the agglomeration effects in the industrial districts in a number of studies in Japan (Yamashita, 1993, 1998, 2001; Nukata, 1998) and in Italy (Inagaki, 2003; Okamoto, 1994; Ogawa, 1998). The concept of 'Ba' sheds light on the ambiguous effect of supply chain members' sharing of a common platform and encoding procedure towards a particular issue, upon directing the common goals and hence collaborative behaviours and a loop of organizational learning at both intra- and inter-organizational interfaces.

This last adds an important element or 'missing piece' to the classic view on Supply Chain Management, which places an emphasis on a rather IT investment-driven systematic approach (Forza and Vinelli, 1996, 1997, 2000; Hunter, 1990; Riddle *et al*, 1999) to achieve efficiency from raw materials to retail sales floors. The traditional supply chain approach focuses on an orderly shift from a transaction-based buyer–supplier relationship to a network-based (Tamura, 2001) partnership (Figure 4.3), which is often explained by a dyadic node of communications between the two parties (Christopher, 1997, 1998; Fernie, 1994, 1998; Azuma and Fernie, forthcoming). The role of 'Ba' is deemed to be a moderating factor in the supply chain in that it facilitates the involved parties with motivations to keep creating a unique value in a seemingly fixed and stabilized partnership environment, which otherwise can become a major inhibitor of continuous innovation. An intra- and inter-organizational learning loop in the supply chain not only deals with the ongoing and latent needs and expectations of the customers, but also serves as an implicit agent to monitor the competition's moves and innovatively copy (Levitt, 1969, 1983; Takeishi, 2001) their operational excellence to gain advantage in the competitive league in the volatile world of fashion.

Figure 4.4 summarizes the relationship between a firm's market-oriented strategy and the role of the supply chain in organically coordinating a series of actions in the external as well as internal processes of market orientation; first, recognition of the market environment; second,

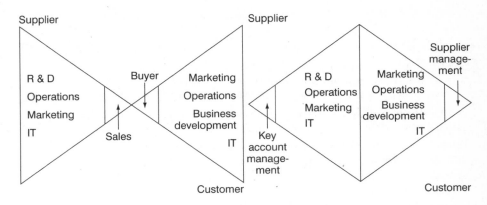

Figure 4.3 Traditional Buyer–Supplier Relationship (Left) and Partnership Buyer–Supplier Relationship (Right)

generation of intelligence on the customer's existing needs and latent/future expectations; third, intra and inter-organizational dissemination of the intelligence; and fourth, responses to satisfy the needs and feedback of the actions (Pelham, 1997; Tamura, 2001, 2003).

The objectives of Quick Response and Supply Chain Management in the fashion industry are far simpler than trade-offs between the size of IT (SCM enablers) investment and the actual impact of SCM on improving the pipeline throughput and financial performance (Fiorito *et al*, 1999; Tamura, 2001). A supply chain, as Porter (1985) describes in the value system concept, is a network of independent firms' value chains that are involved in the production and marketing of particular products and services. This network of value chains targets customer satisfaction, while the traditional value chain approach intends to increase a firm's profit margin (McGee and Johnson, 1987). Supply chain, in this sense, is a fundamental behavioural architecture in which any market-oriented firm may find itself involved, and therefore it is not a system to be configured from scratch, but an existing framework that needs refinement and restructuring in accordance with the degrees of a firm's market orientation. Particularly in the fashion industry where highly fragmented small and medium-sized enterprise (SME) contractors perform many of the supply chain phases, the organizational aspect of supply chain management should be given more credibility than the IT investment versus economies of scale justification.

To put it simply, the goals of supply chain management in the fashion industry are, therefore, in delivering the in-vogue style at the right time in the right place (Fernie, 1994), with increased variety and affordability

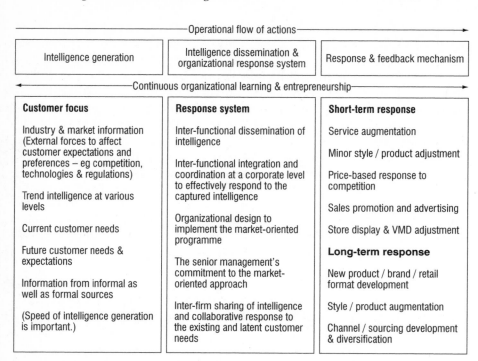

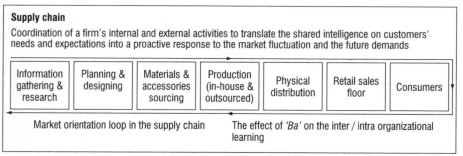

Figure 4.4 The Conceptual Model of the Market Orientation Approach in the Fashion Industry

(Giunipero *et al*, 2001; Lowson, 1998; Lowson, King and Hunter, 1999) and more room for customization (Pine, 1993), thus satisfying both the existing and potential needs of the customers (Slater and Narver, 1999). In other words QR/SCM, in theory, is a medium that induces an organization to create superior customer value, and hence achieve a competitive advantage in the volatile marketplace (Porter, 1985).

At an operational level, the concepts of QR and SCM require a firm and its supply chain partnerships to coordinate their internal and external activities (Chandra and Kumar, 2000) in order to translate their shared intelligence on customers' needs and expectations into a proactive response to the market fluctuation and the future demands. They aim at accurately forecasting the market trends and flexibly synchronizing these with the entire process in the supply chain, based upon an efficient and effective sharing of key information, and the risks and benefits that are embedded in the long and complex pipeline (Christopher, 1997, 1998; Christopher and Juttner, 2000).

Thus it would be reasonable, at least at a theoretical level, to integrate the action flow in the market orientation approach into an extended concept of marketing logistics and Supply Chain Management (Christopher, 1997, 1998; Christopher and Peck, 1998; Christopher and Juttner, 2000), since it is consistent with the intra- and inter-firm coordination mechanism of the supply chain in delivering a flexible and rapid response to the current and foreseen needs of the customer.

MARKET ORIENTATION APPROACH AND SUPPLY CHAIN MANAGEMENT: THE REALITY

Despite such a strong potential for a market orientation being rooted in the SCM philosophy, it is hardly possible for a fashion firm to establish a sustainable competitive advantage solely through its market orientation and supply chain effectiveness. This is due partly to an institutional mechanism in which the fashion trend is set farther ahead of the beginning of each season by a variety of international bodies at various levels, such as colour directions, fibre, yarn, fabric, print and finish, silhouette, styling details, and trims (Jackson, 2001; Chimura, 2001). Even the designs presented on the international catwalks mostly find their origins in design movements, exotic costumes, styles on the street, and other sources that share a continuity from the past, although futuristic as well as contemporary components are always added on to the new collection.

This systematic fashion process of planned creation and obsolescence considerably limits the scope of innovation and thus increases the competitive intensity in the fashion industry towards the state of competitive myopia (Tamura, 1996). No one creation in the history of modern fashion is as epoch-making as the cornerstone innovations in other industries, such as James Watt's and Edison's or more recently the Internet, in terms of the impacts upon the lifestyle of people. Due to its relative simplicity in related technologies and uniformity in the usage of clothes, a breakthrough innovation (Schumpeter, 1934) is unlikely to take place in the fashion industry. While production technologies and consumer preferences in the fashion industry are in a constant change and sophistication, their degree of mutation does not reach the extent that it invalidates or 'de-matures' (Abernathy, Clark and Kantrow, 1983) the existing technological and design paradigm (Kuhn, 1970; Dosi, 1982; Takeishi, 2001).

Fashion is, indeed, a unique phenomenon. It consistently transforms and fluctuates, reflecting the mood of the society. The degree of metamorphosis, however, is within a nominal but a discernable extent in the mind of the consumer. The condition for a fashion firm to differentiate from competition, therefore, is to create a subtle yet appealing difference to the customers in an apparently homogenized environment, where the economy of speed (Minami, 2003) can no longer deliver a sustainable competitive advantage. Compression in the three dimensions of time in marketing the fashion style, serving the customers and reacting to market change (Christopher and Peck, 1998; Hines, 2001) within a supply chain has been becoming a de facto standard in the fashion industry.

If one assumes an entrepreneurial risk and explores ideas to achieve a higher level of intrinsic differentiation by increasing levels of product transformation, the ideal means would be by bringing the decoupling point at the material development stage back up the supply chain (Meijbroom, 1999). It nevertheless involves a significant risk to commit too much to backward speculation (Yahagi, 2001), because a firm is then required to trade off the variety of its fashion offers with the post-ponement benefits. The order lot size is far larger in the materials than in the finished apparel products, and lead times are lengthier in the upstream sector. To narrow down the variety in materials not only deprives a firm of its organizational agility (Tamura, 1996) to effectively respond to market fluctuation but also affects its financial performances, once the trend ceases to be up for the business. The Japanese women's clothing sector, for example, calls for a considerable variety in designs and hence diversity in the choice of materials (Azuma and Fernie, forthcoming). Some of the functions delivered by textile converters, such as assortment in a smaller lot size, risk avoidance, finance, conveyance of market information, and introduction of cutting-edge materials (Tamura, 1975), are indispensable in order to execute market-oriented responses to the ever-changing fragmented needs of the consumer. Thus, there still remains a question regarding this trade-off issue in the fashion supply chain.

Besides, the relationships among the supply chain members in reality tend not to be motivated by common goals and objectives that are based upon an effective sharing of key information and an efficient flow of inventories in the entire supply chain. It is too often the case in the fashion industry that an extreme responsiveness of a firm's fashion supply chain is achieved through an unequal distribution of power. The players who command the creative shrewdness and the marketing function in the mid-to-downstream parts of the pipeline effectually impose a flexible response in the labour-intensive processes on their SME subcontractors who are mostly dependent on their orders (Azuma, 2001; Azuma and Fernie, forthcoming). An effective sharing of 'Ba', in reality, is hard to realize in a power-game relationship (Fernie, 1998; Whiteoak, 1994). Therefore, collaborative creation of a unique value 'from the source' is normally hard to achieve for a fashion firm, coupled with the speculation/postponement issue (Bucklin, 1965; Alderson, 1957) mentioned above.

Thus, the competitive environment in the fashion industry is configured in a somewhat unique way, and this makes it difficult for a fashion firm to differentiate from competition simply via implementing a market-oriented supply chain approach. An integrated programme of market orientation and Supply Chain Management certainly provides a fashion firm and its supply chain partnerships with better visibility of its market orientation activities and helps them deliver a rapid and flexible response to the actual and latent needs in the marketplace. Nevertheless, it does not allow a firm to achieve a concrete differentiation and hence a sustainable competitive advantage. Being locked up itself in a partnership with a smaller number of suppliers, based on a transaction-specific investment, a firm would gradually decrease its capability in satisfying the market needs for variety and in executing effective organizational learning in both official and unofficial settings.

It is indeed paradoxical that an inter- and intra- organizational approach to anticipate and better respond to the changing needs of the customers results in homogenizing firms' responses to the consumers within the restrained scope of innovation in the fashion industry. A rapid and flexible response is often just a prerequisite for a fashion firm to avoid being left out in the midst of harsh competition. Then, what are the real drivers of differentiation in the fashion market?

THE ROLE OF IMITATION AND INNOVATION IN THE FASHION BUSINESS

The fashion industry is an institutional system in which firms' market-oriented commitment can very often result in an apparent homogenization in the fashion retail mix beyond the boundaries of companies as well as brand labels (Azuma and Fernie, forthcoming). In addition to the restraint on the scope of innovation and the degree of product transformation, due to the systematic mechanism of shaping trends and the difficulties in bringing the decoupling point (Meijboom, 1999) up the supply chain, there is a complex set of factors that prohibits a clear-cut fashion differentiation in the marketplace.

While an increasing number of fashion firms have gained much of their time-based competitive capability (Stalk and Hout, 1990; Maximov and Gottschilich, 1993) via a flexible and responsive supply chain, their responses to market change are predominantly short-term oriented. This is partially because there exists a power-game relationship within the inter-firm network in the pipeline (Fernie, 1998; Whiteoak, 1994; Azuma, 2001; Azuma and Fernie, forthcoming). It prevents the creative effect of sharing 'Ba' among the supply chain members from being realized, and reduces the degree of intrinsic differentiation from the materials stage. Stronger members in the supply chain are more prone to gleaning a short-term benefit than pursuing a long-term competitive edge. Their contracted suppliers, on the other hand, are historically highly dependent on their order placements and so have not developed their own innovative function. A truly collaborative market-oriented supply chain in a fast-moving environment is indeed hard to organize for a shared goal and objective.

The influence of fashion media is another factor that inhibits a fashion firm's sustainable competitive advantage. These media, especially the fashion press, persistently feature the upcoming trend and styles, and simultaneously invalidate the trend in the 'near past'. Thus, what is 'in' at present can possibly become an 'out', even overnight, through the power of the media. The positioning of a fashion firm in the marketplace is, by the same token, susceptible to 'what the fashion press says' in addition to 'what the consumers expect'.

Finally, innovation spill-over (Porter, 1985; Takeishi, 2001) is a very conspicuous phenomenon in the fashion industry. Earlier studies have identified a set of inhibitors of imitation (Levin et al, 1998; Teece, 1986; Williams, 1992; Rumelt, 1984; White, 1982; Porter, 1996; Besanko, Dranove and Shanley, 2000):

- legal and regulatory protection;
- superior access to the materials, resources, and customers;
- the size of the market and the economies of scale;
- company-specific intangible capabilities;
- strategic fit.

In the fashion industry, however, most of these barriers are less effective to prevent imitators, due to the nature of the industry. First of all, tangible aspects of the fashion retail mix, such as products and retail formats, can easily be copied through observation and reverse engineering (Von Hippel, 1988), and it is almost impossible to ban the 'me-toos' and the innovative imitators (Levitt, 1969, 1983). In fact, many of the so-called innovative high street retailers, such as The Limited, Zara, and many of the Japanese players have developed their capability to adapt external fashion sources in their own style (Minami, 2003; Levitt, 1969, 1983; Burt, Dawson and Larke, 2003; Azuma, 2002; Fisher, Raman and McClelland, 1999) through their market-oriented supply chain approaches.

Even the know-how and expertise in the backyard of the retail mix is not secure from competitors' intelligence activities (Tamura, 2003). Since firms share common suppliers, interior decorators, consulting firms, sales promotion companies, third-party logistics service providers, credit card operators and IT service providers, a fashion firm's operational secrets are sometimes passed on from one party to another, thus decimating the operational competence of a company. Higher occurrences of job-hopping in the fashion industry too stimulate the leakage of such tacit knowledge from one company to another. This fluid movement of human resources in the entire industry encourages the formation of unofficial human contacts and thus, a tacit knowledge that works within the particular environment at a specific company is translated into a common knowledge among a much larger group of the players in the industry.

Figure 4.5 summarizes the nature of the competition and innovation in the fashion industry, and describes why the market-oriented approach in the fashion business tends to take on a short-term competitive horizon. Taking the institutional and operational characteristics of the fashion industry into consideration, firms' short-termism in their market orien-tation would be logical, as there exist few opportunities to leverage from the fast-mover advantage and establish a sustainable competitive advantage (Levitt, 1969; Schnaars, 1994).

Fashion firms' market-oriented supply chain behaviours are rather sustained by an organizational learning loop of their market operation. As Weerawardena (2003) explains, it is not solely the heterogeneous firm-specific resources (Rumelt, 1984; Montgomery and Wernerfelt, 1988;Barney, 1991), such as all assets, capabilities, organizational processes, firm attributes, information, and knowledge, that determine a firm's source of competitive advantages. Resources do not exclusively determine what the firm can do and how well it can do it (Grant, 1991; Weerawardena, 2003). It is a firm's capabilities to make better use of available resources (Penrose, 1955; Mahoney and Pandian, 1992; Weerawardena, 2003) that help it achieve real rents, although the corporate capability itself is counted as part of the resources.

In the context of the fashion industry, this capability-based approach fits well into the framework of firms' market-oriented supply chain activ-ities. Fashion firms are consistently faced with a situation in which their current competitive excellence is innovatively imitated or leapfrogged by their entrepreneurial competition at any point of time. While this is a natural phenomenon in the volatile world of fashion, such a competitive

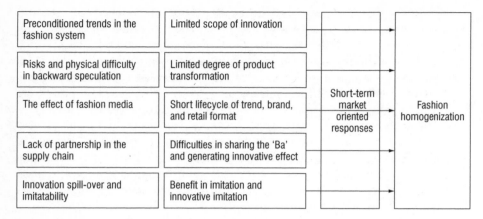

Figure 4.5   The Process of Fashion Homogenization

intensity, coupled with the institutional factors, requires fashion firms to continuously monitor each other as well as their customers' needs and then create a subtle yet a unique 'difference' that better satisfies the customers' expectations than do their rivals. This continuous loop of imitation, continuous subtle innovation, organizational learning and resultant accumulation of new resources, and a firm's capability to utilize its internal and external resources, are deemed the determinants of a fashion firm's competitive advantage in the short-term volatile competitive horizon.

This sequence of imitation and innovation among competitors is persistently taking place within the setting of their integrated market-oriented supply chain. The business that translates the unstated needs of the customer can create a subtle yet an effective difference in a seemingly homogenized market environment. In addition to this, the loop of the short-term market-oriented responses to the marketplace plays a crucial role in turning the wheel of innovation in the fashion industry, although the nature of the innovation is incremental due to the industry's specificity. Figure 4.6 depicts the organizational learning loop within a fashion firm's market-orientation approach.

CONCLUSION AND THE RESEARCH AGENDA FOR FUTURE STUDIES

This chapter has explored the unique nature of competition in the fashion industry from the viewpoint of market orientation and Supply Chain Management. An integrated approach of these two concepts is

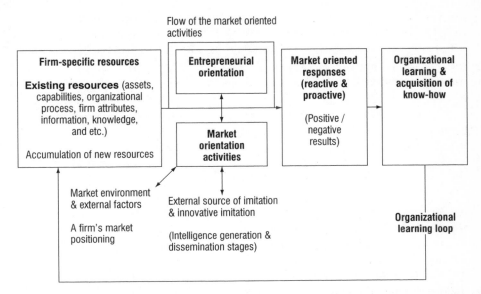

Figure 4.6 Organizational Learning Model in a Fashion Firm's Market Orientation

found, in theory, to create a great potential for a fashion firm (and its supply chain members) to enhance business performances and hence achieve a sustainable competitive advantage by effectively translating latent as well as existing customer needs and expectations into market responses.

The limited scope of innovation in the fashion industry, however, hinders an intrinsic fashion differentiation from taking place, and so fashion firms tend to build their market-oriented activities upon a short-term competitive horizon. Thus, a firm's capability to innovatively copy its competition in the process of the market-oriented supply chain is the determinant of its competitive advantage in the midst of ever-changing needs and expectations of the consumers in the marketplace. An implication is that a firm's long-term success in such an environment is thus dependent on its capability in organizationally learning from the past, present, and future of its market-oriented activities in the restrained but yet volatile environment.

While this study has focused on a theoretical discussion and identified some of the key factors in the fashion industry that affect fashion firms' market-oriented supply chain strategies, there exists a strong need to empirically analyse the nature of the competition, degree of homogenization of the fashion market, and key retail mix components for differentiation in a seemingly homogenized market place. Particularly for the degree of homogenization and key retail mix components, it will be worthwhile to compare and contrast firms' perception of their own retail mix with consumers' relative evaluation of different firms' retail mix, since a fashion firm's retail mix is a major consequence of its market-oriented supply chain activities. An intensive analysis of the gap between the two parties will reveal the conditions for achieving a competitive advantage in the fast-moving yet restricted environment in the marketplace.

REFERENCES

Abernathy, W J (1978) *The Productivity Dilemma: Roadblock to innovation in the automobile industry*, Johns Hopkins University Press, Baltimore

Abernathy, W J, Clark, K and Kantrow, A (1983) *Industrial Renaissance: Producing a competitive future for America*, Basic Books, New York

Abernathy, F H, Dunlop, J T, Hammond, J H and Weil, D (1999) *A Stitch in Time*, Oxford University Press, New York

Alderson, W (1957) *Marketing Behaviour and Executive Action*, Richard D Irwin

Azuma, N (2001) The reality of Quick Response (QR) in the Japanese fashion sector and the strategy ahead for the domestic SME apparel manufacturers, *Logistics Research Network 2001 Conference Proceedings*, pp 11–20, Heriot-Watt University, Edinburgh

Azuma, N (2002) *Pronto moda* Tokyo style: emergence of collection-free street fashion and the Tokyo–Seoul connection, *International Journal of Retail and Distribution Management*, **30** (3), pp 137–44

Azuma, N and Fernie, J (forthcoming) Changing nature of Japanese fashion: the role of Quick Response in improving supply chain efficiency, *European Journal of Marketing*, special issue on Fashion Marketing

Barney, J (1991) Firm resources and sustained competitive advantage, *Journal of Management*, **17** (1), pp 99–120

Besanko, D, Dranove, D and Shanley, M (2000) *Economics of Strategy*, 2nd edn, Wiley, New York

Bucklin, L P (1965) Postponement, speculation, and structure of distribution channels, *Journal of Marketing Research*, **2** (1)

Burt, S L, Dawson, J and Larke, R (2003) Inditex – Zara: rewriting the rules in apparel retailing, *Conference Proceedings, 2nd Asian Retail and Distribution Workshop*, UMDS Kobe, Japan

Chandra, C and Kumar, S (2000) Supply Chain Management in theory and practice: a passing fad or a fundamental change? *Industrial Management and Data Systems*, **100** (3), pp 100–13

Chimura, N (2001) *Sengo Fashion Story* (*Post War Fashion Story*), Heibonsha, Tokyo

Christopher, M (1997) *Marketing Logistics*, Butterworth Heinemann, Oxford

Christopher, M (1998) *Logistics and Supply Chain Management*, 2nd edn, Financial Times, London

Christopher, M and Juttner, U (2000) Achieving supply chain excellence: the role of relationship management, *International Journal of Logistics: Research and Application*, **3** (1), pp 5–23

Christopher, M and Peck, H (1998) Fashion logistics, in *Logistics and Retail Management*, ed J Fernie and L Sparks, Kogan Page, London

Day, G (1994) The capabilities of market-driven organizations, *Journal of Marketing*, **58**, pp 37–52

Deshpande, R (ed) (1999) *Developing a Market Orientation*, Sage, Thousand Oaks, CA

Deshpande, R, Farley, J U and Webster Jr, F E (1993) Corporate culture, customer orientation, and innovativeness in Japanese firms; a Quadrad analysis, *Journal of Marketing*, **57**, pp 23–37

De Toni, A and Nassimbeni, G (1995) Supply networks: genesis, stability and logistics implications. A comparative analysis of two districts, *International Journal of Management Science*, **23** (4), pp 403–18

Dicken, P (1998) *Global Shift: Transforming the world economy*, 3rd edn, Paul Chapman, London

Dickerson, K (1995) *Textiles and Apparel in the Global Economy*, Prentice Hall, New Jersey

Dosi, G (1982) Technological paradigms and technological trajectories: a suggested interpretation of the determinants and directions of technical change, *Research Policy*, **11** (3), pp 147–62

Elg, U (2003) Retail market orientation: a preliminary framework, *International Journal of Retail and Distribution Management*, **31** (2), pp 107–17

Fernie, J (1994) Quick Response: an international perspective, *International Journal of Physical Distribution and Logistics Management*, **24** (6), pp 38–46

Fernie, J (1998) Relationships in the supply chain, in *Logistics and Retail Management*, ed J Fernie and L Sparks, Kogan Page, London

Fiorito, S S, Giunipero, L C and Oh, J (1999) Channel relationships and Quick Response implementation, Conference Paper, 10th International Conference on Research in the Distributive Trades, Stirling University

Fisher, M L, Raman, A and McClelland, A S (1999) *Supply Chain Management at World Co. Ltd*, World Co. Ltd, Tokyo

Forza, C and Vinelli, A (1996) An analytical scheme for the change of the apparel design process towards quick response, *International Journal of Clothing Science and Technology*, **8** (4), pp 28–43

Forza, C and Vinelli, A (1997) Quick Response in the textile–apparel industry and the support of information technologies, *Integrated Manufacturing Systems*, **8** (3), pp 125–36

Forza, C and Vinelli, A (2000) Time compression in production and distribution within the textile–apparel chain, *Integrated Manufacturing Systems*, **11** (2), pp 138–46

Giunipero, L C, Fiorito, S S, Pearcy, D H and Dandeo, L (2001) The impact of vendor incentives on Quick Response, *International Review of Retail, Distribution and Consumer Research*, **11** (4), pp 359–76

Grant, R M (1991) Analysing resources and capabilities, in *Contemporary Strategic Analysis: Concepts, techniques and applications*, ed R M Grant, Blackwell, MA

Hines, T (2001) From analogue to digital supply chain: implications for fashion marketing, in *Fashion Marketing, Contemporary Issues*, ed T Hines and M Bruce, Butterworth Heinemann, Oxford

Hunter, A (1990) *Quick Response in Apparel Manufacturing: A survey of the American scene*, Textile Institute, Manchester

Inagaki, K (2003) *Italia no Kigyouka Network* (*Entrepreneurs Networking in Italy*), Hakuto-Shobo, Tokyo

Itami, H (1999) *Ba no Dynamism* (*The Dynamics of Shared Space and Atmosphere*), NTT Publishing, Tokyo

Jackson, T (2001) The process of fashion trend development leading to a season, in *Fashion Marketing*, ed T Hines and M Bruce, Butterworth Heinemann, Oxford

Jaworski, B and Kohli, A (1993) Market orientation: antecedents and consequences, *Journal of Marketing*, **57**, pp 53–70

Kohli, A and Jaworski, B (1990) Market orientation: the construct, research propositions, and managerial implications, *Journal of Marketing*, **54**, pp 1–18

Kohli, A and Jaworski, B (1999) Market orientation: the construct, research propositions, and managerial implications, in *Developing a Market Orientation*, ed R Deshpande, Sage, London

Kuhn, T (1970) *The Structure of Scientific Revolutions*, University of Chicago Press, Chicago, IL

Levin, R C, Klevorick, A K, Nelson, R R, and Winter, S G (1988) Appropriating the returns from industrial research and development, *Brooking Papers on Economic Activity*, **13** (2), pp 839–916

Levitt, T (1969) *The Marketing Mode*, McGraw-Hill, New York

Levitt, T (1983) *The Marketing Imagination*, Free Press, New York

Lewis, B R and Hawkesley, A W (1990) Gaining a competitive advantage in fashion retailing, *International Journal of Retail and Distribution Management*, **18** (4), pp 21–32

Lowson, B (1998) *Quick Response for Small and Medium-Sized Enterprises: A feasibility study*, Textile Institute, Manchester

Lowson, B, King, R and Hunter, A (1999) *Quick Response: Managing supply chain to meet consumer demand*, Wiley, New York

Mahoney, J T and Pandian, J R (1992) The resource-based view within the conversation of strategic management, *Strategic Management Journal*, **13** (5), pp 363–80

Maximov, J and Gottschlich, H (1993) Time–cost–quality leadership, *International Journal of Retail and Distribution Management*, **21** (4), pp 3–12

McGee, J and Johnson, G. (eds) (1987) *Retail Strategies in the UK*, Wiley, Chichester

Meijboom, B (1999) Production-to-order and international operations: a case study in the clothing industry, *International Journal of Operations and Production Management*, **19** (5/6), pp 602–19

Minami, C (2003) Fashion Business no Ronri – ZARA ni Miru Speed no Keizai (The logic in the fashion business – the impact of economies of speed from Zara experiences), *Ryutsu Kenkyu*, June, pp 31–42

Montgomery, C A and Wernerfelt, J M (1988) Diversification, Ricardian rents and Tobin's Q, *Rand Journal of Economics*, **19**, pp 623–32

Narver, J and Slater, S (1990) The effect of a market orientation on business profitability, *Journal of Marketing*, **54** (Oct), pp 20–35

Nukata, H (1998) Sangyo Shuseki ni Okeru Bungyo no Jyunansa (Flexible division of labour in industrial agglomerations), in *Sangyo Shuseki no Honshitsu (The Essence of the Industrial Agglomeration)*, ed H Itami, S Matushima and T Kitsukawa,Yuhikaku, Tokyo

Ogawa, H (1998) *Italia no Chusho Kigyo (SMEs in Italy)*, JETRO, Tokyo

Ogawa, S (2000a) *Innovation no Hassei Genri (The Process of Innovation)*, Chikura Shobo, Tokyo

Ogawa, S (2000b) *Demand Chain Keiei (Demand Chain Management)*, Nippon Keizai Shimbunsha, Tokyo

Okamoto, Y (1994) *Italia no Chusho Kigyo Senryaku (SMEs' Strategies in Italy)*, Mita Shuppan Kai, Tokyo

Pelham, A J (1997) Market orientation and performance: the moderating effects of product and customer differentiation, *Journal of Business and Industrial Marketing*, **12** (5), pp 276–96

Penrose, E T (1955) *The Theory of the Growth of the Firm*, Wiley and Sons Ltd, New York

Pine II, B J (1993) *Mass Customisation*, Harvard Business School Press, Boston, MA

Porter, M E (1985) *Competitive Advantage*, Free Press, New York

Porter, M E (1996) What is Strategy? *Harvard Business Review*, **74**, pp 61–78

Riddle, E J, Bradbard, D A, Thomas, J B and Kincade, D H (1999) The role of electronic data interchange in Quick Response, *Journal of Fashion Marketing and Management*, **3** (2), pp 133–46

Rumelt, R P (1984) Towards a strategic theory of the firm, in *Competitive Strategic Management*, ed R Lamb, Englewood Cliffs, Prentice Hall, NJ

Schnaars, S P (1994) *Managing Imitation Strategies*, Free Press, New York

Schumpeter, J A (1934) *The Theory of Economic Development: An inquiry into profits, capital, credit, interest, and the business cycle*, Harvard University Press, Cambridge, MA

Siguaw, J S, Simpson, P and Baker, T (1998) Effects of supplier market orientation on distributor market orientation and the channel relationship, *Journal of Marketing*, **63**, pp 99–111

Siguaw, J S, Simpson, P and Baker, T (1999) The influence of market orientation on channel relationships: a dyadic examination, in *Developing a Market Orientation*, ed R Deshpande, Sage, London

Slater, S and Narver, J (1995) Market orientation and the learning organization, *Journal of Marketing*, **59**, pp 63–74

Slater, S F and Narver, J C (1999) Research notes and communications: market-oriented is more than being customer-led, *Strategic Management Journal*, **20**, pp 1165–68

Stalk, G. Jr and Hout, T M (1990) *Competing Against Time*, Free Press, New York

Stern, L, El-Ansary, A and Coughalan, A (1996) *Marketing Channels*, 5th edn, Prentice-Hall, Englewood Cliffs, NJ

Takeishi, A (2001) Innovation no pattern (Patterns in innovation) in *Innovation Management Nyumon* (*Fundamentals of Innovation Management*), Hitotsubashi University Innovation Research Centre, Nihon Keizai Shimbunsha, Tokyo

Tamura, M (1975) *Seni Oroshiuri-Sho no Keiei Kouritsuka no Houkou – Seni Oroshiuri-Sho no Kinou Bunseki Houkoku* (*The Direction towards Textiles and Apparel Wholesalers' Efficient Management: An analysis on the function of textiles and apparel wholesale merchants*), Osaka Chartered Institute of Commerce, Osaka

Tamura, M (1996) *Marketing Ryoku* (*The Power of Marketing*), Chikura Shobo, Tokyo

Tamura, M (2001) *Ryutsu Genri* (*Principles of Marketing and Distribution*), Chikura Shobo, Tokyo

Tamura, M (2003) *Shijoushikou no Jissen Riron wo Mezashite* (*Towards an Operationalization of the Market Orientation Approach*), University of Marketing and Distribution Science Monograph, no 15

Teece, D (1986) Profiting from technological innovation: implications for integration, collaboration, licensing and public policy, *Research Policy*, **15**, pp 285–305

Von Hippel, E A (1988) *The Sources of Innovation*, Oxford University Press, New York

Weerawardena, J (2003) Exploring the role of market learning capability in competitive advantage, *European Journal of Marketing*, **37**(3/4), pp 407–29

White, L (1982) The automobile industry, in *The Structure of American Industry*, 6th edn, ed W Adams, Macmillan, New York

Whiteoak, P (1994) The realities of quick response in the grocery sector a supplier viewpoint, *International Journal of Physical Distribution and Logistics Management*, **29** (7/8), pp 508–19

Williams, J (1992) How sustainable is your advantage? *California Management Review*, **34**, pp 1–23

Yahagi, T (1994) *Convenience Store System no Kakushin-sei (Innovativeness of the Convenience Store System)*, Nihon Keizai shimbunsha, Tokyo

Yahagi, T (2001) Chain Store no Seiki ha Owattanoka (Has the chain store age ended?), *Hitotsubashi Business Review*, August, pp 30–43

Yahagi, T, Ogawa, K and Yoshida, K (1993) *Sei–Han Tougo Marketing (Supplier–Retailer Integrated Marketing Approach)*, Hakuto Shobo, Tokyo

Yamashita, Y (1993) Shijo ni Okeru Ba no Kino (The role of 'Ba' in the marketplace), *Soshiki Kagaku*, **27** (1),pp 75–87

Yamashita, Y (1998) Discounter no Seisui (The rise and fall of discount stores), in *Innovation to Gijutsu Chikuseki (Innovation and Technology Accumulation)*, ed H Itami, T Kagono, M Miyamoto and S Yonekura, Yuhikaku, Tokyo

Yamashita, Y (2001) Shogyo Shuseki no Dynamism (The dynamics of commercial accumulation), *Hitotsubashi Business Review*, August, pp 74–94

5

Fashion logistics and quick response

Martin Christopher, Bob Lowson and Helen Peck

The ability to respond to customer requirements on a timely basis has always been a fundamental element of the marketing concept. However, there has perhaps never been as much pressure as exists today to accelerate further the responsiveness of marketing systems. 'Time-based competition' has become the norm in many markets from banking to automobiles. The challenge to marketing and logistics in the current environment is to find ways in which product development times can be reduced, feedback from the marketplace made more rapid and replenishment times compressed.

Nowhere is this pressure more evident than in markets governed by fashion. Fashion is a broad term which typically encompasses any product or market where there is an element of style that is likely to be short-lived. We have defined fashion markets as exhibiting typically the following characteristics:

- **Short lifecycles.** The product is often ephemeral, designed to capture the mood of the moment; consequently, the period in which it is saleable is likely to be very short and seasonal, measured in
- **High volatility.** Demand for these products is rarely stable or linear. It may be influenced by the vagaries of weather, hit films, television shows or even by pop stars and footballers.
- **Low predictability.** Because of the volatility of demand it is extremely difficult to forecast with any accuracy even total demand during a period, let alone week-by-week or item-by-item demand.

- **High impulse purchase.** Many buying decisions for these products are made at the point of purchase. In other words, the shopper when confronted with the product is stimulated to buy it, hence the critical role of 'availability' and, in particular, availability of different sizes, colours and so on.

The combined effect of these pressures clearly provides a challenge to logistics management. Traditional ways of responding to customer demand have been forecast-based, with the resultant risk of over-stocked or under-stocked situations.

More recently there has emerged another trend that has added further complexity and difficulty to the management of fashion logistics. The growing tendency to source product and materials offshore has led in many cases to significantly longer lead times. While there is usually a substantial cost advantage to be gained, particularly in manufacturing, through sourcing in low labour cost areas, the effect on lead times can be severe. It is not only distance that causes replenishment lead times to lengthen in global sourcing. It is the delays and variability caused by internal processes at both ends of the chain as well as the import/export procedures in between. The end result is longer pipelines with more inventory in them, with the consequent risks of obsolescence that arise.

Much of the pressure for seeking low-cost manufacturing solutions has come from retailers. At the same time there have been moves by many retailers in the apparel business to reduce significantly the number of suppliers they do business with. This supply base rationalization has been driven by a number of considerations, but in particular by the need to develop more responsive replenishment systems – something that is not possible when sourcing is spread over hundreds, if not thousands, of suppliers.

MANAGING THE FASHION LOGISTICS PIPELINE

Conventional wisdom holds that the way to cope with uncertainty is to improve the quality of the forecast. Yet, by definition, the volatility of demand and the short lifecycles found in many fashion markets make it highly unlikely that forecasting methods will ever be developed that can consistently and accurately predict sales at the item level. Instead ways must be found of reducing the reliance that organizations place upon the forecast and instead of focusing on lead time reduction. Shorter lead times mean, by definition, that the forecasting horizon is shorter – hence the risk of error is lower. In the same way that the captain of a supertanker has a planning horizon that is determined by the vessel's stopping distance (many miles), so too in business the forecast period is determined by the time it takes to design, make and ship the product – lead time, in other words.

There are three critical lead times that must be managed by organizations that seek to compete successfully in fashion markets:

- **Time to market.** How long does it take the business to recognize a market opportunity and to translate this into a product or service and to bring it to the market?
- **Time to serve.** How long does it take to capture a customer's order and to deliver the product to the retail customer's satisfaction?
- **Time to react.** How long does it take to adjust the output of the business in response to volatile demand? Can the 'tap' be turned on or off quickly?

Time to Market

In these short lifecycle markets, being able to spot trends quickly and to translate them into products in the shop in the shortest possible time has become a prerequisite for success. Companies that are slow to market can suffer in two ways. First, they miss a significant sales opportunity that probably will not be repeated. Second, the supplier is likely to find that when the product finally arrives in the marketplace, demand is starting to fall away, leading to the likelihood of mark-downs. Figure 5.1 illustrates the double jeopardy confronting those organizations that are slow to market. New thinking in manufacturing strategy which has focused on flexibility and batch size reduction has clearly helped organizations in their search for quick response. The use of highly automated processes such as computer aided design (CAD) and computer aided manufacturing (CAM) has revolutionized the ability to make product changes as the season or the life cycle progresses.

Time to Serve

Traditionally in fashion industries orders from retailers have had to be placed on suppliers many months ahead of the season. Nine months was not unusual as a lead time. Clearly, in such an environment the risk of both obsolescence and stock-outs is high, and a significant inventory carrying cost is inevitably incurred somewhere in the supply chain as a result of the lengthy pipeline.

Why should the order to delivery cycle be so long? It is not the time it takes to make or ship the product. More often the problem lies in the

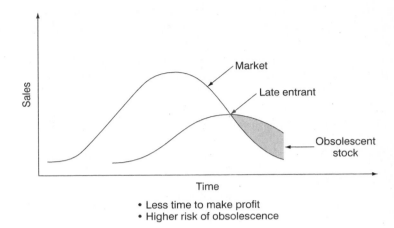

Figure 5.1 Shorter Lifecycles Making Timing Crucial

multiple steps that occur from the point at which a decision is taken to place an order, through the generation of the accompanying documentation (particularly in overseas transactions involving quota approvals, letters of credit and so forth), into the suppliers' processes – which themselves are likely to be equally lengthy. Often the total time in manufacture is considerable because of the traditional, batch-based production methods. In other words each step in the total manufacturing cycle is managed separately from the others, and the quantities processed at each step are determined by so-called economic batch quantities. Furthermore, when manufacture takes place offshore, considerable time is consumed in preparing documentation, in consolidating full container loads and in-bound customs clearance after lengthy surface transportation.

The underpinning philosophy that has led to this way of doing things is cost minimization. Primarily the costs that are minimized are the costs of manufacture, and secondly the costs of shipping. In fact, this view of cost is too narrow and ultimately self-defeating. The real issue is the total supply chain cost including the costs of obsolescence, forced mark-downs and inventory carrying costs.

Time to React

Ideally in any market, an organization wants to be able to meet any customer requirement for the products on offer at the time and place the customer needs them. Clearly, some of the major barriers to this are those highlighted in the previous paragraphs: time to market and time to serve.

However, a further problem that organizations face as they seek to become more responsive to demand is that they are typically slow to recognize changes in real demand in the final marketplace. The challenge to any business in a fashion market is to be able to see 'real' demand. Real demand is what consumers are buying or requesting hour by hour, day by day. Because most supply chains are driven by orders (that is, batched demand) which themselves are driven by forecasts and inventory replenishment, individual parties in the chain have no real visibility of the final marketplace. As Figure 5.2 suggests, inventory hides demand. In other words the fact that there are usually multiple inventories from the retail shelf back through wholesalers, to suppliers means that upstream parties in the chain are unable to anticipate the changing needs of the customers other than through a forecast based as much upon judgment and guesswork as it is upon actual consumer demand.

THE LEAD-TIME GAP

The fundamental problem that faces many companies – not just those in fashion industries – is that the time it takes to source materials, convert them into products and move them into the marketplace is invariably longer than the time the customer is prepared to wait. This difference between what might be called the 'logistics pipeline' and the customers' order cycle time is termed the 'lead-time gap'. Conventionally, this gap was filled with a forecast-based inventory – there was no other way of attempting to ensure that there would be product available as and when customers demanded it.

The problem was that often it would be the 'wrong' inventory: for example, sizes, colours or styles that were not those actually demanded. Figure 5.3 highlights the problems of the lead-time gap which in the fashion industry was traditionally measured in months rather than weeks.

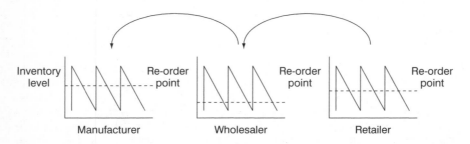

Figure 5.2   Inventory Hides Demand

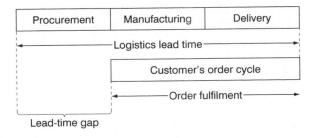

Figure 5.3 Lead Times

These lengthy supply pipelines often result in revenue losses in the final market. Table 5.1 provides an indication of the size of these losses, and of note is the cost of carrying inventory. The biggest item is forced markdowns – mainly at retail – with the total losses amounting to over 14 per cent of retail sales. A distinction is made between promotional markdowns, that is, special sales, and the marking down that occurs out of necessity when a season ends and unwanted goods must be moved to make way for new merchandise – forced markdowns.

It is against this background that the Quick Response (QR) movement originated in 1984 from a textile industry research programme in the United States. Studies at the time revealed a clothing industry pipeline in which inventories and work in progress had reached alarming levels (see Table 5.2), and it is a situation that can still be seen in many industries. More information concerning the history of QR can be found in Hunter (1990) and Gunston and Harding (1986).

Today, QR is now a recognized operations strategy (Lowson, 2002) and as such, it continues to attract considerable interest for two additional, yet closely related reasons: first, the ability of this strategy to cope with the complexity of fashion logistics; and, second, as a method to combat the relentless shift toward offshore sourcing from low-wage economies.

In all fast-moving consumer goods (FMCG) industries, demand is now more fragmented and the consumer more discerning about quality and

Table 5.1 Revenue Losses in the Apparel Pipeline (% Retail Sales)

	Fibre and Textile	Apparel	Retail	Total
Forced markdowns.	0.6%	4.0%	10.0%	14.6%
Stock-outs.	0.1	0.4	3.5	4.0
Inventory @ 15% carrying cost	1.025	2.9	6.4	
Total	**1.7%**	**6.9%**	**16.4%**	**25.0%**

Source: Lowson, King and Hunter, 1999

Table 5.2 Clothing Pipeline Inventories and Work in Progress (Weeks)

	Inventory	WIP
Fibre		
Raw material	1.6	
WIP		0.9
Finished fibre @ fibre	4.6	
Fibre @ textile	1.0	
Total	8.1	0.9
Fabric		
WIP – greige		3.9
Greige goods @ greige	1.2	
Greige goods @ finish	1.4	
Finishing		1.2
Finished fabric @ textile	7.4	
Fabric @ apparel	6.8	
Total	16.8	5.1
Apparel		
WIP		5.0
Finished apparel @ apparel	12.0	
Ship to retail	2.7	
Apparel @ retail Distribution centre	6.3	
Apparel @ store	10.0	
Total	31.0	5.0
Total	**55.0**	**11.0**

Source : Lowson, King and Hunter, 1999

choice. There is also an increasing fashion influence: no single style or fashion has dominated for any length of time. For many consumer sectors, demand is approaching the chaotic in its insatiable appetite for diverse services and goods. 'Mass customization' and individualized products with shorter season lengths; micro merchandising and markets segmented at the individual level; large numbers of products chasing a diminishing market share; are all evidence of the inexorable movement toward a sea change, and mark the folly of firms expecting to operate as they have in the past. One of the most important findings from the early studies was the ability of QR to compress time in the supply system. If the pipeline is condensed to about one-third of its traditional length, not only did the design of goods better reflect more accurate consumer information, it is possible for the retailer to reassess the demand for products while the season is under way and receive small, frequent reorders from the supplier, provided reorder lead times are short enough (of the order of 2–4 weeks) (Gunston and Harding, 1986).

The effect on sales forecast errors of compressing the supply system is shown in Figure 5.4. Here, the central horizontal axis shows the number of months ahead of the season that predictions are made, and the upper and lower curves show estimates of the forecast error. Twelve-month lead times are common in many FMCG sectors, and yet significant improvements are available if these times can be reduced.

QUICK RESPONSE STRATEGIES

Quick Response (QR) can be defined as:

> A state of responsiveness and flexibility in which an organization seeks to provide a highly diverse range of products and services to a customer/consumer in the exact quantity, variety and quality, and at the right time, place and price as dictated by real-time customer/consumer demand. QR provides the ability to make demand–information driven decisions at the last possible moment in time ensuring that diversity of offering is maximized and lead-times, expenditure, cost and inventory minimized. QR places an emphasis upon flexibility and product velocity in order to meet the changing requirements of a highly competitive, volatile and dynamic marketplace. QR encompasses an operations strategy, structure, culture and set of operational procedures aimed at integrating enterprises in a mutual network through rapid information transfer and profitable exchange of activity.

(Lowson, King and Hunter, 1999)

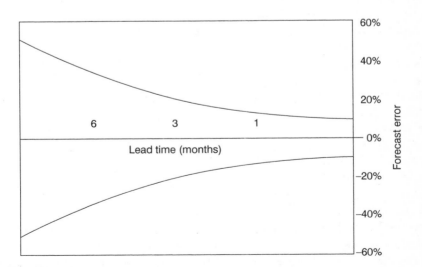

Figure 5.4 Lead Time and Forecast Error

QR has a number of strategic implications for the organization. Research has shown that mere implementation of technology or particular procedures without the strategic underpinning leads to sub-optimal performance (Lowson, 2002).

The Alignment of Organizational Activity to Demand

This is a fundamental principle of QR. All activities within an enterprise should be paced to demand and customer behaviour. Products and services are produced and delivered in the variety and volume that match demand. The activity within a company moves to the beat of this drum. Swings in demand are closely monitored: too little or too much leads to waste and inefficiency. Whether it is marketing, purchasing, new product development or operations, all endeavours follow the market tempo, and the realization that this alignment may necessitate a change in corporate culture. Consequently, it is important that senior management recognizes and understands these demand patterns. Resources need to be deployed that can undertake this vital externally focused role.

Linkages Between Demand and Supply

Given the importance of the alignment activity mentioned above, a strategic understanding of the drivers of demand and its synchronized connection with supply is imperative for QR. In the past much attention has, quite rightly, been placed upon improvements in supply. However, demand is the target – no matter how sophisticated the supply weaponry, it is ineffectual if the target is not understood. Only when the value and benefits sought by the customer/consumer are appreciated in all their complexity, can a strategy to supply them be developed. This involves detailed assessment of supply and demand processes and sub-processes by customer or consumer grouping. Together with the supply of a tangible product, there are myriad other dimensions peculiar to the customer/consumer. These include varying information content, timeframes, physical arrangement for logistics, service support, marketing campaigns, and information systems.

Demand Relationships

QR recognizes that both customers/consumers and products are dynamic and place unique demands on the organization. Identical products, jeans for example, will have unique product flows depending upon customer/consumer buying behaviour and QR needs (whether a department store, speciality store, supermarket, wholesaler, independent corner store, or whatever). Similarly, product attributes will vary by product, for example, volume and flow characteristics, demand patterns, seasonality, promotional strategy, cyclical needs, information content, credit terms and customer incentives and repeat purchase patterns. These attributes can be aligned with the QR product categories of 'basic', 'seasonal', 'fashion or short season' and 'ultra-short season'. These different customer/consumer and product behaviours will customize and tailor QR channels in line with the requirements. Once this assessment is done, it is possible to apply specific QR components or systems that can be tied into the unique supply pipeline.

Resource Configuration

Conventional strategy looks long-term for some form of advantage by configuration of activities and resources to the environment of the operation: a strategic fit between strengths and weaknesses and opportunities and threats. In the QR world, this strategic architecture is inter-organizational. Strategy and strategic thinking are at a network level, encompassing many external interconnections. In addition, within this configuration must fit the mapping of customer/consumer values and perceived benefits onto operations, in order to underpin the link between demand and activity (as above).

Time

Time as a strategic weapon is vital to QR operation, but like any weapon its effectiveness depends on the circumstances of its use. Strategies of time compression have gained much popularity of late. Unfortunately, as with many such movements, the application has been widespread but often ill considered. A time-based strategy is subtle and above all else, must be well thought out. Mere slashing of time for the sake of it misses the point. As with demand, time-based competition requires careful assessment as to where best it can serve customers/consumers.

Fast and accurate adaptation to market change is perhaps the most important element of the QR strategy. The adroitness and dexterity to move to satisfy unplanned demand or previously unrecognized market niches, require any organization to be strategically configured for such a response. However, this architecture will only be effective if the operational environment is understood and the opportunities for time compression assessed. Accuracy and flexibility will reduce time delays, and postponement strategies will enable products, indeed all activity, to be tailored to known and exact needs rather than those forecast. It should also be remembered that the use of time for advantage will be inter-organizational: gains made internally will rapidly be lost if not carried through by network partners.

Primacy of Information

Data and information are the foundation of QR – every business is an information business. Here, we are not dealing with information technology (IT), but a strategy for information systems (IS). Technology is merely the vehicle used to carry vital data resources. The links between demand and successful, accurate and flexible supply are data and the resulting information. For any operation in the 21st century, the prime strategic consideration is the use of information as a resource. Timely and accurate flows will enable fast and accurate responses without waste and unnecessary cost.

Partnerships and Alliances

Perhaps one of the most significant developments in recent management and business thinking has been externalization: the recognition that performance relies increasingly upon a series of alliances and relationships with other enterprises in the environment as the most effective way to deal with constantly changing market conditions. Competition is now between networks rather than individual firms. The coordination and relationships between these various entities are matters for strategic consideration. From a QR perspective, the web of relationships and mutual networks upon which the organization depends requires a professional management approach, and increasingly firms are devoting staff and other resources to this task. The use of outsourcing, the concept of virtuality, and a focus on core value-adding processes have heightened this pressure for proper external organization and management with commercial partners. This requires a greater understanding of organizational behaviour and communication beyond traditional boundaries, particularly power and culture, in order to manage the growing number of strategically significant relationships that impact on the modern firm.

GLOBAL SOURCING AND QUICK RESPONSE

As highlighted earlier, consumer demand is becoming more volatile. QR is designed for such an environment. The clothing industry is perhaps one of the most demanding challenges for logistics management, with hundreds of colours, thousands of styles and millions of stock-keeping units (SKUs) on the retail shelves at any one time. Further, the average shelf lives of these merchandise items shortens with each passing year.

A key factor in the value of QR is its ability to deal with uncertainty or variance. There are numerous sources of uncertainty in a supply pipeline, starting with demand through to the reliability on the part of suppliers and shippers, and Quick Response offers the ability to counter the negative impacts of uncertainty. Speed and flexibility are the key, but it is important to realize that the level of uncertainty associated with the product dictates the optimal level of speed and flexibility required. The type of supply chain needs to fit the characteristics of the product as well as the uncertainty associated with it.

Many fashion or fast-moving goods sell in distinct seasons, and are on the shelf for just one season and almost totally replaced in the following year. Figure 5.5 represents sales of a typical product subject to pronounced seasonal fluctuation.

The normal practice is to manufacture as much as possible of the finished goods inventory required before the season starts and then deliver half to two-thirds of the necessary products before the beginning of the season (point A) and ship the balance of the inventory at pre-agreed times (say, point B), or wait re-orders (points B to C). QR takes a different route. Although it may pose manufacturing capacity problems, as little as possible is made or shipped before the season. From day one, PoS data are gathered, analysed, and then used to understand demand preferences. Manufacturing is then guided by the continuing (daily or weekly) PoS data. Re-order and re-estimation and replenishment approaches are then used for frequent re-orders (points A to B). This QR approach can be

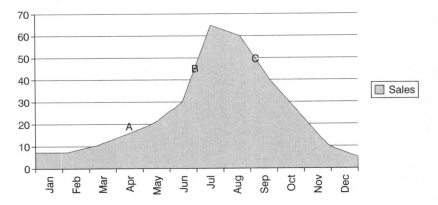

Figure 5.5 Seasonality Profile

better appreciated when applied to a particular demand situation such as global or offshore sourcing.

THE COSTS OF OFFSHORE SOURCING

As earlier discussed, a Quick Response operations strategy offers a high degree of speed, flexibility and responsiveness in supply pipelines. This has substantial implications for sourcing decisions, particularly those involving offshore sourcing. Empirical research has established that sourcing offshore to secure lower cost inputs (typically from low-wage, underdeveloped regions) can have negative consequences; once the hidden and inflexibility costs are quantified (Lowson, 2001).

Hidden costs are those that are not typically anticipated by the buying organization, but almost always occur. Some examples include the various initial investments to establish the new source of supply, control of quality and delivery variables; high initial training costs, coupled with a high staff turnover affecting both throughput and quality; significantly lower operator efficiency offshore; irrevocable letters of credit charges; delays at the port of entry, last minute use of air freight and other logistics costs; expensive administrative travel to correct problems; process inefficiencies and quality problems; long lead times and the need for large buffer inventories; and finally, the not insubstantial human cost involved in the conditions endured in many foreign factory environments often employing child labour and over-using natural resources.

Inflexibility costs are the costs of using suppliers that are inflexible and unresponsive to changes in demand (before, during and after a product selling season), leading to disproportionate levels of demand amplification across a longer supply network and a number of considerable cost implications.

It is only when these two cost categories can be properly quantified that the advantages and disadvantages of low-wage, foreign purchasing can be fully understood, and a method for their true representation becomes apparent. Once the hidden costs are categorized, sourcing from sources on the basis of low cost alone becomes far less attractive. Further, when the costs of inflexibility are added, it becomes clear that using a domestic Quick Response supplier may be a far better option due to the added velocity and flexibility that is provided.

THE QUICK RESPONSE ALTERNATIVE

Collapsing the product pipeline can reduce time and provide a more efficient response to rapidly changing consumer demand. In this way, a QR operations strategy will encourage the cross-enterprise re-engineering of business processes, from product development to replenishment, with resulting improved stocking points, lower inventory, lower cost and increased sales. The value chain is reconfigured to reflect speed of response, flexibility and differentiation. Table 5.3 compares two different sourcing alternatives: the Quick Response domestic supplier and the offshore counterpart.

In this initial scenario two possible buying decisions are reviewed using QR and then offshore sources of supply. First, end-consumer purchases, whether bought from a retailer or manufacturer, are assumed to be £100,000. It is then assumed that the customer (a manufacturer or retailer) has bought the goods for the same price (£60,000). An averaged gross margin is also assumed of 40 per cent on these sales. The only difference between the two sourcing alternatives is the flexibility and speed of response. The ability of the QR supplier to rapidly replenish the stock of the customer (manufacturer or retailer) to real-time consumer demand allows the customer to turn inventory of the product six as opposed to 2.5 times a year. This faster turnover rapidly increases the customer's gross margin return on each pound invested in inventory from £1.67 to £4.00, more than twice that of the offshore competition. Because of this inventory turnover advantage the manufacturer or retailer could afford to pay a premium for the product and still get a better return (Table 5.4).

In the table the price paid for goods by the customer has increased by one-third, but because of the flexibility and responsiveness of the supplier, the return on inventory has increased by 1.2 percent or from £1.67 to £1.69.

Table 5.5 views the sourcing decision from another perspective: the decision to move sourcing offshore to a competitor with lower unit cost but a slower response. In this situation the foreign supplier would need to reduce the purchase price by nearly 35 per cent to retain a comparative gross margin return on investment (GM ROI) to that of the QR supplier.

Table 5.3 QR and Faster Turnover

	QR supplier	Offshore supplier
Consumer purchase price (£)	100,000	100,000
Customer purchase price (£)	60,000	60,000
Gross margin (£)	40,000	40,000
Average inventory (£)	10,000	24,000
Gross margin (%)	40.00	40.00
Inventory turns (pa)	6.02	2.5
GM ROI (%)	400	167

Table 5.4 QR and a Higher Cost of Goods

	QR supplier	Offshore supplier	Cost advantage applicable
Consumer purchase price (£)	100,000	100,000	
Customer purchase price (£)	78,000	60,000	30.33%
Gross margin (£)	22,000	40,000	
Average inventory (£)	13,033	24,000	
Gross margin (%)	22.00	40.00	
Inventory turns (pa)	6.02	2.5	
GM ROI (%)	169	167	

The more flexible and higher velocity supplier proves more competitive than the lower-cost one, even without taking into account the other hidden and inflexibility costs.

Product velocity also produces other benefits. Replenishing stock in response to real-time demand ensures that the right goods are available, reflecting what is being demanded. Revenue will rise as products in demand are sold at the expected price rather than marked down as unwanted. Table 5.6 shows the combined effect of velocity, faster inventory turns and reduced markdowns.

As product velocity increases, so too will revenue, as there is less need to sell goods below optimum price points. The customer's (manufacturer or retailer) return on investment grows to over three times that of a competitor.

Finally, Quick Response also has an impact on strategic pricing decisions. Velocity and flexibility in the supply system will allow an original equipment manufacturer (OEM) or retailer to reduce the price of the finished goods below that of the competition and capture greater market

Table 5.5 A Move to Offshore Supply

	QR supplier	Offshore supplier	Cost advantage applicable
Consumer purchase price (£)	100,000	100,000	
Customer purchase price (£)	60,000	38,448	35.92%
Gross margin (£)	40,000	61,552	
Average inventory (£)	10,000	15,379	
Gross margin (%)	40.00	61.55	
Inventory turns (pa)	6.02	2.5	
GM ROI (%)	400	400	

Table 5.6 The Effect of QR Velocity

	QR supplier	Offshore supplier
Consumer purchase price (£)	113,000	100,000
Customer purchase price (£)	60,000	60,000
Gross margin (£)	53,000	40,000
Average inventory (£)	10,000	24,000
Gross margin (%)	40.00	40.00
Inventory turns (pa)	6.02	2.5
GM ROI (%)	530	167

share (Table 5.7). Because of QR flexibility and responsiveness, the retailer or manufacturer can reduce the purchase price to the consumer by 32 per cent and still earn a slightly better return in terms of GM ROI than competitors.

THE IMPORTANCE OF AGILITY

Successful companies in fashion markets seem not just to be able to capture the imagination of the consumer with their products, but are often characterized by their agility. In other words, they have the ability to move quickly, uninhibited by cumbersome processes and lengthy supply chains. Many organizations are finding that it is possible to make significant improvements by adopting a twin strategy of simultaneously reducing the logistics lead time and capturing information sooner on actual customer demand.

Table 5.7 QR and Strategic Pricing

	QR supplier	Offshore supplier	Cost advantage applicable
Consumer purchase price (£)	76,840	100,000	−32.00
Customer purchase price (£)	60,000	60,000	
Gross margin (£)	16,840	40,000	
Average inventory (£)	10,000	24,000	
Gross margin (%)	21.91	40.00	
Inventory turns (pa)	6.0	2.5	
GM ROI (%)	168	167	

* Based upon purchase price of £113,000 as seen in Table 5.6

The Spanish-based apparel company Zara provides a good example of how an integrated design, manufacturing and retail group is successfully managing its international supply chains. The first Zara shop opened in La Coruna, Northern Spain in 1975. In under 30 years the business had grown to become one of Spain's leading textile and apparel companies, with sizeable production facilities in Spain, purchasing operations in south-east Asia and the Caribbean, a finance holding company in the Netherlands and around 200 retail outlets (owned by the company) in Europe and the Americas.

Like Italian fashion giant Benetton, Zara produces a single global product range, designed to appeal to an international target market, in this case fashion-conscious 18 to 35-year-olds (the same market segment as is targeted by The Limited and The Gap in the United States, and Next in the UK). The whole process of supplying goods to the stores begins with cross-functional teams – comprising fashion, commercial and retail specialists – working within Zara's design department at the company's headquarters in La Coruna. The designs reflect the latest in international fashion trends, with inspiration gleaned through visits to fashion shows, competitors' stores, university campuses, pubs, cafes and clubs, plus any other venues or events deemed to be relevant to the lifestyles of the target customers. The team's knowledge of fashion trends is supplemented further by regular inflows of EPOS data and other information from all of the company's stores and sites around the world.

Fashion specialists within the design department are responsible for the initial designs, fabric selection and choice of prints and colours. It is then up to the team's commercial management specialists to ascertain the likely commercial viability of the items proposed. If the design is accepted, the commercial specialists proceed to negotiate with suppliers, agree purchase prices, analyse costs, margins and fix a standard cross-currency price position for the garment. The size of the production run – the number of garments required – and launch dates (the latter vary between countries in accordance with custom and climate) are also determined at this point.

Raw materials are procured through the company's buying offices in the UK, China and the Netherlands, with most of the materials themselves coming in from Mauritius, New Zealand, Australia, Morocco, China, India, Turkey, Korea, Italy and Germany. This global sourcing policy using a broad supplier base provides the widest possible selection of fashion fabrics, while reducing the risk of dependence on any source or supplier. Approximately 40 per cent of garments – those with the broadest and least transient appeal – are imported as finished goods from low-cost manufacturing centres in the Far East. The rest are produced in Spain, using Zara's own highly automated factories and a network of smaller contractors. Two guiding principles underlie all of its operations: quick response to market needs and working without inventory. Here lies the company's principle source of competitive advantage.

Zara's manufacturing systems are in many ways similar to those developed and employed so successfully by Benetton in northern Italy, but refined using ideas developed in conjunction with Toyota. Only those operations that enhance cost-efficiency through economies of scale are conducted in-house (such as dying, cutting, labelling and packaging). All other manufacturing activities, including the labour-intensive finishing stages, are completed by networks of more than 300 small subcontractors, each specializing in one particular part of the production process or garment type. These subcontractors work exclusively for Zara's parent, Inditex SA. In return they receive the necessary technological, financial and logistical support required to achieve stringent time and quality targets. Inventory costs are kept to a minimum because Zara pays only for the completed garments. The system is flexible enough to cope with sudden changes in demand, though production is always kept at a level slightly below expected sales, to keep stock moving. Zara has opted for undersupply, viewing it as a lesser evil than holding slow-moving or obsolete stock.

Finished goods are forwarded to the company's huge distribution centre in La Coruna, where they are labelled, price-tagged (all items carry international price tags showing the price in all relevant currencies) and packed. From there they travel by third-party contractors by road and/or air to their penultimate destinations. The shops themselves receive deliveries of new stock on a twice-weekly basis, according to shop-by-shop stock allocations calculated by the design department. The whole production cycle takes only three or four weeks. In an industry where lead times of many months are still the norm, Zara has reduced its lead-time gap for more than half of the garments it sells to a level unmatched by any of its European or North American competitors.

CONCLUSION

Fashion retailing, and the manufacturing sector that supports it, are clearly highly dependent on an agile logistics capability. The ability to capture new design ideas, to convert these into products and to bring them to market in the shortest possible timescale has become a prerequisite for success in the fashion business. Paradoxically many retailers in this sector have actually seen their design-to-store lead times increase as a result of so-called low-cost sourcing strategies.

To compete successfully in short lifecycle and volatile markets requires that a wider definition of cost be adopted. The real cost is the total end-to-end pipeline cost, which includes not only the manufacturing cost of the product, but also the inventory carrying cost, the cost of mark-downs as well as the cost of loss of sales through stock-outs. The key to the minimization of this total supply chain cost is the adoption of agile strategies, which focus on time compression and quick response. Retailers and manufacturers that recognize the importance of agility will out-perform those that do not.

REFERENCES

Gunston, R and Harding, P (1986) Quick Response: US and UK experiences, *Textile Outlook International*, **10**, pp 43–51

Hunter, N A (1990) *Quick Response for Apparel Manufacturing*, Textile Institute, UK

Lowson, R H (2001) Retail sourcing strategies: are they cost effective?, *International Journal of Logistics*, **4** (3), pp 271–96

Lowson, R H (2002) *Strategic Operations Management: The new competitive advantage*, Routledge, London

Lowson, R H, King, R and Hunter, N A (1999) *Quick Response: Managing the supply chain to meet consumer demand*, Wiley, Chichester

6

Logistics in Tesco: past, present and future

David Smith and Leigh Sparks

INTRODUCTION

The business transformation of Tesco in the last 25 or so years is one of the more remarkable stories in British retailing. From being essentially a comparatively small 'pile it high, sell it cheap' downmarket retailer, the company has become one of Europe's leading retail businesses, with retail operations in countries as far-flung as Ireland, Poland, Malaysia and Japan. In the United Kingdom its loyalty card and its e-commerce operations are generally considered to be world-leading, and its expertise in these fields is much in demand (Humby, Hunt and Phillips, 2003).

Accounts of this transformation by those involved are widely available (Corina, 1971; Powell, 1991; MacLaurin, 1999). Tesco is the focus of much academic, analyst and commentator consideration (for instance Seth and Randall, 1999; Burt and Sparks, 2002, IGD, 2003a). Some aspects of the Tesco operations have been discussed in public by their executives (such as Kelly, 2000; Mason, 1998; Jones, 2001; Jones and Clarke, 2002; Child, 2002). This literature points to the fundamental transformation of the retail business to meet changing consumer demands and global opportunities. Tesco has become dominant in its home market (Burt and Sparks, 2003) and closely watched on the international stage.

The visible component of this transformation is in the location and format of the retail outlets and in the range of products and services that the company offers in-store and online. Customers are also aware of the change through the constant reinforcement of the corporate brand. Less visible however is the logistics transformation that has underpinned this retail success story. It should be obvious that the supply chain required to deliver to lots of small high-street stores in the 1970s, selling comparatively simple products, was vastly different to the current supply chain in delivery of the breadth of products in a modern Tesco Extra hypermarket, or in the availability required to run Tesco Express convenience stores, or the warehouse worlds and weekly shopping on Tesco.com. This logistics and supply chain transformation has received far less public consideration, although some academic analysis is available (Sparks, 1986; Smith and Sparks, 1993; Smith, 1998; Jones and Clarke, 2002).

This chapter presents a summary of this logistics and supply chain transformation in Tesco. It draws heavily on this public literature, although a series of interviews with managers and directors at different levels in the company has also informed the work. The paper aims to describe, analyse and draw lessons from the logistics journey Tesco has undertaken.

TESCO IN THE PAST: ESTABLISHING CONTROL OVER DISTRIBUTION

The current retail position of Tesco is far removed from the origins of the company. Tesco made its name by the operation of a 'pile it high, sell it cheap' approach to food retailing. Price competitiveness was critical to this and fitted well with the consumer requirements of the time. The company and its store managers were essentially individual entrepreneurs. The growth of the company saw considerable expansion until by the mid-1970s Tesco had 800 stores across England and Wales. This entrepreneurial approach to retailing, epitomized by Sir Jack Cohen, was put under pressure however as competition and consumer requirements changed. Tesco itself had therefore to change.

The emblematic event signifying the beginning of this transformation was Operation Checkout in 1977 (Akehurst, 1984). Dramatically, trading stamps were removed from the business, prices were cut nationally as a grand event and the business received an immediate considerable boost to volume. Stores were re-merchandized as part of Operation Checkout, and consumers began to see a different approach to Tesco retailing. After this initial repositioning event and phase, Tesco began to better understand its customers, control its business, and move away from its solely down-market image (Powell, 1991). This retail transformation brought into sharp focus the quality and capability of Tesco supply systems and the relationships with suppliers.

Such concerns have remained critical during the almost irresistible rise of Tesco in the 1980s and 1990s. By moving away from its origins, Tesco changed its business. Initially the focus was on conforming out-of-town superstores, but since the early 1990s a multi-format approach has developed, encompassing hypermarkets, superstores, supermarkets, city centre stores and convenience operations. The Tesco corporate brand has been strongly developed (Burt and Sparks, 2002) and international ambitions have emerged. In all this, the distribution and supply of appropriate products to the stores has been fundamental.

There have been four main phases in the reconfiguration of the distribution strategy and operations. First, there was a period primarily of direct delivery by the supplier to the retail store. Second, there was the move, starting in the late 1970s, to centralized regional distribution centres for ambient goods and the refinement of that process of centralized distribution. Third, a composite distribution strategy developed, starting in 1989. Fourth, the 1990s witnessed the advent of vertical collaboration in the supply chain to achieve better operating efficiency.

Direct to Store Delivery

Tesco in the mid-1970s operated a direct to store delivery (DSD) process. Suppliers and manufacturers delivered directly to stores, almost as and when they chose. Store managers often operated their own relationships (Powell's 'private enterprise', 1991: 185) which made central control and standardization difficult to achieve. Product volumes and quality were inconsistent. This DSD system fell apart under the pressures of the volume increases of Operation Checkout.

As Powell comments, quoting Sir Ian MacLaurin:

> Ultimately our business is about getting our goods to our stores in sufficient quantities to meet our customers' demands. Without being able to do that efficiently, we aren't in business, and Checkout stretched our resources to the limit. Eighty per cent of all our supplies were coming direct from manufacturers, and unless we'd sorted out our distribution problems there was a very real danger that we would have become a laughing stock for promoting cuts on lines that we couldn't even deliver. It was a close-run thing.

(Powell, 1991: 184)

Powell continues:

> How close is now a matter of legend: outside suppliers having to wait for up to twenty-four hours to deliver at Tesco's centres; of stock checks being conducted in the open air; of Tesco's four obsolescent warehouses, and the company's transport fleet working to around-the-clock, seven-day schedule. And as the problems lived off one another, and as customers waited for the emptied shelves to be refilled, so the tailback lengthened around the stores, delays of five to six hours becoming commonplace. *Possibly for the first time in its history, the company recognized that it was as much in the business of distribution as of retailing.*

(Powell, 1991: 184, emphasis added)

The company began to gain control of the problems through operational 'fire fighting', and while problems occurred, melt-down was avoided. It was clear however that changes to distribution would be needed as the new business strategy took hold.

Centralization

The decision was taken to move away from direct delivery to stores and to implement centralization. The basis of this decision (in 1980) was the realization of the critical nature of range control on the operations. Store managers could no longer be allowed to decide ranges and prices and to operate mini-fiefdoms. If the company was to be transformed as the business strategy proposed, then head office needed control over ranging, pricing and stocking decisions. Concerns over quality of product also suggested a need to relocate the power in the supply chain. Centralization of distribution was the tool to achieve this.

Tesco adopted a centrally controlled and physically centralized distribution service (Kirkwood, 1984a, 1984b) delivering the vast majority of stores' needs, utilizing common handling systems, with deliveries within a lead time of a maximum of 48 hours (Sparks, 1986). This involved an extension to the existing company distribution facilities and the building of new distribution centres, located more appropriately with the current and future store location profile. Investment in technology, handling systems and working practices allowed faster stock-turn and better lead times. Components of the revised structure were outsourced, allowing comparisons between contractors and Tesco-operated centres, to drive efficiency.

This strategy produced a more rationalized network of distribution centres, linked by computer to stores and head office. The proliferation of back-up stock-holding points and individual operations was reduced.

These centres were the hubs of the network, being larger, handling more stock, more vehicles and requiring a more efficient organization. Centralization produced the necessary control over the business and fitted with the changed retail strategy of the 1980s (larger company superstores). Figures 6.1 and 6.2 show the changing store profile and the impact of the distribution changes on corporate stock-holding.

From 1984 the percentage of sales via central facilities has increased from under 30 per cent to over 95 per cent in 2002. By 2003, the annual distribution volume had increased to more than 1 billion cases delivered, out of 25 distribution centres, covering 7 million square feet of warehouse area, holding 9.9 days' stock for stocked products. The scale of the ambient distribution centre increased: for example Thurrock, which opened in 2002, is 500,000 sq ft with a weekly assembly capacity greater than 1 million cases. A similar very large non-food national distribution centre is located in Milton Keynes with automation for selected product lines.

Composite Distribution

Centralization proceeded on a product line basis. By 1989 Tesco had 42 depots, of which 26 were temperature controlled. While this was a massive reduction from the plethora of small locations in the 1970s, it was still capable of improvement. Fresh foods were basically handled through single temperature, single-product depots. These were small and ineffi-

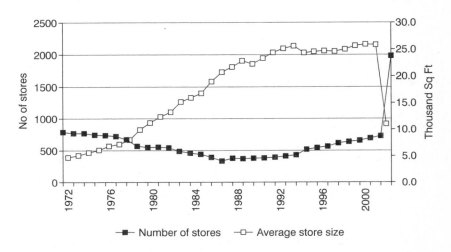

Figure 6.1 Number of Stores and Average Size of Stores, Tesco Plc (UK only)

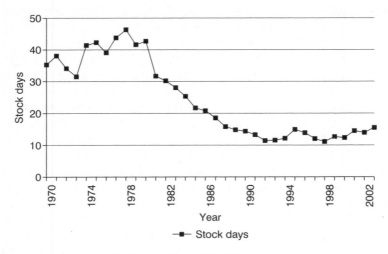

Figure 6.2 Inventory in Tesco Plc, 1970–2003

cient and were subject to only tactical operational improvements, allowing for example more frequent store deliveries and a more accurate idea of the cost of product distribution.

While stores received some improvements in the mid-1980s, there remained some disadvantages of the centralized network. For example, each product group had a different ordering system. Individual store volumes were so low that delivery frequency was less than desired and quality suffered. Delivery frequency was maintained, leading to high empty-running costs and increased store receipt costs. It was prohibitively expensive to have on-site Tesco quality control inspection at each location, which meant that the standards of quality desired could not be rigorously controlled at the point of distribution. It was also realized that this network would neither cope with the growth Tesco forecast in the 1990s nor, as importantly, be ready to meet expected high legal standards on temperature control in the chill chain.

The produce depot at Aztec West in Bristol opened in 1986 and represented the best of the centralized network. Tesco could have made further investment in single-product distribution systems, upgraded the depots and transport temperature control and put in new computer systems, but would still have achieved overall a less than optimal use of resources and cost-efficiency. A strategy of composite distribution was planned in the 1980s to take effect in the 1990s. A subsidiary requirement was the importance of ensuring continuity of service during the changeover period.

Composite distribution enables temperature-controlled product (chilled, fresh and frozen) to be distributed through one system of multi-temperature warehouses and vehicles. Composite distribution uses specially designed vehicles with temperature-controlled compartments to deliver any combination of these products. It provides daily deliveries of these products at the appropriate temperature so that the products reach the customers at the stores in the peak of freshness. An insulated composite trailer can be sectioned into up to three independently controlled temperature chambers by means of movable bulkheads. The size of each chamber can be varied to match the volume to be transported at each temperature. The composite distribution network in the UK, including Northern Ireland, now has ten centres, replacing the 26 single temperature centres in the 'centralized' network. Half these centres are operated by specialist distribution companies, again enabling comparison of performance.

Composite distribution provides a number of benefits. Some derive from the original process of centralization, of which the composite system is an extension. Others are more directly attributable to the nature of composite distribution. First, the move to daily deliveries of composite product groups to all stores in waves provides an opportunity to reduce the levels of stock held at the stores, and indeed to reduce or obviate the need for storage facilities at store level. The result of this is seen at store level in the better use of overall floorspace (more selling space) and in stock terms by a continuous reduction (see Figure 6.2).

The second benefit is the improvement of quality, with a consequent reduction in wastage. Products reach the store in a more desirable condition. Better forecasting systems minimize lost sales due to out-of-stocks. The introduction of sales-based ordering produces more accurate store orders. More rigorous application of code control results in longer shelf life on delivery, which in turn enables a reduction in wastage. This is of crucial importance to shoppers who demand better quality and fresher products. In addition, however, the tight control over the chain enables Tesco to satisfy and exceed the new legislation requirements on food safety.

Third, the introduction of composite delivery provided an added benefit in productivity terms. The economies of scale and enhanced use of equipment provide greater efficiency and an improved distribution service. Composite distribution strategically provides reduced capital costs and operationally reduces costs through for example less congestion at the store. Throughout the system there is an emphasis on maximizing productivity and efficiency of the operations, enabled by tactical involvement in various new technologies.

The introduction of composite delivery was not a simple procedure. Considerable problems were encountered, requiring Tesco to work closely with suppliers and distributors. The move to composites led to the further centralization of more product groups, the reduction of stock holding, faster product movement along the channel, better information sharing, the reduction of order lead times and stronger code control for critical products. Such changes are easy to list but hard to implement and achieve.

There were also issues that existed post-composite. The need to maintain continuity of service to retail stores, which means that the implementation of improvements must be invisible, affects abilities to change. The cost of primary distribution remained within the buyer's gross margin and was not identified clearly and separately. This cost had to be substantiated indirectly by talking to suppliers and hauliers. In other words clarity and transparency were not achieved. Finally and most importantly, certain sectors of the supplier base were fragmented and not fully organized for the needs of retail distribution, despite the concomitant development of retail brand products. That fragmentation made the task of securing further permanent improvements difficult. While many suppliers could reorganize their procedures to meet the changed timing demands of composite delivery, some could not.

This composite structure is essentially the backbone of the current network. In order to increase the volume capability of the composites, Tesco implemented a change to its frozen strategy by commissioning a new automated frozen distribution centre at Daventry. This national frozen centre services Tesco stores by delivering through the composite distribution centres. This enabled the composite frozen chambers to be converted to chill chambers, thus releasing extra volume capability to service Tesco business growth.

Vertical Collaboration

The discussion of the phases of supply chain reconfiguration thus far has essentially focused on structural change to the distribution network. Implicit in this is some alteration to the linkages with suppliers and distribution specialists, but in many ways this was ancillary to the internal changes. Once the basic network outline was settled, however, attention turned more fundamentally to vertical collaboration in the supply chain. Information sharing, electronic trading and collaborative improvements have become critical.

This sharing of information was part of a wider introduction of electronic trading to Tesco. In particular, Tesco built a Tradanet community with suppliers (Edwards and Gray, 1990; INS, 1991). Improvements to scanning in stores and the introduction of sales-based ordering enabled Tesco better to understand and manage ordering and replenishment. Sales-based ordering automatically calculated store replenishment requirements based on item sales, and generated orders for delivery to stores within 24 to 48 hours. This information was used via Tradanet to help suppliers plan ahead both in product and distribution. Delivery notes, invoices and other documentation were also be sent by Tradanet.

In 1997 Tesco gave a commitment to share information with its suppliers. Suppliers could obtain information provided they dedicated resources to focus on Tesco customer wishes and provided appropriate product offerings. This commitment complemented the change in commercial structure to focus on category management and ECR principles. Tesco moved from the traditional single point of contact with suppliers (the buyer and the national account manager) to a more complex interaction in which functions collaborated. A commercially secure data exchange system based on the Internet (Tesco Information Exchange – TIE) was established.

This concern with information provision for collaborative purposes inevitably turned attention on to the practices of primary distribution. The changes to control the supply chain had been concentrated mainly on the distribution centre to the retail store component, but realization began to emerge of opportunities elsewhere.

The purpose of examining primary distribution (manufacturer to distribution centre) was to identify and implement changes that were profitable to the supply chain as a whole. Frequently opportunities occurred through shared user solutions, which are different from the mainly dedicated solutions found in secondary distribution. Primary distribution required some change in approach and style, with Tesco letting go of direct control and allowing appointed hauliers and consolidators greater freedom over the shape of the least-cost, good service solutions.

Once the cost of primary distribution had been calculated, there was business motivation to apply logistics resources to identify opportunities to make improvements in the organization and structure of the inbound flow of goods. The purpose was to reorganize UK, European and worldwide sourcing and distribution networks. Tesco was then able to be proactive in negotiating more competitive distribution rates as a result of the negotiation scale, the command of the sourcing of products and its own expertise in distribution operations. These factors all contributed to enhanced operational efficiency and supply chain profitability. There was a valuable cost contribution that could be made by involving the operators in identifying more efficient ways of organizing primary distribution, and then helping bring those insights to the surface and create solutions that worked for all the segments of the supply chain. It was important in achieving this to work in a cross-functional style, and the primary distribution managers sat in the commercial areas with which they were working. This created a united focus on achieving good results for the business.

The restructuring, information sharing and primary distribution also focused attention on using assets more completely. Tesco's 3D logistics programme sought to achieve a total supply chain perspective. This inevitably involved considering the flow of goods on shorter time horizons, allowing delivery and distribution to be reconfigured, creating more capacity in existing centres and aligning primary and secondary distribution.

An important part of this alignment relationship development has been the supplier collection programme. Tesco vehicles collect supplier products on their way back to the depot following a store delivery, saving costs and reducing emissions (DETR, 1997). Additionally, suppliers' vehicles that had delivered to depots or were conveniently in the area were routed to take goods to Tesco retail stores on their way back to their home base. Such collaborations involve three-way partnerships among suppliers, logistics service providers and Tesco.

The overall objective was to create conditions in which the unit cost of distribution reduced year on year, and at the same time, the return on the capital invested in vehicles and centres increased through better coordination and stronger confidence in the information. The result was an important strategic alliance between primary and secondary distribution which examined the peaks and troughs in utilization to find those that were complementary. Alignment of time has been noted above, but other changes also brought full supply chain benefits. One specific opportunity was in the handling and movement of goods, with product increasingly ordered, produced and delivered in merchandise-ready units.

These phases of reconfiguration of the supply chain took Tesco from a position of being at the mercy of suppliers and inconsistent practice to the very leading edge of logistics expertise. Tesco distribution and supply chain was recognized as world class (McKinsey, 1998).

THE PRESENT: TESCO SUPPLY CHAIN TODAY

The Changing Business

As Jones and Clarke (2002) point out, the process of change outlined above made huge strides towards modernizing Tesco's supply chain. As a consequence of this, lead times to stores and from suppliers had been cut radically and stock holding reduced enormously (Figure 6.2). Massive progress had been made. However this progress was achieved at a time when Tesco had moved from a standardized, conforming, domestic retailer to one where the retail and supply challenges were multiplying.

These challenges involved internationalization, the development of successful home shopping and operational alterations at store level.

The real process of becoming an international retail operation started in the mid-1990s, when Tesco embarked on a long-term strategy of building a profitable large-scale international business. By 2003, Tesco had successfully established that retail presence in Northern Ireland, the Republic of Ireland, Hungary, Poland, Czech Republic, Slovakia, Thailand, South Korea, Taiwan and Malaysia. Tesco has recently purchased retail chains in Japan and Turkey. It has become the market leader in five of those international countries, in addition to being number one grocery retailer in the UK. That overseas operation now accounts for almost half the Tesco Group retail space and 20 per cent of retail sales (Tesco plc Annual Report, 2003). The approach is to use local knowledge to tailor the operation and not to spread the business too widely, although other markets remain possible (such as China and the United States – Child, 2002).

One of the lessons in internationalization that Tesco does not have to relearn is the importance of expertise in supply chain logistics. Its UK experiences have provided a solid base for supply chain operations in these international markets. While the extent and the approach vary depending on market circumstances (IGD 2003a), the core processes are being introduced and allowing efficiencies to be gained.

In 1995 Tesco conducted a home shopping pilot scheme at a single store. Customers could use a variety of methods to order, with these orders picked at the store by Tesco staff, and collected or delivered to the customer's home or drop-off point. This pilot was extended to 10 stores in 1997, and a store-based picking operation was expanded nationally from 1999. By 2003 Tesco.com covered 96 per cent of the UK population geographically and had annual sales of £447 million. A fleet of 1,000 temperature controlled vans was delivering 110,000 orders per week, which is a 65 per cent share of the UK Internet grocery market. A similar approach is now established in the Republic of Ireland and in South Korea, where over 70 per cent of the population has Internet access. Grocery Works, which is a partnership between Tesco.com and Safeway Inc, has established coverage in parts of the western United States.

This store-based model was not the common approach adopted by competitors, and criticism of the approach was 'vitriolic' (Child, 2002). Jones (2001) in an interview with John Browett (CEO of Tesco.com) points to three key elements of the decision to use store-picking. First, Tesco realized that warehouse picking schemes could not make money. Second, customers wanted the full range of products, and economics showed Tesco needed the wide range to drive basket size. Third, geographic coverage from warehouses is insufficient. The Tesco.com experiment is now profitable, and has shown to some extent how supply chain systems can add value to the business in new ways. The Internet however places pressure on the accuracy of speed of supply chain systems, forcing even Tesco to look again at the processes (see later).

The retail base of Tesco has also changed domestically from the 1980s. The present-day Tesco is a multi-format retailer with formats ranging from Extra hypermarkets to small Express convenience stores. This variation has been compounded by retail operational changes. Store opening hours have been extended in many locations to encompass 24-hour opening. Service levels and quality thresholds have been enhanced. Non-food has become a much greater proportion of even standard store offers than before. Product ranges, operating times and service standards all combine to pressurize a supply system that was essentially developed for a simpler, more standard situation.

The extension to non-food lines, the growing internationalization of the business (including product sourcing) and the consumer demand for fresh products also come together to internationalize the supply chain. From being heavily domestic in nature, the procurement of products from overseas has become a key feature of the business. This breadth of supply again demands efficiency in the supply chain.

The Current Network

The current Tesco supply chain network is well documented (IGD, 2003b). This report shows that there are 25 distribution depots with a warehouse area of 7.3 million square feet and annual total case volumes of 1.17 billion. Centralized distribution accounts for 95 per cent of the volume. Of these 25 depots, 15 are run in-house by Tesco and the remainder are contracted to Wincanton (five), Exel Logistics (two), Tibbett and Britten (two) and Power Europe (one). National Distribution Centres (four) are combined with Regional Distribution Centres (ambient) (nine, of which four are 'mega-sites', three fast-moving sites and two medium-moving sites), Composite Distribution Centres (one) and Temperature Controlled Depots (11, including seven fresh foods, three fresh and frozen and one new frozen site). In additional there are 24 consolidation centres run by a variety of operators which feed into this system. The system operates almost 3,000 vehicles, covering 224 million km per annum. In short, this is an extensive, large-scale network of supply.

The operations of the components of this network have also undergone radical change. Performance is now much more rigorously monitored, mainly through the 'steering wheel' approach widespread throughout Tesco. Any distribution centre steering wheel focuses on Operations (safety and efficiency), People (appointment, development, commitment and values), Finance (stock results, operating costs) and the Customer (accuracy, delivery on time). Through such performance measuring at all levels, quality standards are maintained and enhanced.

Current Initiatives

Jones and Clarke (2002) point out that despite the successes of the reconfiguration of the Tesco supply chain in the 1980s and 1990s noted above, analysis of the chain pointed to a number of areas where benefits could still be achieved. In a much quoted example, a can of cola was followed in the supply chain from a mine (for the metal to make the can) to the store. It was discovered that it took 319 days to go through the entire chain, of which time only 2 hours was spent making and filling the can. This process involved many locations, firms and trips (Jones and Clarke, 2002; Jones, 2002, Jones, 2001). As Jones and Clarke note, 'even in the best-run value streams there are lots of opportunities for improvement' (2002: 31).

This can example is one illustration of the first step in a process undertaken by Tesco (Jones and Clarke, 2002). This first step involved the mapping of the traditional value stream. This mapping process demonstrated the stop–start–stop nature of the value stream (Figure 6.3). Second and consequently therefore, value streams that 'flowed' were created/designed (Figure 6.4). Third, arising from flow principles, Tesco began to look at synchronization and aspects of lean manufacturing by its suppliers. Finally, Tesco utilized its consumer knowledge from its loyalty card to rethink what products and services should be located where in the value stream (Humby *et al*, 2003). Jones and Clarke (2002) describe this process as the creation of a 'customer-driven supply chain'. Others might use the term 'demand chain'. This process is essentially where Tesco is currently in terms of its supply chain.

Clarke (2002) describes the five big supply chain projects that Tesco is currently engaged in (see also IGD, 2003a) and which derive essentially from the process outlined above:

Continuous Replenishment (CR)

CR was introduced in 1999 and has two key features. First, there is a replacement of batch data processing with a flow system, and second, using the flow system, multiple daily orders are sent to suppliers allowing for multiple deliveries, reducing stockholding through cross-checking and varying availability and quality. This approach has been extended since 1999 (Table 6.1) and has further potential both domestically and internationally.

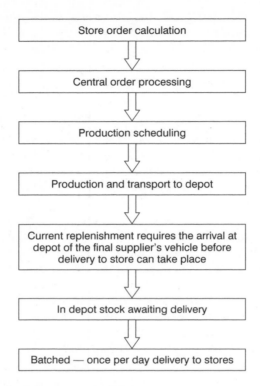

Figure 6.3 Replenishment – As Was

In-Store Range Management

Based on customer behaviour data and stock-holding capacity analysis at store, Tesco can now produce store-specific planograms and store-specific ranging. The system is designed to improve store presentation as well as stock replenishment and availability. Tesco is able to provide the exact stock requirement for specific shelves in specific stores to its out-replenishment system. This system is being rolled out in 2003/5.

Network Management

Network management attempts to integrate and maintain the network assets and extend the life of the system. Two new sites in 2001 added 18 per cent to the capacity of the system. The frozen element of the composite system has been centralized in a new frozen centre, allowing chill and ambient expansion in the released space. Cross-docking is used at the regional centres for frozen and slow-moving lines. Consolidation centres provide fresh produce for cross-docking. These changes have

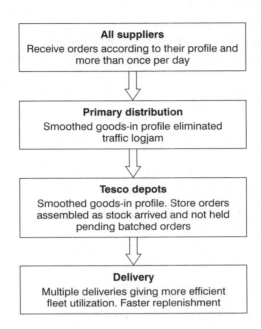

Figure 6.4   With Continuous Replenishment

Table 6.1   Tesco Development of Continuous Replenishment

Year	Development
1999	Work with external provider (RETEK) on trade management and merchandise planning
2000	Continuous replenishment in ambient grocery
2001	Continuous replenishment in fresh foods
2002	Continuous replenishment in clothing, direct store deliveries and bread and moving goods
2003	Drill into the production planning and develop store-specific ranging

Sources: IGD, 2003a; Clarke, 2002

produced a more integrated network which has made better use of the assets, extended the life of centres and improved performance by selecting the right 'value stream' for appropriate products.

Flow-Through

As noted above, flow-through or cross-docking is now more extensive. Product storage is now much reduced and increasingly distribution centres have no racking and do not store product. The importance of cross-docking is set to increase, given the substantial savings delivered from reduced stock holding. A different but nonetheless important aspect of flow-through is the use of merchandisable ready units to allow product to be put on sale in stores without extra handling. Such units (often called 'dollies') are increasingly common in fast-moving items, but can be used for many other items as well.

Primary Distribution

Primary distribution and factory gate pricing (FGP) is the area of focus for cost reduction in inbound logistics. Primary distribution is the term Tesco prefer, seeing the process as a 'strategic change in the way goods flow... (and about) achieving efficient flows and not a pricing process' (Wild, quoted in Rowat, 2003: 48). However cost reduction is a key driver behind the interest in primary distribution. Essentially, primary distribution is about control (and pricing) of the supply chain from the supplier despatch bay to the goods in bay of the retail distribution centre. It separates out the cost of transportation from the purchase price of the product itself, and by putting it into a separate primary distribution budget, it allows direct control and analysis by Tesco. By March 2003, 30 per cent of all Tesco inbound freight was under such agreements, which amounts to 300 million cases annually or 10,000 deliveries a week from 500 suppliers.

Prior to this initiative, the commercial buyer used to purchase products at a price which included the delivery by the supplier into the retail distribution centre. The gross margin, on which buyers are measured for performance, is the difference between this purchase price and the price charged to the consumer at the retail store. Hence, as can be imagined, removing the transport cost element from that purchase price impacts on the way the gross margin is calculated, and the commercial buyers have to adjust their targets accordingly. It is a major financial development within a retail organization to implement such a change and still retain strict control over the disciplines of making individual buyers accountable for achieving the new level of gross margins during the period of transition. Primary distribution is a strategy that requires the cooperation of the whole of the supply chain including the retail buyers. This Tesco achieved by bringing together cross-functional teams and by the full endorsement of the policy from senior directors including the chief executive.

Naturally the suppliers, and their transport service providers, went through quite major changes to their arrangements for the delivery of their goods to the retail distribution centres, as they implemented this policy planned by the primary distribution team at Tesco. It was now the retailer, not the supplier, that appointed which transport and distribution companies would do this work, at a price negotiated directly between the retailer and the logistic service provider. It is not surprising, therefore, that there was some adverse reaction in the industry, especially from those transport operators that had lost work as a result. As a result the remaining volume from those suppliers and manufacturers, which they still had to deliver to other retailers, was no longer at a volume and delivery pattern that was economical without raising costs. This, they said, was the direct result of the primary distribution decisions made by the retailer to reorganize the consolidation of product delivery.

The case put forward by the retailer was that to maximize competitive advantage, the whole supply chain needed to be aligned with the demand patterns of consumers, and that this must now include primary distribution. It further argued that it saw no justification for other retailers to benefit from the economies of scale derived from the major retailers, which ordered the majority of the volume. Factory gate pricing is a sign of a very mature retail supply chain. It provides both full visibility of the costs and the accountability to organize how the primary network is structured. It requires a high level of co-operation between suppliers and retailers to leverage the benefits of a fully controlled supply chain. The result for Tesco is significant cost savings and thus lower prices for consumers. For those involved with Tesco in this there are major opportunities for the most efficient distributors, and the manufacturers may see their jobs becoming simpler, through changed collection and back-hauling procedures. Tesco's vision for primary distribution is an in-bound supply chain which is visible, low-cost, efficient and effective.

The current position for Tesco's supply chain is therefore again one of change. The reconfiguration of the 1980s and 1990s has now been modified by the conceptual and intellectual approaches of the recent years. The ideas of how a supply chain should look, perform and be costed are sweeping through the existing system and those that supply product into it. In the same way that Tesco itself does not stand still, so too the supply system is having to adapt and change.

THE FUTURE: EVOLUTION OR REVOLUTION?

It is impossible to fully predict the future and to state categorically what the Tesco supply chain will look like in the coming years. Some things are known, however. The processes and procedures described above that have been put in place by Tesco have at least five more years to run. They will change the supply chain but represent the continuing evolutionary influence of developments already known. Likewise, work in the area of environmental aspects of logistics will continue to place pressure on retailers and suppliers to improve their performance. Key performance indicators at government and other levels are becoming more fundamental (for example DETR, 1999; DfT, 2003a, 2003b). Concerns about the environment and about aspects of recycling and reuse will continue to be influential.

Perhaps however the future could be more radical? While the concerns above will undoubtedly be maintained and influence supply systems, the processes put in place may also have more wide-reaching consequences. Tesco is at the beginning of understanding all the issues in primary distribution. Manufacturers likewise are only now getting to grips with some of these issues. Is the scene set therefore for a more fundamental examination of the supply relationships? Jones (2002) puts forward a variety of scenarios for grocery supply chains. All have at their heart a move away from the current system of bigger, centralized and dispersed to a model of faster, simpler and local. Such a system focuses on moving value creation towards consumers and eliminating non-value creation steps in supply. Information systems are simplified so as to avoid order amplification and distribution. The supply chain is thus compressed in space and time, producing and shipping closer to what is needed just in time. As Jones (2002) concludes, 'We can not predict exactly what forms these developments will take.... Nevertheless there are huge opportunities for improving the performance of the grocery supply chain, for those willing to think the unthinkable.'

SUMMARY

This chapter aimed to understand and account for the changes in logistics in food retailing by examining changes in Tesco logistics. The basic premise was that the transformation of retailing that the consumer sees at store level has been supported by a transformation of logistics and supply chain methods and practices. In particular, there has been an increase in the status and professionalism in logistics as the time, costs and implications of the function have been recognized. Professionalism has been enhanced by the transformation of logistics through the application of modern methods and technology. For all retailers, the importance of distribution is now undeniable. As retailers have responded to consumer change, so the need to improve the quality and appropriateness of supply systems has become paramount.

The Tesco study demonstrates many aspects of this transformation. In response to a clear business strategy, logistics and supply chains have been realigned. From a state of decentralization and poor control, the company has moved through centralization and composites which enabled control to be exercised stringently. These in turn have led to new methods and relationships in supply systems, both within Tesco and throughout the supply chain. Logistics does not stand still, and recognition of the need to think clearly about supply pervades the case study. The developments outlined above and the transformation described are not the ultimate solutions. As consumers change their needs, so retailing must and will respond. As retailing responds, companies will modify their operations, not least their logistics, or be placed at a competitive disadvantage.

REFERENCES

Akehurst, G (1984) Checkout: the analysis of oligopolistic behaviour in the UK grocery retail market, *Service Industries Journal*, **4** (2), pp 198–242

Burt, S L and Sparks, L (2002) Corporate branding, retailing and retail internationalisation, *Corporate Reputation Review*, **5** (2/3), pp 194–212

Burt, S L and Sparks, L (2003) Power and competition in the UK retail grocery market, *British Journal of Management*, **14**, pp 237–54

Child, P N (2002) Taking Tesco global, *McKinsey Quarterly*, 3, pp 135–44

Clarke, P (2002) Distribution in Tesco. Presentation for Tesco UK Operations Day 2002 [Online] www.tesco.com/corporateinfo/ (accessed 20 Sep 2002)

Corina, M (1971) *Pile It High, Sell It Cheap*, Weidenfeld and Nicolson, London

Department of Environment, Transport, and the Regions (DETR) (1997) *Good Practice Case Study 364: Energy savings from integrated logistics management, Tesco plc*, HMSO, London.

DETR (1999) *Energy Consumption Guide 76: Benchmarking vehicle utilisation and energy consumption, measurement of Key Performance Indicators*, HMSO, London

Department for Transport (DfT) (2003a) *Benchmarking Guide 77: Key Performance Indicators for non-food retail distribution*, HMSO, London

DfT (2003b) *Benchmarking Guide 78: Key Performance Indicators for the food supply chain*, HMSO, London

Edwards, C and Gray, M (1990) Tesco case study, in *Electronic Trading*, DTI, HMSO, London

Fernie, J (ed) (1990) *Retail Distribution Management*, Kogan Page, London

Fernie, J (1997) Retail change and retail logistics in the UK: past trends and future prospects, *Service Industries Journal*, **17** (3), pp 383–96

Humby, C, Hunt, T and Phillips, T (2003) *Scoring Points: How Tesco is winning customer loyalty*, Kogan Page, London

Institute of Grocery Distribution (IGD) (2003a) *The Tesco International Report*, IGD, Watford

IGD (2003b) *Retail Logistics 2003*, IGD, Watford

INS (1991) *Tesco: Breaking down the barriers of trade*, INS, Sunbury-on-Thames

Jones, D T (2001) Tesco.com: delivering home shopping, *ECR Journal*, **1** (1), pp 37–43

Jones, D T (2002) Rethinking the grocery supply chain, in *State of the Art in Food*, ed J-W Grievink, L Josten and C Valk, Elsevier, Rotterdam [Online] www.leanuk.org/articles.htm (accessed 30 Oct 2003)

Jones, D T and Clarke, P (2002) Creating a customer-driven supply chain, *ECR Journal*, **2** (2), pp 28–37

Kelly, J (2000) Every little helps: an interview with Terry Leahy, CEO, Tesco, *Long Range Planning*, 33, pp 430–39

Kirkwood, D A (1984a) The supermarket challenge, *Focus on PDM*, **3** (4), pp 8–12

Kirkwood, D A (1984b) How Tesco manage the distribution function, *Retail and Distribution Management*, **12** (5), pp 61–65

MacLaurin, I (1999) *Tiger by the Tail*, Macmillan, London

Mason, T (1998) The best shopping trip? How Tesco keeps the customer satisfied, *Journal of the Market Research Society*, **40** (1), pp 5–12

McKinsey Global Institute (1998) *Driving Productivity and Growth in the UK Economy*, McKinsey, London

Powell, D (1991) *Counter Revolution: The Tesco story*, Grafton Books, London

Reynolds, J (2004) An exercise in successful retailing: the case of Tesco, chapter 26 of *Retail Strategy: The view from the bridge*, ed J Reynolds and C Cuthbertson, Elsevier Butterworth-Heinemann, Oxford

Rowat, C (2003) Factory gate pricing: the debate continues, *Focus*, Feb, pp 46–48

Seth, A and Randall, G (1999) *The Grocers*, Kogan Page, London

Smith, D L G (1998) Logistics in Tesco: past, present and future, in *Logistics and Retail Management*, ed J Fernie and L Sparks, pp 154–83, Kogan Page, London

Smith, D L G and Sparks, L (1993) The transformation of physical distribution in retailing: the example of Tesco plc, *International Review of Retail, Distribution and Consumer Research*, **3** (1), pp 35–64

Sparks, L (1986) The changing structure of distribution in retail companies, *Transactions of the Institute of British Geographers*, **11** (2), pp 147–54

7

Temperature-controlled supply chains

David Smith and Leigh Sparks

INTRODUCTION

Consumers expect food in retail stores to be of good quality, to have a decent shelf life and to be fit for purpose. If a retailer can present products attractively and provide good shelf life, then there is more chance of the products being purchased and satisfying consumer needs. Managing the supply chain to maintain quality and 'fitness' of food products therefore has direct cost and service implications. Many dimensions have to be managed. One of these dimensions is the need for an appropriate temperature regime. Many food stores contain products supplied and retailed at a number of different temperatures. Failure to maintain an appropriate temperature control can adversely affect the product's appearance or shelf life at one end of the spectrum, or could potentially make consumers ill or even kill them at the other end. Temperature-controlled supply chains (TCSCs) could be said to be a matter of life or death.

WHAT IS A TEMPERATURE-CONTROLLED SUPPLY CHAIN?

At its simplest, a TCSC is a food supply chain that requires that food products be maintained in a temperature-controlled environment, rather than exposing them to whatever ambient temperatures prevail at the various stages of the supply chain. This basic description hides however an essentially complex and potentially expensive process. The length and complexity of such supply chains are determined by the natures and sources of the products, the legal and quality assurance requirements on food safety, and the distribution facilities available from production to consumption. Recently they have been affected by the need to deliver food safety and integrity throughout the supply chain (Deloitte/Cmi, 2003).

There are several food temperature levels to suit different types of products: for example we could identify frozen, cold chill, medium chill and exotic chill. Frozen is −25° Celsius for ice-cream; −18° for other foods and food ingredients. Cold chill is 0° to +1° for fresh meat and poultry, most dairy and meat-based provisions, most vegetables and some fruit. Medium chill is +5° for some pastry-based products, butters, fats and cheeses. Exotic chill is +10–15° for potatoes, eggs, exotic fruit and bananas. If a food supply chain is dedicated to a narrow range of products, the temperature will be set at the level for that product set. If a food supply chain is handling a broad range of products, an optimum temperature or a limited number of different temperature settings is used. Failure to maintain appropriate temperature regimes throughout a product's life can shorten the life of that product or adversely affect its quality or fitness for consumption.

It should be immediately obvious that the management process in TCSC is a complicated one. Chilling and freezing products is in itself hard, and maintaining appropriate temperatures throughout a product's life, in both storage and transit, is complicated. How, for example, can a retailer ensure that products are always under the appropriate temperature regime when they travel from a field in New Zealand to a refrigerator in a shop in Tobermory?

THE IMPORTANCE OF TEMPERATURE-CONTROLLED SUPPLY CHAINS

The TCSC in food is a significant proportion of the retail food market and one that has been increasing steadily (McKinnon and Campbell, 1998). CH Robinson/Iowa State University (2001) suggest that over half the spend in American supermarkets is on temperature-controlled products. Frozen food in the UK has been increasing in volume by 3–4 per cent on average per annum for the last 40 years. Developments in products such as ready meals and prepared salads have further expanded the market.

Analysts see the meal solution sector continuing to increase very rapidly (Gorniak, 2002). 'Fast food' chains have captured a huge market share and are reliant on frozen product. The importance of products requiring temperature control, to both consumers and retailers, has thus been increasing, and seems set to increase further.

Even products that we often take for granted may require some form of temperature control. Prepared sandwiches for example require chilled storage of ingredients. These are then combined to make the finished product, which in turn requires temperature-controlled storage, distribution and display (Smith, Davies and Bent, 2001). Failure to maintain adequate control (for example placing prawn sandwiches in the sun) generates obvious risks. More subtly, an inability to maintain temperature control will reduce shelf life in the product, which is any case often very limited. This increases wastage and complicates the supply dynamics, adding costs. Similarly, much of the bread in supermarket in-store bakeries is brought to the store frozen, and baked/heated on the premises.

On the supply side, changes in the location of product sources and the removal of wholesalers from the channel have had major effects. Technological changes in production and distribution have also allowed a transformation of the supply network. As production and distribution technological capabilities have developed, so the ability for national and international, rather than local, sourcing and distribution has emerged. Products can be brought across the world to satisfy demands for products 'out of season' or of an exotic nature, as well as for reasons of lower purchase or cost price. Internationalization of supply of even indigenous products is common. The system developments needed to meet the demands for quality and consistency, including temperature control aspects, do impact on the channel composition (eg Dolan and Humphrey, 2000). The handling systems to manage the air freighting of for example tomatoes from the Canary Islands, baby sweetcorn from Egypt or flowers from Malaysia require a considerable technological development. They also however represent a fundamental organizational and relationship shift.

CH Robinson/Iowa State University argue that TCSC are more important than 'ordinary' retail supply chains as they have inherently more complexity and complications:

> The (Logistics) challenge is more formidable when the materials and products require temperature control. The shelf life is often short for such products, placing even greater importance on the speed and dependability of the transportation and handling systems. Temperature controlled products also require specialized transportation equipment and storage facilities and closer monitoring of product integrity while in the logistics system.

Adding to the logistics complexity is the seasonal demand for many temperature controlled products ... arising from natural production conditions and consumer demand.... In addition, carriers of temperature controlled products confront unique requirements and incur greater costs than carriers of dry products.

(CH Robinson/Iowa State University, 2001: 1–2)

Some of the uniqueness and increased costs derives from this need to ensure temperature control. There is extra cost incurred in the requirements for handling temperature-controlled products, and also in the need to monitor temperature regimes in the supply chain.

As the number and range of temperature-controlled products have increased, and a number of market failures have occurred, so the issue of food safety has become more central (Henson and Caswell, 1999; Lindgreen and Hingley, 2003). Failures of food safety in the UK (not all of course associated with failures of temperature control) are common on a localized and individual level. For example there is a high level of personal food poisoning in the UK, although the extent to which this is a result of product or channel failure rather than an individual consumer's lack of knowledge or care is unclear. More publicly notable however have been national events ('food scares') such as Listeria in cheese, Salmonella in eggs and chickens, BSE in cattle and E coli 157 in meat. These national events raise concern and comment about food safety. There is thus a perception over the safety of supply of food and food chains, which in turn has focused attention on risk assessment and risk management. Such concerns are not of course restricted to the UK. Deloitte/Cmi (2003) point to similar issues in the United States, and note that the issue of food safety has been ranked first in a CIES survey of food retailing issues in 2002, compared with not being ranked at all in 1999. TCSCs gain importance therefore from the risks associated with failure and from the steps necessary to minimize these risks. Some of the steps are voluntary and company-specific, others are required by recent legal developments (see later).

As a consequence of risk assessments and the major problems in food safety, TCSCs have become a focal point for the development of food safety legislation across Europe. Although such legislation introduces requirements that cover a broad range of issues, one key aspect is the temperature conditions under which products are maintained. Such legislation combined with increasing retailer liability for prosecution has put great pressure on the standards of control throughout the food supply chain, particularly in the case of temperature control. For these reasons, TCSCs are often seen as a specialist discipline within logistics. To some extent this is understandable given the need for specialist facilities such as warehouses, vehicles and refrigerators to operate chilled or frozen distribution channels. This specialist market however is itself increasing in scale and scope, both as the market expands and as operational and managerial complexity increases.

However, it is not all cost and regulation, as there are operational and commercial benefits to be gained from proper TCSC management. These benefits might include an increase in shelf life and freshness and thus better customer perception of products and the retailer. This increase in product quality and perception is the direct result of maintaining the correct temperature for that product group steadily and constantly throughout its supply chain journey. One major effect of an increase in shelf life and freshness has been that consumers can notice the difference between product supplied through a fully temperature-controlled supply chain and that supplied through a partially temperature-controlled supply chain, and make product and retailer choices accordingly. While it is generally the case today that the major food retailers maintain chill and cold chain integrity and thus have totally controlled TCSCs, this has not always been the case.

CHANGES IN TEMPERATURE-CONTROLLED SUPPLY CHAINS

The TCSC has developed and changed since the 1980s. In the past in the UK, the supply chain often consisted of single temperature warehouses dedicated to narrow product ranges of food, such as butters, fats and cheeses at +5° Celsius, dairy-based provisions, meat-based provisions, fresh meat and poultry, fruit and vegetables and frozen products. The design, equipment and disciplines were only partially implemented so that there was incomplete integrity of the temperature control. Products were exposed to periods of high ambient temperature, which affected the shelf life and the quality of the product. Single temperature systems also meant that many more deliveries were needed. Such systems were essentially inefficient and ineffective.

Such a situation existed in the 1980s in Tesco (see Sparks, 1986; Smith and Sparks, 1993; Smith, 1998). In the mid-1980s the Tesco TCSC consisted of a large number of small single-temperature warehouses, each specializing in the storage, handling and delivery of a narrow product range. Examples of these sets of product ranges were fresh produce; fresh meat and poultry; butters, fats and cheeses; chilled diary provisions; chilled meat provisions; and frozen foods. Each set was managed by a different specialist logistics service provider organized on behalf of the manufacturer and supplier. The deliveries to the retail stores took place two or three times a week, with the temperature-controlled vehicle going from one store to another delivering the appropriate number of pallets of products. The delivery notes and product checking were conducted at the back door of the store, and the cost of delivery was included in the price of the product. Fresh meat and poultry was controlled on an individual case basis and charged by weight as each case had a different weight.

There are several limitations of this model of a TCSC. It was expensive to expand to meet large increases in overall growth in volume as it requires the building of more and more single-temperature warehouses. The retail delivery frequency was limited. The delivery volume drop size per store was small and vehicles used were under-sized because of problems over retail access. At that time there also was not full awareness of the importance of maintaining total integrity of the chill chain.

The strategy that Tesco decided upon was to build a small number of new large multi-temperature 'composite' warehouses that would store, handle and deliver the full range of product sets, all from the same location. The manufacturers and suppliers of all the product sets made daily deliveries into the composite distribution centre. The composite delivery frequency to the retail stores increased to daily. The delivery vehicles had movable bulkheads and three temperature-controlled evaporators so that up to three different temperature regimes could be set on the one vehicle. The benefit was improved vehicle utilization and improved service to retail. Chill chain integrity disciplines were implemented rigorously from supplier to retail shelf.

There are other aspects to this change. Distribution and retail agreed a policy of not checking the goods at the retail back door, which improved the speed with which the goods could be transferred into the temperature-controlled chambers at the store. This improved chill chain integrity. The goods were delivered in green reusable plastic trays, on 'dollies', or on roll cages, which improved handling at store, in terms of both speed and quality. New store designs permitted the use of full-length vehicles, so improving efficiency.

Another major change in supply chains between the 1980s and 2000s has been the increasing pace of the order and replenishment cycle (McKinnon and Campbell, 1998). Today with many fresh products there is no stock held in the retail distribution centre overnight (IGD, 2001). Stock holding in frozen products has also declined to below 10 days (IGD, 2001). Lead times have continued to be reduced.

One of the key drivers of this increase in pace has been the development of information technology, which has enabled a large volume of data to be collected, processed and transmitted at faster speeds. Today data are collected from the point of sale and used in calculating future customer demand, which in turn forms the basis of the orders placed on suppliers. The scale, control and skill of the retail logistics operation has improved so that even distance-sourced products can be rapidly transported to their destinations at the regional distribution centres. The move to centrally prepared meat and poultry rather than having butchers at the retail stores is one example of this (Lindgreen and Hingley, 2003). Another example is the sourcing of produce from Spain direct from the growers into the distribution centres (see box). These changes, encouraged by information technology among other factors, require changes in supply chain facilities and operations to ensure chill chain integrity.

Produce Direct from Spain

Spain has become one of the major providers of produce to the rest of Europe. In the late 1990s, major UK supermarkets started to purchase produce direct from Spanish suppliers rather than through UK wholesalers. The total direct flow of produce from Spain solely to UK is over 1,000 vehicles per week.

For example, iceberg lettuce is grown in large volumes between October and May in Murcia and Almeria in south-east Spain under direct contract between the retailer and the growing cooperatives. The retailers' quality assurance and technical departments provide the grower with the product specification and transport temperature-control requirements from Spain to UK.

There are two methods of direct delivery into the UK supermarket distribution network. The first is to fill the vehicle in Spain solely with iceberg lettuce. The delivery is split once it arrives in the UK by sending the vehicle to two distribution centres. The second method is to combine several produce products, for instance iceberg lettuce and courgettes, while the vehicle is still in its originating region in Spain. This combined product volume fills the vehicle, which then delivers the whole load to a single distribution centre in the UK.

The distance from Murcia to central England is 1,500 miles. The deliveries flow through daily. The total process from harvesting to customer is four days:

- Day one: the iceberg lettuce is harvested, cooled, packaged and loaded into temperature-controlled vehicles set at $+3°$.
- Day three: the iceberg lettuce arrives direct at the UK supermarket temperature-controlled distribution centre where it is checked in. Within 3 hours it is allocated and picked for a retail store, ready to go out on the next delivery.
- Day four: the iceberg lettuce is on display in the retail store, available for the consumer to purchase.

The code life on direct iceberg lettuce is one day above 'normal' deliveries. This extra day can be used for rolling stock in the distribution centre. The ability to roll stock means that full loads of iceberg lettuce can be delivered direct to the distribution centre. Any stock that is not allocated to a store and picked immediately (due to demand) can be rolled over to supply the next day's orders.

The range of products delivered direct has increased from the original Golden Delicious and Granny Smith apples to now include Braeburn and Royal Gala on top fruit; white seedless grapes, nectarines, peaches, iceberg lettuce, galia melons and broccoli.

The seasons of other products direct from Spain are December/January: soft citrus; January/May: tomatoes and broccoli; June/August: galia and honeydew melons.

Source: author interviews

Following the implementation of centralized distribution, attention turned to the condition of TCSC for the inbound product sets from the supplier and manufacturer into the regional distribution centres. The examination of the logistics of the inbound supply chain revealed that there were huge opportunities to improve transport efficiency. The increasing pace of the retail supply chain had resulted in most suppliers of temperature-controlled product sets sending their vehicles long distances, but only partly filled, to the various retailers' regional distribution centres. So for example, suppliers' vehicles carrying fruit and vegetables from a supplying region like Kent were following each other to distant regional distribution centres in northern England and Wales, each with a partially full vehicle to the same destination. Clearly there was an opportunity for the consolidation of supply.

This process of consolidation saw the appointment of designated logistics service providers in the appropriate regions to manage and operate temperature-controlled consolidation centres, accumulating full vehicle loads of temperature-controlled products to despatch to the composite distribution centres. These consolidation centres also conducted quality assurance testing of the product. There were two benefits of placing the quality assurance function in the consolidation centres. The first was that they were close to the suppliers so that any problems could be dealt with face to face where required. The second benefit was that these vehicles did not then need to undergo quality assurance checking when they arrived at the distribution centre. This improved the turnaround time of the inbound vehicle, increasing its productivity and profitability, and also enabled the handling operation to commence earlier and so keep the goods-in bay clear for the next set of deliveries. This was especially important in the early evening when a very high volume of produce harvested that same day is delivered.

Some of the effects of these changes to the Tesco supply chain are considered in Table 7.1. This summarizes the last 15–20 years of temperature control supply and the ways in which this has changed. Over the time period the shelf life for these products has increased considerably. In the case of vegetables, it has doubled and for top fruit the increase is even greater. This provides better product for longer for the consumer, and is more efficient for the retailer. It does, as the table indicates, require a major reorientation of the supply chain and a dedication to standards. The overall effect however has been to provide fresher product more quickly and cheaply to the retail store, and to lengthen the shelf life and quality time of a product for the consumer.

The discussion above is centred on developments in Tesco. Similar operations and developments have been introduced in other major food retailers. These have been needed to handle the massive expansion of demand in the temperature-controlled sector in recent years and to compete with the market leader.

ISSUES IN TEMPERATURE-CONTROLLED SUPPLY CHAINS

The discussion above and comments in the introduction allow the identification of a number of key issues in TCSC. Here, three are identified for further discussion: the issues of costs, food safety and HACCP, and partnerships.

The basic supply configuration in the temperature-controlled channel is not really much different from those in ordinary retail distribution channels. The demands placed on the components however are far more extreme, and thus the issue of costs of facilities and operations is important.

TCSCs place strict conditions on the design, equipment and discipline of the operation, which makes the cost greater than for ambient products. Temperature-controlled storage facilities need to be maintained at the appropriate temperature with accurate recording equipment and cooling equipment, including the capacity to cope with high ambient temperatures especially in the summer. Vehicle docking bays need air bags that inflate around the vehicle to prevent exposure to ambient temperatures. For frozen storage facilities, the loading and unloading bays should be at 0°C.

Table 7.1   Tesco Case Study: Enhancements in Shelf Life

Stage	Soft fruit	Top fruit	Veg	Temperature-controlled supply chain status and improvement action
Pre-1980				Single temperature produce centres (three). Ambient and +5° Celsius. Code dates not a legal requirement. Shelf life managed at retail. Retail ordered from local suppliers without any technical support.
1980–6				Two further produce centres. Operating procedures remained the same. Suppliers normally loaded in yard or from ambient bays. Many vehicles have curtain sides.
1986				Notice that code dates to become a legal requirement for produce. Produce technical team established shelf life and introduced QC checks at distribution centres. 78/48-hour ordering cycle to retail.
1987	2 CD + 2 CL = 4 days total	5 CD + 2 CL = 7 days total	3 CD + 2 CL = 5 days total	Code dates CD introduced for loose and pre-packed produce. In addition to the selling code dates there were additional days where product would be at its best. This time was called Customer life (CL). QC in produce depots to enforce specification. Two further produce centres. Code of practice introduced for suppliers included distribution centre controls and vehicle standards, eg no curtain siders.
1989	2 CD + 4 CL = 6 days total	5 CD + 9 CL = 14 days total	3 CD + 5 CL = 8 days total	Six composite distribution centres opened. Separate temperature chambers of +3, +10, +15 for produce. Composite multi-temperature trailers deliver at +3 and +10° Celsius loading from sealed temperature-controlled loading bays. Customer life extended by 2 days for soft fruit, by 5 days for top fruit and 3 days for vegetables. No increase in code dates. Consumer demand for Fruit and Vegetables doubled as a consequence of the introduction of strict temperature control disciplines throughout the supply chain.

Table 7.1 *continued*

Stage	Soft fruit	Top fruit	Veg	Temperature-controlled supply chain status and improvement action
1990				**Food Safety Act**: To meet due diligence HACCP (Hazard Analysis Critical Control Points) analysis introduced throughout the supply chain. The result was more consistent shelf life but no increase in days. Retail stores only allowed to buy from suppliers with technical approval.
1995	2 CD + 5 CL = 7 days total	5 CD + 10 CL = 15 days total	3 CD + 6 CL = 9 days total	Produce temperature controlled consolidation hubs introduced. Six further hubs added over next three years. QA control introduced at hubs so quality checked before produce despatched to the composites. Hubs located close to supplier regions so prompt resolution of problems with supplier management. Shelf life review shows increase of 1 day across all vegetables, soft fruit and stone fruit. Salads become inconsistent because of harvesting during the night before dew point. But there was a greater benefit of starting despatch earlier, especially from Spain. Retail order lead time 48/24 hours
1997				Composite distribution centres change produce chamber temperatures to +1 and +12° Celsius with tighter variation of +/–1° from +/–2° before. No change to shelf life because the supply chain disciplines fully in place.
1998	2 CD + 5 CL = 7 days total	6 CD + 10 CL = 16 days total	4 CD + 6 CL = 10 days total	Technical departments given targets to increase produce shelf life. One potential improvement was to introduce US-type variety control. The benefit is only possible because of the very strict total supply chain temperature control. One extra day of code life for stores.
2000				Continuous replenishment introduced. The benefit is split deliveries into retail stores with different code dates for retail without any loss of customer shelf life.

Table 7.1 *continued*

Stage	Soft fruit	Top fruit	Veg	Temperature-controlled supply chain status and improvement action
2002	2 CD + 5 CL = 7 days total	7 CD + 10 CL = 17 days total	5 CD + 6 CL = 11 days total	Further supply chain improvements in shelf life to extend code dates by one day, no change to customer life to improve availability on selected lines: core vegetables, top fruit, stone fruit but not salads or soft fruit. Three potential methods are: a) atmospheric control especially during the three-day delivery from Spain; b) humidity control; c) ethylene control.

Source: author interviews

Vehicles require appropriate insulation and refrigeration and control panels to set and to maintain the product at the correct temperature. An important facet of this transport refrigeration is that it is not designed to remove heat from the product (as in 'normal refrigeration'), so it is essential that the heat is taken out of the product before it is loaded onto a vehicle. If not, heat will transfer to other products causing them to be exposed to a temperature outside the designated range. Some vehicles have bulkheads and several evaporators so that different sections can be set at different temperatures. The benefit of this is that vehicle utilization is improved, but operating procedures are made more complicated. This also affects costs. The cost of a multi-temperature refrigerated trailer is about £100,000 compared to around £30,000 for an ambient trailer. The cost of warehousing is about £20 per square foot compared to about £10 for ambient. Warehouse operatives and drivers must behave in accordance with the requirements for chill chain integrity to protect the product. Losing a trailer load of product through overheating is not only expensive but also severely impacts on service level to retail and the consumer, because the pace of the supply chain does not leave time to recover with alternative product. Such cost considerations have enabled niche operators to enter and develop the market for frozen and chilled distribution. There is also a specialist association in the UK to assist this sector of the logistics industry (Cold Storage and Distribution Federation – http://www.csdf.org.uk/) and to liaise with government on regulations in this sector.

As noted earlier, the integrity of TCSCs is important for food safety (see Deloitte/Cmi, 2003). This places an obligation of care and duty of implementation on the supplier, retailer and logistics. In the UK, for example, the Food Safety Act of 1990 defined the storage, handling and transportation requirements for food products, including temperature control for certain categories. One of the provisions of the Food Safety Act 1990 makes it an absolute offence to sell food that is unfit for human consumption. Food that has 'gone off' due to inadequate temperature control falls into this category. The Act however allows for a defence of 'due diligence' against any charges. Thus a business may be able to mount a defence based on evidence that all reasonable precautions had been exercised to avoid the commission of the offence. In terms of temperature control, this implies that there needs to be a system of control, maintenance, monitoring and recording (for evidence) of the temperature regimes in the supply chain.

The Food Standards (Temperature Control) Regulations of 1995 made it an offence to allow food to be kept at temperatures that could cause risk to health. This again implied a tightening of systems in the chain. This was effectively codified by the General Hygiene Act of 1995, which required all food businesses to adopt a risk management tool such as Hazard Analysis Critical Control Point (HACCP). Loader and Hobbs (1999) see this as a change in philosophy, representing a move away from an end-product food safety inspection approach to a preventative, scientific focus with the responsibility for risk management placed on the food business proprietor. As a result, HACCP and other systems (Sterns, Codron and Reardon, 2001) have been vital to establish process controls through the identification of critical points in the process that need to be monitored and controlled (see box).

Hazard Analysis Critical Control Points (HACCP)

It is important in the application of the disciplines of an integrated temperature-controlled supply chain to understand the principles of the obligations of suppliers, retailers and logistics service providers.

All have a duty of care for the product. In order to meet this duty of care they must demonstrate that they have applied due diligence in the structure and execution of their operation: that is, that they have taken all reasonable methods to ensure the care of the product.

One of these reasonable methods is Hazard Analysis Critical Control Points (HACCP), which is central to the discipline of chill chain integrity in logistics. The Quality Assurance department conducts a survey of the supply chain under its control, with the objective of identifying those circumstances where the product might be exposed to unsuitable conditions, or hazards. They rank these hazards according to the importance of their risk, for example as high, medium or low. Procedures are then put in place at an appropriate level to prevent that risk. To express this differently: identify the hazards, analyse their importance, identify which are critical and set up control procedures at these points. Once HACCP is put in place it becomes a strong argument that due diligence is being practised.

For temperature-controlled supply chains, there are big benefits from putting the physical and operational procedures in place along the whole length of the supply chain. This investment reduces a high risk to a low risk. By stabilizing the temperature throughout the life of the product, suppliers and retailers can concentrate on other aspects that can add value to the product, such as growing varieties.

If we take the example of the movement of chill goods from distribution centre to retail stores on multi-temperature vehicles, then the risk to food safety is high and the risk of occurrence is high. The Critical Control points for loading at the distribution centre are:

- The temperature setting is stated on the load sheet and run sheet.
- The loader checks the load sheet and sets temperatures for compartment.
- The loader secures the bulkhead.
- The loader switches refrigeration on and ticks the relevant temperature on the load sheet.
- Once loading is complete a supervisor checks settings and switches against load sheet and signs off if correct.
- The load sheet is handed into the goods out office.
- The driver checks digital readings (usually at the front of unit, visible in the rearview mirror) against the run sheet and if correct, signs off and hands it in to the goods out office.
- The goods out clerk checks if the temperatures on the load sheet and run sheet match, and if correct, allows the vehicle to leave.
- The goods out supervisor undertakes daily checks to assure compliance.

Source: author interviews

These Acts in the UK were in essence national responses to approaches being recommended in Europe and codified in the EU legislation. The food scares in the UK of the late 1990s also brought forward a response. The Food Standards Act 1999 created the Food Standards Agency (FSA) in April 2000. The Act was intended to induce all those involved in the food supply chain to improve their food handling practices, including temperature control. There is no doubt that as the FSA becomes more established, it will have a stronger role to play in TCSC than we have seen to date (http://www.foodstandards.gov.uk).

This onus on due diligence and the responsibility of businesses had a major effect on systems of control and monitoring of performance. It also however had an effect on the business relationships and governance in place. If a retailer for example wishes to be protected from claims, it must ensure that its suppliers are undertaking good practices, in addition to its own practice. This is not only true for retailer brand products, but for all sourced products. As such, traceability and tracking become more fundamental and good partnerships become crucial. As costs rise in introducing new systems, increasing the depth and quality of partnerships is both a safeguard and offers possible cost benefits. As a result, partnerships expanded considerably after 1991 in the UK (Wilson, 1996. Loader and Hobbs, 1999; Fearne and Hughes, 2000; Lindgreen and Hingley, 2003). Food retailers today are keen to have such partnerships and to use them in their marketing, as seen in the numerous 'farm assured' type schemes. Such partnerships and changes in organization of the supply chain are not restricted to UK suppliers. Dolan and Humphrey (2000) show how in Africa, the requirements of the leading UK retailers have transformed the horticultural sector in scale and operational terms, leaving smaller producers in a precarious position. This scale dimension is linked closely to the legal requirements and the costs of compliance and potential chain failure.

FUTURE DEVELOPMENTS AND CONSTRAINTS

TCSCs have undergone considerable changes in recent decades. This process is likely to continue, driven as it is by tightening legislation and risk awareness, the increased costs of supply and the demands on the chain from increased volume and pace of operation. A number of future issues can be explored.

First is the question of risk and integrity. There are a number of gaps in the typical current TCSC. For example, at the retail outlet, few stores have a chilled reception area that docks with the incoming distribution vehicle. The majority have an ambient delivery bay that is exposed to the outside temperature. The delivery reception area requires an operational discipline such that chilled and frozen product is not left exposed to ambient temperature for more than 20 minutes. The retail operational staff have to move the chilled and frozen pallets, roll cages and the like promptly into the relevant temperature-controlled chambers. Finally, when the product is being taken to the chilled or frozen retail shelf or cabinet within the store for replenishment, the same 20-minute rule applies. The potential for problems is clear. Another gap occurs in the 'forgotten' segment of the supply chain: the length of time from selection of product by a consumer to purchase and then transport home could be considerable, and affect the product adversely. As electronic commerce expands, so issues of home delivery confront much the same problem. If the home owner has always to be present, such services are more limited and/or costly. But 'dropped' deliveries of temperature-controlled products increase the risks for the consumer.

Second, there is likely to be further technological development. In the future, electronic temperature tagging could become the norm, so that operators throughout the TCSC will be able to monitor current and previous conditions. Such monitoring could be real-time online for some products, or could be packaging-based for others: for example, colour-coded packaging changing colour if temperatures go outside allowable ranges. Advances in packaging environments leading to enhanced shelf-life time may also accompany such monitoring advances. Associated developments in technologies such as Radio Frequency Identification (RFID) will bring additional data management and control issues.

Finally, there are issues brought about by globalization and partnership trends. While there have been benefits to the introduction of current procedures and practices, concern is mounting about the environmental costs of monocultures and the extreme distribution distances that are travelled. Given the costs of compliance to meet western food safety concerns, it might be more beneficial to look for more local sourcing. The internationalization of retailing acts as a counter to this however, and may allow retailers to build deeper partnerships across the globe and to utilize their experience to enhance the quality of the local supply chain. However consumer demands may not allow time in the supply chain for such global solutions. The future organizational shape, and the role of partnerships, remain therefore subject to change (Zuurbier, 1999).

REFERENCES

CH Robinson Worldwide Inc/Iowa State University (2001) *Temperature Controlled Logistics Report 2001–2002*, CH Robinson Worldwide

Deloitte Consulting/Cmi Consulting (2003) *Delivering Integrity in the End-to-End Food Supply Chain*, Deloitte Consulting/Cmi Consulting, London

Dolan, C and Humphrey, J (2000) Governance and trade in fresh vegetables: the impact of UK Supermarkets on the African horticultural industry, *Journal of Development Studies*, **37** (2), pp 147–76

Fearne, A and Hughes, D (2000) Success factors in the fresh produce supply chains, *British Food Journal*, **102**, pp 760–72

Gorniak, C (2002) *The Meal Solutions Outlook to 2007*, Reuters Business Insight, London

Henson, S and Caswell, J (1999) Food safety regulation: an overview of contemporary issues, *Food Policy*, **24**, pp 589–603

Institute of Grocery Distribution (IGD) (2001) *Retail Logistics 2001*, IGD, Watford

Lindgreen, A and Hingley, M (2003) The impact of food safety and animal welfare policies on supply chain management: the case of the Tesco meat supply chain, *British Food Journal*, **105** (6), pp 328–49

Loader, R and Hobbs, J E (1999) Strategic response to food safety legislation, *Food Policy*, 24, pp 685–706

McKinnon, A C and Campbell, J (1998) *Quick Response in the Frozen Food Supply Chain* [Online] www.som.hw.ac.uk/logistics/salvesen.html (accessed 10 July 2002)

Smith, D L G (1998) Logistics in Tesco, Chapter 8 of *Logistics and Retail Management*, ed J Fernie and L Sparks, pp 154–83, Kogan Page, London.

Smith, D L G and Sparks, L (1993) The transformation of physical distribution in retailing: the example of Tesco plc, *International Review of Retail, Distribution and Consumer Research*, **3**, pp 35–64

Smith, J L, Davies, G J and Bent, A J (2001) Retail fast foods: overview of safe sandwich manufacture, *Journal of the Royal Society for the Promotion of Health*, **121** (4), pp 220–23

Sparks, L (1986) The changing structure of distribution in retail companies, *Transactions of the Institute of British Geographers*, **11**, pp 147–54

Sterns, P A, Codron, J-M and Reardon, T (2001) *Quality and Quality Assurance in the Fresh Produce Sector: A case study of European retailers*, American Agricultural Economics Association Annual Meeting, Chicago, August [Online] http://agecon.lib.umn.edu/ (accessed 11 July 2002)

Wilson, N (1996) The supply chains of perishable products in northern Europe, *British Food Journal*, **98** (6), pp 9–15

Zuurbier, P J P (1999) Supply chain management in the fresh produce industry: a mile to go? *Journal of Food Distribution Research*, **30** (1), pp 20–30

8

Rethinking efficient replenishment in the grocery sector

Phil Whiteoak

ECR – A FAD OR THE FUTURE?

The idea of Efficient Consumer Response (ECR) is sweeping through the board rooms of most fast-moving consumer goods manufacturers and retailers in the advanced economies of the world. The vision of ECR Europe, 'Working together to fulfil consumer wishes better, faster and at less cost', is driving a unique initiative by suppliers, distributors and retailers that claims to provide European consumers with the best possible value, service and variety of products through a collaborative approach to improving the supply chain. Debate still rages as to whether ECR is, at best, a philosophy which can genuinely improve consumer value or, at worst, simply a new management fad. Alternatively, it may be seen as a tactic for gaining control in a trading relationship or simply as a toolkit for tinkering with the complex balances of the supply chain. Indeed, in a provocative address to the 39th CIES Annual Executive Congress in Paris in June 1996, Professor Lou Stern of Northwestern University, USA, remarked, 'ECR is a short-term survival tactic, a mandatory set of tactics which may allow the business to buy time . . . it does not ask the question "How do people really want to shop for food?"'

Rather, it assumes that the answer is the existing supermarket . . . and goes on from there to address value chain logistics.' He also decried the notion of collaboration: 'partnership as it's practised today is manipulation. . . we'll be partners if it benefits me.'

There is no doubt that today's grocery markets are intensively competitive. The internationalization of trade and the rapid pace of technological development are creating major challenges, even for well-established businesses. Globally, increasingly sophisticated consumers are driving both manufacturers and retailers into developing extended product ranges and into trading in more countries and distribution channels. These trends tend to dilute traditional economies of scale. Supply chains are becoming longer and more complex as a result of the need for sourcing the materials to support these markets. Environmental legislation, the pressure of reducing cycle times and a focus on customer service are constraining the drive for efficiency and cost reduction. Addressing value chain logistics is thus not to be disparaged and offers the logistics community a worthwhile opportunity to improve its performance within this dynamic environment, notwithstanding other breakthroughs in fulfilling consumer needs, such as home tele-shopping. In any event, there will always remain the need to move goods efficiently from the point of production to the point of consumption. In short, there will always be a 'supply chain'. In grocery, the opportunity is indeed worthwhile: the retail value of European grocery markets is in excess of €700 billion (1998 prices), with supply chain costs estimated to be around 10 per cent of sales. Small improvements in logistics efficiency across this market can thus generate huge cash savings. The building of a critical mass of businesses that share the vision and that co-operate and exchange information to employ a number of 'improvement concepts' is the key to unlocking this benefit.

The improvement concepts within the ECR initiative embrace Category Management (which aims to optimize the range of products stocked in store, the efficiency of promotions and new product introductions), Product Replenishment and Enabling Technologies. Broadly, these address 'demand side' and 'supply side' activities and the information systems necessary to support them, and consist more or less of a catalogue of techniques and a guide for their application. No single technique is universally effective and, while the application of any one technique may generate benefits for one supply chain player, it may have adverse consequences for the other. This chapter reviews the facts and myths behind current 'efficient replenishment' thinking and proposes a supplementary approach to the current practice.

EFFICIENT REPLENISHMENT

Both in the United States and in Europe the initial focus of the ECR movement was product replenishment, or, as it has come to be known, Efficient Replenishment. The reasons for this are simple: first, the size of the prize to be won in streamlining grocery supply chains is huge – in the United States it was first estimated that the total grocery supply chain inventory could be reduced from more than 100 days of sales to around 60 days by the application of ER techniques. Although in European supply chains the stock is on average already substantially below the American aspiration, their annual operating costs of €70 billion (1998 prices) offer tempting opportunities. Second, so far, the subject of ER has been relatively non-contentious. Hitherto, it has not figured greatly in trading debates between retailers and their suppliers about range, promotions and profitability and has frequently been left to the logistics functions of either business to resolve.

However, there is now a growing awareness across Europe that ER is a strategic tool for improving margins and reducing cash tied up in working capital. The danger is that the pursuit of these benefits by any one party without consideration of the possible impacts on other players in the supply chain can significantly disturb the balance of costs between manufacturers and retailers. Despite setting out to create a climate of collaboration in which all parties should benefit, the ECR movement may add to this risk of destabilization by promoting a particular technique without adequate explanation of the most appropriate criteria for its application. This idea is explored below.

What is efficient replenishment? Figure 8.1 illustrates the concept as a smooth, continual flow of product, matched to consumption and supported by a timely, accurate and paperless information flow.

The techniques often described for delivering this vision are illustrated in Figure 8.2. Of these, Continuous Replenishment and Cross-Docking are probably amongst the most frequently discussed, and perhaps the least well understood.

CONTINUOUS REPLENISHMENT PROGRAMMES (CRP)

CRP comes in many forms. The most commonly described is Vendor Managed Inventory (VMI) in a Fixed Order Quantity (FOQ) environment. This requires *daily* review of the retail sales and stock position, with an order only suggested when necessary to meet previously agreed

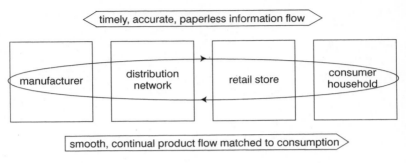

Figure 8.1   Concept of Efficient Replenishment

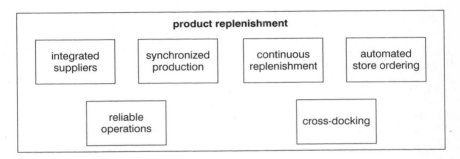

Figure 8.2   Techniques for Efficient Replenishment

target stocking levels. The replenishment algorithm uses actual retail sales information for forecasting future sales, on the basis of which a new order is calculated. In order to work effectively, this must have Electronic Data Interchange (EDI) communication from the retailer to the supplier and probably needs intervention or examination by the supplier's customer service department every day.

What is the objective of this sort of CRP? By gaining *control* of retail replenishment processes a manufacturer aims to manage ordering behaviour towards more efficient load building. The manufacturer is also responsible for managing product availability at the point to which goods are delivered (which presupposes the manufacturer can do this better than the retailer), hence assuring support for his promotional and feature activity and thereby moving towards preferred supplier status. The manufacturer does gain the benefit of market intelligence about sell-through, but overall the information is of little further value unless it can be obtained from a sufficiently large population of customers to enable its use in the modification of sales forecasts and production plans. In any case, this is likely to be most suitable for retail outlets where there are store back-room stocks and where orders are still raised directly on the supplier. It is also suitable for retail regional distribution centres (RDCs) which are responsible for their own replenishment and which are prepared to relinquish control to the supplier. It is most likely to be suitable for lines with large volume sales and forecastable promotional impact.

A variant on this is called Co-Managed Inventory (CMI) where retailers share information about promotional programmes of all suppliers in the category with vendors participating in the scheme. There may well be legal limitations on this under European competition law. In the United Kingdom, there are few applications of this sort of VMI with the major multiple retailers.

VMI may also run in a Fixed Order Cycle (FOC) environment. Typically, this is used to service smaller outlets which are not capable of managing their own inventories well and where it is only cost-effective for a supplier to make a sales call or a delivery weekly or fortnightly at most. In this situation, either the supplier's representative or merchandiser counts stock or, prompted by a small discount as an incentive, the customer counts it and returns a balance for each stocked product by telephone or fax to the supplier's office where it is keyed into the VMI system. The movement between the current and previous stock balance is used to calculate the retail sales. Otherwise the mathematics are the same as before. This approach is suitable for use where customers are not sufficiently well-advanced to be able to support EDI connections. The prime aim of this style of application is to be a sales support tool for gaining control of in-store availability to support display and feature selling. Real examples of this exist in the independent wholesale sector. The key elements in the replenishment here are the order review cycle, the replenishment lead time and the target safety stock level.

Both FOQ and FOC VMI systems could also be run by suppliers upstream of grocery product manufacturers to keep factories supplied on a similar basis. There are also some radical approaches now in existence where suppliers are expected to keep factory input buffers full or topped-up with no formal communication of expected requirements.

In the case of the large multiple retailers in the United Kingdom, their aim is very much to run a CRP process in which they retain control of the replenishment (in order only to have to deal with a single uniform process) and move towards a daily call off on very short lead times. This is undoubtedly continuous replenishment but not VMI. However, there are initiatives running in the United Kingdom on joint promotional planning and, although these may be part of a CRP initiative, they are not what is commonly understood to be CRP in the industry.

Very generally, in retailer CRP programmes a number of functions are required: aggregation of store demand (via Automated Store Ordering) to a total demand on an RDC, calculation of the RDC replenishment requirement, conversion of the RDC replenishment need into a supply instruction (sales order process/despatch preparation). These processes need to be carried out regardless of whether they are done by the customer or the supplier. In some applications in the United States, retailers have delegated the responsibility for both store and RDC replenishment to vendors, giving them access to store scanning data. The reason for transferring responsibility for, for example, RDC replenishment from retailer to manufacturer is either about gaining control or demonstrating a mutual advantage. In many cases supply chain partners may not be willing to relinquish control, irrespective of the quality of the case argued.

CROSS-DOCKING

Cross-docking is a technique in which goods arriving at an RDC are unloaded from the inbound vehicle and moved from the goods receiving area 'across the dock' for marshalling with other goods for onward despatch without being put away into stock. This technique has long been a necessity for very short-life, perishable products. There are broadly two types: full pallet and case level cross-docking. The former is often used in large geographic areas (such as the United States) where a full vehicle of full pallets moves from the production source to a regional cross-dock point. The full pallets are then off-loaded and moved across the dock for consolidation with full pallets from another source to enable the building of a full vehicle load for onward transfer to the final destination, which is likely to be a warehouse local to a number of stores where the full pallets are put away into stock for subsequent let-down, picking and delivery to store. Typically, the picking at this stage is the traditional 'pick-by-store' technique.

Case level cross-docking embraces a new concept – pick-by-line to zero. The key elements here are timely delivery and just the right quantity. In this case, there is usually only one move between the manufacturer and the store. At the RDC, lanes are set out containing roll-cages to be delivered to each store served by the RDC. As the goods arrive, they are broken down and the appropriate quantity of each product line is loaded into the roll cages for each store. Full pallets of single products are no longer necessarily appropriate – only the quantity of product required by the stores need be delivered in order to avoid having to put a surplus away into stock. A strategy of pick-by-line cross-docking has obvious appeal to retailers. Not only is working capital freed-up from inventory holding, but also the assets and people required for managing warehouse stocks (put-away, let-down, etc.) are no longer required. These represent approximately 30 per cent of the operating costs of a conventional stock-holding retail RDC. Most importantly, though, the freeing-up of buildings previously occupied by racking and stock creates space. This space in turn enables throughput capacity to be created. Thus, from a simple change in supplier delivery behaviour, a retailer can generate significant increases in its capacity to process volume growth in the business without major investment in buildings, plant and equipment.

From a manufacturer's perspective, the implications of such a change are that it has to be able to supply on short lead times, to support daily review of order requirements, to make deliveries scheduled to meet retailer receiving requirements and, above all, to maintain consistently reliable service levels.

SYNCHRONIZED PRODUCTION

This technique aims to match manufacturing production cycles with retail sales and in many batch-oriented packeted grocery production processes remains a pipe dream. Canning, bottling and carton-filling lines are expensive to install and are often used to produce many different finished products. Inherently, they are designed to run in cycles and therefore to 'make for stock'. Often, too, their upstream supply chains are extended, with material availability constrained by crop yields. To move closer to 'making to order' requires clear communication and effective implementation of customer marketing plans to achieve predictable consumer offtake. Retail buying behaviour must be synchronized with offtake levels and there needs to be adequate instantaneous logistics capacity to accommodate the peaks and troughs in demand. This all needs to be allied to shorter manufacturing cycles and run lengths and faster change-overs to support the burgeoning number of product lines necessary to keep pace with increasingly demanding consumers. As order-to-delivery lead times continue to be squeezed by retailers at a rate not matched by corresponding improvements in manufacturing cycle and response times, the possibility of 'making-to-order' remains unattainable. The reality in most packeted grocery plants remains that of 'making-for-stock'. This requires an accurate sales forecast to be made, which, in an environment of increasing promotional activity, continues to be a prerequisite of efficient replenishment.

Notwithstanding these difficulties, it should go without saying that Reliable Operations (that is, the ability to produce the planned product at the right time, at the right quality and in the right quantity) are fundamental to being able to fulfil retail demand reliably and at the minimum level of stock. Integrated Suppliers are part of a concept in which the suppliers of manufacturers are part of the same 'virtual enterprise' as the manufacturer. Often they are responsible for keeping factories supplied with materials on a continuous replenishment basis along exactly similar lines to those outlined above for CRP activity between manufacturers and retailers. The idea of integration as a supply chain development tactic is discussed in more detail later.

SUPPLY CHAIN TYPES

An alternative way of assessing the use of these techniques is to consider the different types of grocery supply chains in which they might be used. Figure 8.3 sets out the four main types which characterize 80 per cent of European grocery supply.

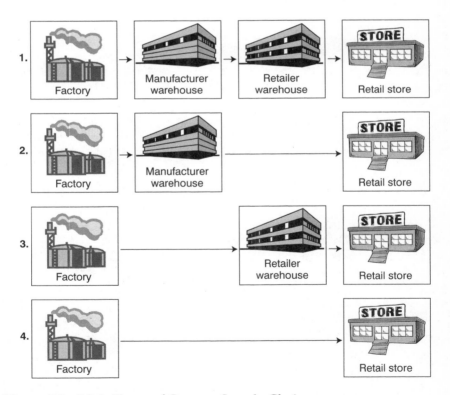

Figure 8.3 Main Types of Grocery Supply Chain

These generally have the following characteristics:

1. Make to stock production with RDC delivery.
2. Make to stock production with direct store delivery.
3. Make to order production with RDC delivery.
4. Make to order production with direct store delivery.

The first is the routine method of distribution in the greater part of European grocery markets, typically applicable to large volumes of ambient temperature chain goods, produced in cyclical batch processes, and where retail stores have little or no back-room stock. The second is typically used in less advanced markets, where stores retain stock back-rooms or in markets where large deliveries can be made to very large hypermarkets. The third applies in perishable goods chains where volumes are insufficient for efficient delivery direct to store and a consolidation is necessary in the retail RDC to drive up vehicle utilization. The last also applies in perishable chains, typically where large volume, very short life items are sourced locally for stores (eg milk, bread). Exceptionally, this route may be used for 'specials' such as display pallets direct from factory to store.

The key replenishment processes are

- Retail store with automated (computer assisted) store ordering (CAO);
- Retail RDC with Purchase Order Management (POM) based on aggregated store orders;
- Retail RDC with Continuous Replenishment Programmes (CRP) by supplier;
- Supplier warehouse or supplier factory with order processing/ despatch preparation.

Note that even if suppliers undertake CRP, there will remain a need for order processing to convert requests for a delivery into a vehicle despatch and to apply pricing. The only processes which potentially overlap or are duplicated are RDC POM and supplier CRP.

Note also the role of the retail RDC. This may be to hold stock, but is primarily to consolidate store deliveries across a range of suppliers. In the event that the RDC is stockless, then its supply is more likely to be closely coupled with the store CAO, suggesting that vendor-managed CRP is less likely to be attractive to retailers. Retailers will wish to remain in control of store replenishment. Thus CRP programmes are not likely to represent the long-term trade direction.

In summary, retail distribution of ambient goods will in the main be focused through RDCs, not principally via direct store delivery.

These RDCs will continue to destock via lead time reductions and increased order frequency. Suppliers will see the effects of this in smaller, more frequent orders, more order picking and reduced vehicle utilization.

Principles already successfully applied to fresh food and private label distribution will be applied to ambient and frozen branded goods. Stock will only be held in store and will be eliminated in retail RDCs by daily ordering and same-day delivery seven days per week driven by checkout scanning data and significant investment in replenishment systems and technology. Order quantities will no longer be governed by achieving best terms conditions but rather will aim to provide 'just the right quantity'. Stock at RDCs will be eliminated as products are 'picked by line' on arrival, moved 'across the dock' and assembled for store delivery. Deliveries to RDCs will therefore be scheduled to optimize RDC resource utilization and to consolidate store delivery transport into fewer vehicles. Ultimately, deliveries arriving at RDCs will be required to have been pre-assembled into roll-cages. Quality of manufacturer service (in terms of delivery accuracy and timing) will be the key to maintaining product availability in store. This will lead to peaking of picking and vehicle loading activity in manufacturer warehouses (ie more instantaneous spare distribution capacity will be required), 'real-time' processing of orders, automatic allocations of stock and more responsive supply systems. Electronic Data Interchange (EDI) will be a prerequisite to enable the achievement of the necessary fast cycle times of the replenishment process. Bar-coded product identification and case marking will be essential to facilitate the automation of goods handling and the elimination of errors. Visibility of stock available to commit becomes essential. There will be no time to replan or redeploy. The role of the manufacturer's customer service clerk will therefore be much reduced because there will no longer be the opportunity to participate directly in the order management process.

A fundamental strategy for countering such trends will be the use of genuine cost-related price cards which identify and pass on the costs of such added-value servicing arrangements and which promote the type of ordering behaviour better suited to the nature of the manufacturer's production process. This will enable manufacturers to limit the erosion of their lead times so that the peaking of the requirements for distribution capacity can be smoothed. However, requests to expose manufacturer logistics costs will increasingly become a component of the trading debate. Activity- based costing in the logistics network will thus be the key to price card determination and for providing the information for these discussions.

In parallel there will be a retail focus on the efficiency of vehicle utilization, featuring requests for customer collection, use of consolidators for smaller volume business and pooling with third parties in intermediate warehouses. This will lead to demands for ex-works pricing, cherry-picking of routes by retailers and loss of control of vehicles by suppliers. However, there will be a potential for the creative use of shared fleets to increase vehicle utilization. These practices will be applied to routine replenishment. Exceptionally, different practices and routes to store may be used for special or promotional lines.

Finally, downstream of the supplier warehouse, and from a supplier viewpoint, replenishment consists of two parallel processes. The *physical response* (ie moving goods through the supply chain) and *planning* the availability of the appropriate stock. The ECR work to date has tended to focus on the inventory replenishment and ordering processes between manufacturer–retailer pairs and, other than cross-docking, little attention has been paid until now to improving the physical aspects of moving the goods.

IMPACT OF LEAD TIME REDUCTIONS ON MANUFACTURER INVENTORY LEVELS

The foregoing discussion identifies areas where manufacturers will need to increase their response capability within the physical distribution network. Will these changes also impact their stock holding? Since, in the main, large producers of packaged goods manufacture in cycles, they will have to continue to manufacture for stock, but the uncontrolled erosion of lead time described above will reduce their opportunity for 'make-to-order' production and increase their dependence on sales forecasts to plan cycle stocks to meet the service requirements. Changes in retail physical distribution practice could transfer inventory holding and handling activity upstream to manufacturers and potentially have an adverse impact on the capacity and efficiency of supplier distribution warehouses and transport utilization. Business processes and systems will therefore need to be developed to support parallel activities in fast-cycle operational distribution and the planning and scheduling of the necessary inventory and logistics resources.

However, this analysis relates mainly to developments in large-scale retail grocery. Clearly, the situation in other channels is varied and dynamically changing. The logistics networks manufacturers provide must be able to adapt to the needs of these other channels as well as providing the capacity to respond to the grocery trends.

Most packeted goods manufacturers are primarily 'make-for-stock' organizations. Generally, customer order-to-delivery lead times are already less than production cycle times and, broadly, further reductions in delivery lead time will not materially affect cycle stocks. However, as lead times are reduced, the 'actual' component of immediate future sales (the order bank) is also reduced, increasing the forecast component. Therefore, the element of safety stock which covers forecast accuracy is likely to increase.

Manufacturer programmes for stock reduction must therefore hinge on reducing cycle times and improving forecast accuracy. Cycle times are determined by the following:

- economic run lengths (a trade-off of material batch efficiencies with changeover and downtime costs, together with achievable line output rates thus determines the amount to be made in one run);
- rate of sale (determining how often this amount should be made);
- available line capacity.

Militating against shorter run lengths are loss of capacity through downtime, increased costs due to changeovers and reduced efficiency. However, increasing range complexity within a fixed plant configuration will *demand* shorter run lengths and thus more frequent cycles.

A branded product manufacturer has to supply many different channels and individual retailers. The manufacturer must therefore balance capacity across a multiplicity of customers and thus efficient consumer response with an individual customer cannot extend into the daily scheduling of production.

THE BRANDED MANUFACTURER'S RESPONSE

Manufacturers are already beginning to provide support for these fast cycle requirements by increasing the capacity and efficiency of their distribution networks and by providing new order management systems. However, these only provide the capability to deliver more efficiently whatever stock is available. Manufacturers therefore also need to provide support for improved planning processes to assure supply availability to meet customer service performance targets and to establish lowest target stock levels to achieve this service level. This has to be achieved whilst making the appropriate trade-offs with manufacturing and supply chain operating costs.

This suggests a number of information strategies as shown in Table 8.1.

Table 8.1   Information Strategies to Support Improved Planning Processes

Objective	Strategy
to improve in-market forecasting	customer-level activity management and joint forecasting initiatives based on point of sale, data; category
to improve efficiency of transport	develop new approaches to shared transport management
to improve factory scheduling	implementation of Master Production Scheduling (MPS) and Manufacturing Resource Planning (MRP) programmes (these address having the right stock in total although not necessarily in the right place)
to improve in-market stock deployment	implementation of Distribution Requirements Planning (DRP) systems; use of vendor-managed CRP programmes
to improve financial processes	use of Electronic Funds Transfer techniques
to improve administrative efficiency	development of new EDI transactions (eg confirmation of proof of delivery); use EDI price or promotion databases; adoption of 'green lane' delivery arrangements (no checking of supplier deliveries at retail RDGs)

SUPPLY CHAIN INTEGRATION

Supply chain integration between trading partners is often cited as an essential technique to achieve improvements in the efficiency of the replenishment processes. It is important to understand what is meant by the concept – integration can be a technique for aiding optimization of the supply chain but it can also be a means whereby one participant in the chain gains control over a greater part of the chain. So far, the integration activity reported in the ECR literature has been mainly focused on execution level processes, typically operating between manufacturer and retailer pairs, or *along* the chain. For example, the principal techniques described are CRP and cross-docking. Few examples have been seen of *across* the chain integration and there has certainly been little evidence of integrated planning. Now, given that one manufacturer supplies many customers and one customer is supplied by many manufacturers, the idea of considering the replenishment process in this context as a chain is erroneous. Supply chains are in fact supply *networks* in which complexity is increasing rapidly.

So far, improvements in efficiency have come from the application of techniques, none of which is universally beneficial. Integration *along* a chain is a technique to enable one partner to gain *control*; integration *across* the network will help overall *optimization*. Some consequences of 'along the chain' integration are considered below.

CONSEQUENCES OF ALONG-THE-CHAIN INTEGRATION

Figure 8.4 illustrates the evolution of UK retail grocery distribution practice. The x-axis of the graph considers the period of time since the 1970s. The y-axis uses as its measure of efficiency the rate of retail inventory turn.

Over the last 20 years or so there have been four stages in this evolutionary process. The first, 'Store Control', typical during the 1970s, is characterized by direct delivery from manufacturers to stores, with store inventory levels controlled by the branch manager, often 'assisted' by the manufacturer's representative. Usually, one order was placed each week on a week's delivery lead time, with up to five weeks' stock held in store. Improvements in inventory turnover during this period were relatively slight. The second stage, 'Depot Control', saw the establishment of retail RDCs in the early 1980s and the gradual transfer of stock and stock control from stores to the

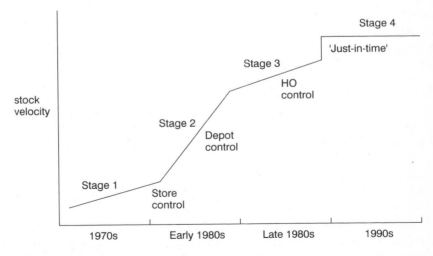

Figure 8.4 Evolution of UK Grocery Distribution

RDCs. Generally, orders were still taken on a weekly basis, but there were several deliveries made each week, and lead times were beginning to edge down. Stock levels were significantly reduced by this centralization process. The RDCs still operated on a put-away and let-down basis, with order pickers touring the picking face to assemble complete orders for branches on a pick-by-store basis. This period also saw the increasing introduction of computerized branch replenishment systems.

In the third stage, 'Head Office Control', the control of replenishment was transferred from the RDCs to retail head offices, with further increases in order review frequency and reductions in lead time. Stock in the system fell further, to between one and three weeks. A further innovation was the initial introduction of ordering based on data obtained from the checkout scanners. The new concept of composite, multi-temperature storage and distribution began to appear.

In the United Kingdom, retail grocers are already in the final stage, 'Just-In-Time', for perishable goods and are fast moving there for frozen and non-perishable packaged grocery products. Here, there can only be a final step change as RDC stock is reduced to the minimum to support pick-by-line cross-docking. The features of this phase are the extension of the composite networks supported by accurately-timed, daily deliveries on very short lead times.

In summary, the period of this overall evolution features a centralization of warehousing, inventories and inventory control, coupled with a trend towards advanced JIT replenishment methods, supported by massive retail investments in information technology support.

By transferring the four stages of development to the x-axis, a generalized picture of distribution evolution may be obtained (see Figure 8.5). The state of development of a market in general or an individual retailer in particular may be mapped on to this model by positioning it at the appropriate stage. However, fundamental to progress up this curve is the presence or absence of a number of the enabling technologies illustrated in Figure 8.6.

In order to move from Stage 1 to Stage 2 and operate via an RDC, it is necessary for the RDC to have some sort of warehouse management system. For the inventory to be controlled at the RDC, an RDC level stock control needs to be introduced. The centralization of the control of inventories at Head Office requires central visibility of RDC stocks and a process and system for managing them. To progress effectively to Stage 4, a retailer ideally needs the goods received to be bar-coded with the appropriate identifiers, as well as a computerized point-of-sale data capture system and computer-assisted store ordering processes. For the communications to work effectively, EDI links have to be established with suppliers. The significance of this simple model is that the enabling tech-

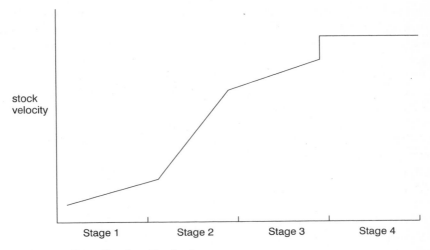

Figure 8.5 Distribution Evolution

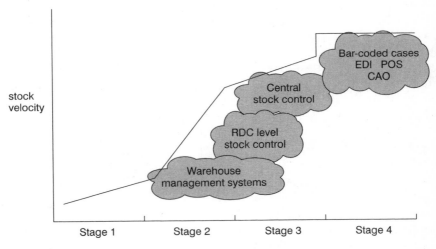

Figure 8.6 Prerequisite 'Enabling' Technologies

nologies up to the end of Stage 3 require only implementation by the retailer. There is no impact on the manufacturer. However, in order for a retailer to implement EDI and to scan bar-coded cases, its suppliers have to modify their own systems and processes to conform to these new requirements. This is a case of integration 'forced' on to a manufacturer as a requirement for doing business.

Another aspect of this evolution of replenishment processes is the concept of 'opportunity' technologies which can be introduced at various stages of the development curve. Figure 8.7 illustrates this. Here it may be seen that Vendor Managed Inventory offers an opportunity for retailers still at Stage 2 in the evolution curve. Technologies such as cross-docking and automated goods-in vehicle scheduling at retail RDCs are increasingly propounded as methods of further driving down costs. However, each of these approaches demands a systems and business process change on the part of the other players in the supply chain. These will certainly generate one-off implementation costs and quite likely ongoing operational cost increases for one partner which will not always outweigh the overall benefit, even though the initiator of the change may himself gain. These are further examples of integration as a means of gaining control or driving benefits for one party only.

EXAMPLE OF ACROSS-THE-CHAIN INTEGRATION

However, an example of an opportunity technology which can offer benefits across the whole of the evolution curve is transport pooling (see Figure 8.7), although this has to be based on cross-sectoral collaboration in which the day-to-day management is vested in disinterested third parties, rather than vested in any one supply chain partner. This is explored further below. Figures 8.8 to 8.13 illustrate the concept. In simple terms the supply chain is often viewed as a flow of information

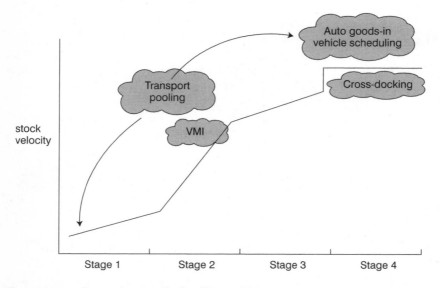

Figure 8.7 Opportunity Technologies Transport Policy

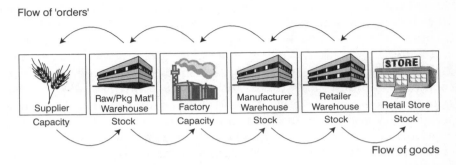

Figure 8.8 Supply Chain Characteristics

Figure 8.9 Networks of Third Parties

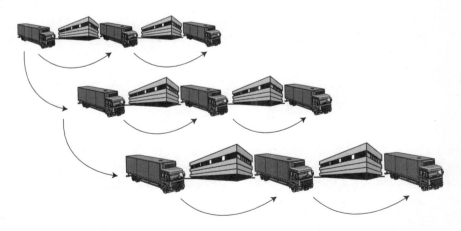

Figure 8.10 Consolidation Opportunities Along and Across Many Supply Chains

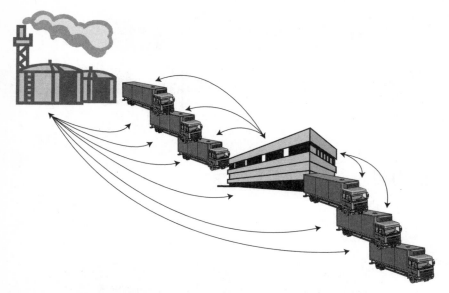

Figure 8.11 Complex Communications Via an Added-Value Network Service

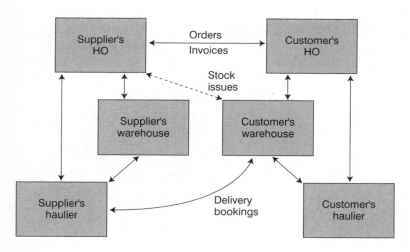

Figure 8.12 Replenishment Interfaces

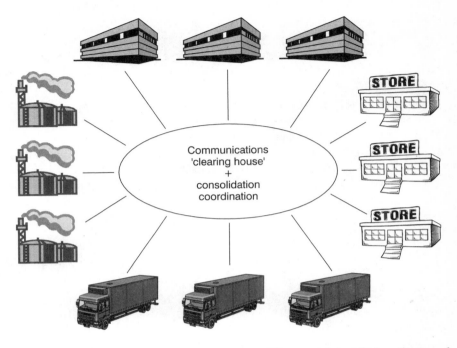

Figure 8.13 Simplified Communications Via an Added-Value Network Service

and goods between suppliers and retailers (Figure 8.8). In reality, there are many third parties involved in the chain, notably many separate transport and warehousing operators (Figure 8.9). On the basis that the use of opportunity technologies such as transport pooling derives greater benefit from a larger number of participants, then there are likely to be at least as many opportunities for consolidation *across* many supply chains as there are *along* single ones. Here, across the chain integration affords a genuine chance of optimization (Figure 8.10). However, complex communications and the absence of standards inhibit the achievement of synergy opportunities (Figure 8.11). For example, Figure 8.12 illustrates the communication flows that take place between the parties involved. In addition to the routine exchange of orders and invoice data between the supplier and customer head offices and, potentially, the exchange of warehouse stocks and issues data in a CRP relationship, there are many instructions issued between both the supplier and retailer and their logistics operators – transport movement instructions, warehouse order picking and assembly instructions, etc. Further, each haulier may have to make collection and delivery bookings at each warehouse. These instructions are not often issued in any sort of industry standard format, nor are they visible to other parties. The opportunity for improving synergy must stem from simplifying and standardizing these communications, using a third party added-value network service to act as a communications clearing house and a consolidation coordinator (Figure 8.13).

Integration across the chain is thus about integrating replenishment processes with the other parties involved, such as transport and warehousing suppliers, and communicating with them via electronic means. This integration needs to address what processes should be included, what should be communicated, with whom, when, how and why, and how the activity should be organized to optimize its efficiency together with what new software and services will be needed to facilitate this way of working.

FACILITATING ACROSS-THE-CHAIN INTEGRATION

Current grocery industry logistics thinking across Europe is increasingly dominated by activity in ECR. Much of this is now retailer-led and, as is evident from the foregoing analysis, not always in the best interests of manufacturers. There are four principles which should drive logistics development and ECR. These should aim to do the following:

1. To reduce total supply chain costs.
2. To enhance consumer value and community benefit.
3. To obtain an equitable division of any benefits resulting from change.
4. To maintain a fair balance of control in the supply chain.

The thesis explored above is that growing retailer power and significant retailing developments in internationalization, new store formats, own label, information technology and distribution are characterized by a trend towards not only centralization of control of their own supply chains by retailers but also attempts to acquire greater control over manufacturer supply logistics. Retailers are currently driving supply chain development towards their own goals and not always in the interests of the above principles. Their initiatives are sometimes detrimental to the interests of branded manufacturers (current 'best practice' ideas such as more frequent deliveries, cross-docking and pick by line are not necessarily in the best interests of the principals). There is a clear danger of transfer of control downstream and transfer of costs upstream. This situation may be redressed through promoting awareness of the real consequences and developing new initiatives rather than trying to redirect existing ones such as ECR. Hence there is a need to develop new initiatives in cost-effective distribution to the consumer. This can best be managed via a new collaborative approach. An outline of the objectives of collaboration and a method for establishing it is set out below.

A NEW COLLABORATIVE APPROACH

The broad principle here is that the greater the number of participants, the greater the synergy opportunities and the greater the chance of levering action within the logistics and network services provider community. By centralizing common activities and 'leapfrogging' the current thinking, this will also help to avoid the proliferation of multiple communication and operating standards which add costs. This is envisaged as operating within a free market environment in order to drive synergies and reduce redundancy, therefore leading to lower costs.

A collaborative approach between manufacturers, their suppliers and customers is envisaged, aimed at optimizing physical flows, executed via a community of service providers, working to common commercial principles. This could feature combined purchasing and operations in physical distribution and sharing of physical logistics resources. This would be supported by a common set of enabling systems and technologies, based upon common standards and a set of common cost measures. This will require an open, competitive market of a large number of service providers (logistics, finance, IT) covering all supply chain functions. (See Figures 8.14 and 8.15.)

The approach to this collaboration is to establish a shared view on how best to achieve the principles above, to promote change to deliver the principles, to support only changes which support the principles and to resist changes which contravene them. The benefits of such collaboration would be that a free market approach fosters choice and competition and the common use of the service providers and common standards reduces redundancy and prevents the proliferation of multiple data formats. In addition, the opportunity for benefit grows with the number of participants and, overall, this is a better way to drive synergies and reduce supply chain costs equitably.

The service provider would manage the pooling of information and provide added value services, such as providing visibility and tracking of transport movements, optimizing transport circuits, managing the disposition of transport assets, consolidation activities, and returnables flows. In addition, central data base applications such as operational analyses and freight bill management could be offered.

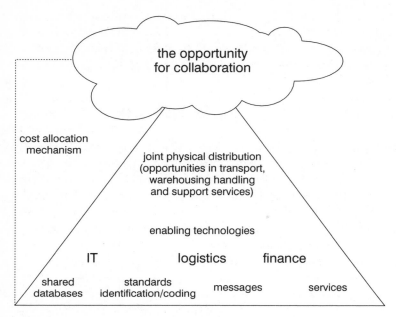

Figure 8.14 Opportunity for Collaboration

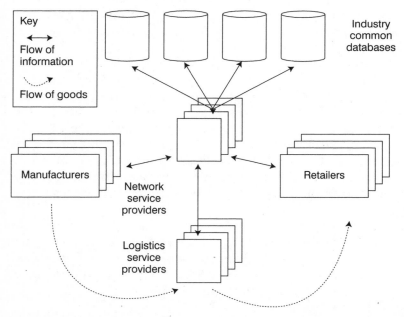

Figure 8.15 Open Market Solution

PRINCIPLES FOR COLLABORATION

Members of such a working approach will need to obtain agreement on the vision, scope and objectives of collaboration, to develop common principles for commercial dealing and operations, and to build a shared terminology and working standards. They will need to be able to demonstrate consistency and sustainability of performance, transparency of information and mutual trust. Membership should be restricted to parties who have compatible physical characteristics in their supply chains (temperature, product compatibility – non-injurious characteristics such as odour taint). They must be prepared to pool information and be willing to change their current practices. They must be able to exchange data electronically and be prepared to commit both adequate business volumes to the joint enterprise and sufficient human resources to ensure successful participation.

OUTLINE METHOD FOR COLLABORATION

The methodology is based upon a matrix approach. This consists of first identifying focus areas for collaboration and then building a programme based on a number of process steps.

The focus areas are:

- commercial principles;
- network strategy;
- warehouse facilities;
- full vehicle trunking;
- store deliveries;
- IT support.

The process steps are:

- common mind-set;
- communications;
- development;
- planning;
- performance targets;
- performance evaluation;
- process effectiveness;
- continuous development.

Establishing a common mind-set is the process of understanding the mutual objectives of participating businesses. A communication channel and the processes for communication then need to be set up. The development stage is aimed at agreeing the programme of work within which mutual expectations and performance targets will be determined and the resources necessary for implementation and operation agreed. Operating performance needs to be reviewed frequently and appropriate adjustments made. The effectiveness of the process needs to be monitored regularly and a programme for continuous improvement run. The matrix may then be completed and a set of tasks confirmed for each cell (see Figure 8.16).

CONCLUSION

UK replenishment practice is in advance of much of the ECR theory and retailers are in the driving seat. Models of development trends may be built, on to which the position of suppliers and their customers may be mapped. The characteristic features of each stage of each of these evolutionary models determine a number of prerequisite enabling technologies and consequential opportunity technologies. Such an approach can provide valuable insight into possible future retail developments. However, control of the supply chain has long been essential, for short shelf life and private label products. A source of retailers' competitive advantage is the efficiency of 'their' supply chain across the total product range. Logistics efficiency via a single supply chain is therefore their main priority. Consumers judge retailer value (for stock-up shopping) across the total shopping basket but the presence of major brands is also a 'benchmark of value'. Thus multiple retailers will continue to press for control of the supply chain across their range, including packeted goods, and branded manufacturers must seek a mutually acceptable basis for supply chain development and operations with them in order to remain listed. Managing this together with handling the different supply chains of other trade channels to maximize availability efficiently is the key to growing consumer value.

Common terminology, measures and communication standards are fundamental to industry progress. Manufacturers must therefore focus on and clearly define the processes at the interfaces between their own and retailers' businesses. They must set up appropriate performance measures and build enabling systems to support the evolution of these interfaces. They must explore 'opportunity' technologies and their impacts and prerequisites and creatively re-engineer their use of assets and systems to lever the

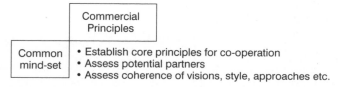

Figure 8.16 Template for Collaboration

benefits of these opportunities. EDI should become a strategic thrust of doing business. This will require new EDI message exchanges and standards to be confirmed. Across the chain consolidation opportunities should be explored and wider support sought for such approaches.

There are a number of other implications for manufacturers: they must provide a variety of solutions for different channels and customers. They must have the skill, resources and information available to manage their category in-store, supported by activity-based costing to give internal (and possibly external) transparency to their cost structures. They need to be able to synchronize customer plans with their manufacturing and logistics capability. They must recognize the role of information and information technology in creating this new transparency and in enabling these new methods of working.

There needs to be a new integration of sales and market planning and logistics operations in which visible in-store activity planning can be linked to production scheduling and stock deployment. More responsive physical distribution networks need to be established which can accommodate lead-time compression with the appropriate capacity. Opportunities for resource sharing require the development of the necessary IT capability supported by EDI, traded unit and pallet bar-coding and conformity with standard industry data exchange formats. This should be underpinned by cost-related pricing based on activity-based costing. There needs to be clear communication of promotional activity, effective sales forecasting and clear, effective stock management policies supported by flexible manufacturing operations and advanced logistics capability, flexibility and efficiency.

Logistics service providers should be directly involved in the development of these opportunities. This will recognize the prevailing practice of using contract logistics and move the capability of the logistics industry forward by involving third party service companies in ECR initiatives to drive opportunities for synergy and consolidation. This will also increase the accessibility of efficient replenishment opportunities for smaller businesses. It will therefore require the development of standards in terminology, processes and messages between logistics service providers. A huge opportunity awaits the providers of value-added network service vendors in offering the communications infrastructure and management software to facilitate shared-resource operations.

In the United Kingdom the real future for the 'supply-side' component of ECR lies in rationalizing and revitalizing the approach to managing transport and consolidation on an industry basis. This will genuinely benefit all parties, including the consumer, but is dependent upon a radical rethink of the way the transport industry currently operates. Is the industry fit for the challenge?

9

The development of e-tail logistics

John Fernie and Alan McKinnon

INTRODUCTION

Non-store shopping is not new. Traditional mail order goes back over a century. The 'big book' catalogues have experienced slow decline with the advent of more up market 'specialogues'. Nevertheless, the tradition of selling to friends and family continues with party plans, most notably Ann Summers, and door to door selling through Avon and Betterware catalogues. These 'low tech' forms of selling have accounted for around 4–5 per cent of all retail sales in the UK and the US for many years but this was forecast to change dramatically in the new millennium when 'higher tech' options would dominate the market place. The 'hype' exceeded reality and after the dot.com boom in the late 1990s, a considerable shakeout of the industry has occurred since 2000 with the prospect of a more stable pattern of development occurring until 2010. This chapter will discuss growth of e-commerce, the evolving market and consumer responses to online retailing. The challenges faced by the grocery sector will be discussed in some depth, especially the 'killer costs' of picking and delivering to customers' homes.

THE GROWTH OF E-COMMERCE

While it is generally accepted that e-commerce has grown considerably in the 1990s and the early part of this century, accurate, reliable figures are difficult to ascertain because of the need to agree upon a widely accepted definition. Most research has focused on business to consumer (B2C) transactions, although few companies in this sector have made a profit. It has been the business to business (B2B) and consumer to consumer (C2C) sectors that have produced real benefits to customers and hence increased profitability for the partners involved. In C2C markets, intermediaries such as eBay are online auctioneers brokering deals between bidders and sellers. Similarly B2B exchanges, such as GlobalNetXchange and WorldWide Retail Exchange, promote online auctions and collaborations between partners to reduce costs. Businesses involved in these e-commerce markets are infomediaries in that they are trading information, and are facilitators in reducing transaction costs between buyer and seller.

The problem with the B2C model compared with C2C and B2B models is the requirement to trade goods and services that are tangible and need to be stored and transported to the final consumer. Additionally, a market presence and brand identity are necessary ingredients to wean customers away from their traditional methods of buying behaviour. Yet despite these apparent drawbacks, the 'hype' associated with this new form of trading led many analysts to discuss the notion of disintermediation in B2C markets. Traditional retail channels were to be disrupted as new players entered the market with online offers. Not surprisingly conventional retailers reacted passively to the new threat in view of their investment in capital assets. Pure e-tailers, with the exception of niche players, sustained losses, with numerous bankruptcies and others such as Peapod being taken over by major retail groups (Ahold in this case). With hindsight, a multi-channel strategy is the obvious route to success, especially for companies with a mail order presence. Some multi-channel retailers, such as Eddie Bauer, indicate that customers shopping at all channel alternatives (stores, catalogues and online sites) spend more than single or dual channel customers. This 'clicks and bricks' approach gives a customer greater flexibility, including in the case of clothing products, the opportunity to return goods to their nearest stores.

This approach is confirmed by research in the United States undertaken by the Boston Consulting Group (see Ganesh, 2004). In a survey of 63 retailers of various sizes and categories, it found that the most valued customer is the multi-channel customer. Retailers are utilizing cross-channel coordination whereby Web sites promote stores and catalogue offers. It is not unusual for customers to walk into stores with Web site printouts. More importantly to our later discussion here is the whole issue of returns management. Around 25 per cent of all goods purchased online are returned, hence the ability to handle returns can improve customer retention.

THE MARKET

One of the reasons for over-optimistic forecasts for e-commerce growth in the 1990s was consumer acceptance of the Internet and widespread adoption of PC usage. By 2002 it was estimated that the number of Internet users numbered 450 million, with over half of this market coming from five countries: the United States, China, the UK, Germany and Japan (Table 9.1). Over 90 per cent of Internet users are English-speaking, with a similar percentage of 'secure' commercial sites (those that can perform 'secure' credit card transactions) on offer. Growth has been greatest in North America partly because of the relative cheapness of transaction costs: telephone charges there are lower than in other parts of the world. In Europe, however, deregulation of national monopolies, such as in the UK, will facilitate growth in the future. The increased sophistication of mobile phones with WAP applications also offers potential opportunities.

The technology for delivering e-commerce solutions is much more sophisticated and reliable than a decade earlier. Unfortunately, forecasts of online retail sales were strictly technological rather than behavioural-

Table 9.1   The Largest Users of the Internet Worldwide: A Comparison of Estimates for 2002 (millions)

Country	Estimate	Country	Estimate	Country	Estimate
1. USA	149.0	14. Brazil	6.1	27. Czech Republic	2.2
2. China	33.7	15. Australia	5.6	28. Norway	2.2
3. UK	33.0	16. India	5.0	29. Finland	2.1
4. Germany	26.0	17. Poland	4.9	30. Argentina	2.0
5. Japan	22.0	18. Thailand	4.6	31. Philippines	2.0
6. South Korea	16.7	19. Sweden	4.5	32. Malaysia	2.0
7. Canada	14.2	20. Hong Kong	3.9	33. Chile	1.8
8. France	11.0	21. Turkey	3.7	34. Denmark	1.6
9. Italy	11.0	22. Switzerland	3.4	35. South Africa	1.5
10. Russia	7.5	23. Portugal	3.1	36. Greece	1.3
11. Spain	7.0	24. Belgium	2.7	37. New Zealand	1.3
12. Netherlands	6.8	25. Austria	2.7	38. Singapore	1.3
13. Taiwan	6.4	26. Mexico	2.3	39. Israel	1.2

Source: Michalak and Jones, 2003

based. This should present a warning to those who see WAP technology as the new medium for e-commerce in the next 5 to 10 years.

To give an indication of the optimism exhibited by commentators in the mid-1990s with regard to the scale of online retail sales penetration, the *Financial Times* produced a conservative estimate of sales in Europe by 2000 in 1995. The author estimated that 10 to 15 per cent of food sales and 20 to 25 per cent of non-food sales would be made by home shopping (Mandeville, 1995). In reality, online grocery sales throughout Europe were around 0.24 per cent in 2000, with non-food sales only making an impact in computer software, CDs, books and videos. The position is much the same in the United States where online sales accounted for around 1 per cent of all retail sales in 2000 and 2001 (Reynolds, 2001). This slow growth in sales can be attributed to consumers using the Web for informational rather than transactional purposes, in addition to purchasing other services rather than retail. For example, Forrester Research show that of the US $20–30 billion estimate of the online consumer market in the United States in 1999, only 60 per cent accounted for the physical distribution of goods (Laseter *et al*, 2000). The other 40 per cent accounted for digital delivered goods, such as airline and event tickets, banking services and auctions.

More recent research indicates that retail sales online have been buoyant in 2001–3 in the United States and Europe. Whereas conventional retail sales in the United States grew 3.1 per cent throughout 2002 to US $3.26 trillion, online sales grew 26.9 per cent to US $45.6 billion during the same period, thereby accounting for 1.4 per cent of all retail sales. Forecasts for the years to 2005 suggest that a figure of 4–5 per cent will be reached. Similar trends are evident in Europe, where total EU e-commerce sales increased from 1,195 billion euros to 2,660 billion, a 123 per cent increase. Retail sales doubled, with notable increases in household (214 per cent) and supermarket categories (123 per cent) relative to more established e-tailing sections, books/music (40 per cent) and electronics (86 per cent). Furthermore, the digital delivered products continue to exhibit strong growth, especially in airlines (666 per cent) and car rental (586 per cent).

THE E-COMMERCE CONSUMER

Internet connectivity, as revealed in Table 9.1, depicted an English-speaking, developed country phenomenon. This concealed the different stages of development of these markets and the geodemographic profile of Internet consumers. It is generally accepted that most European countries lag behind the United States, which had more than 80 per cent of households connected to the Net in 2001. As the market matures, the profile of the consumer begins to be more representative of the population it serves. In the early stages of development the profile of the e-commerce shopper was a young male professional living in a middle-class neighbourhood. As the technology becomes more accepted the gender and socio-economic mix has changed. CACI (2000), the market research group, has undertaken an analysis of online behaviour and buying activity of adults (over 18 years of age) in the UK. Table 9.2 provides a detailed classification of e-Types, combining CACI's core database of 30 million lifestyle records with Forrester Research's UK Internet Monitor. This shows an online lifecycle from infrequent online purchases – virtual virgins, chatters and gamers and dot.com chatters – to frequent online purchases – surfing suits and wired living.

When this classification of online shopping categories is applied to 3,000 retail catchment areas, a more detailed picture of online geodemographics is evident. As would be expected, London and the south-east of England lead the way in terms of online shopping. Nevertheless, there are 'hot spots' across the UK with Edinburgh, Aberdeen and Bristol scoring highly despite poor overall representation in Scotland and the south-west. Areas with a poor score are north of England cities with a mixed income profile, and rural towns and centres.

In Canada, Statistics Canada has undertaken a Household Internet Use Survey since 1997. This provides a comprehensive data source to monitor e-commerce trends on a longitudinal basis. Michalak and Jones (2003) have analysed data from these surveys and show that the Internet adoption rate has grown from 29.4 per cent to 51.3 per cent from 1997 to 2000. Similar geodemographic trends are evident in Canada to those of the UK. The spatial distribution of e-commerce sales is strongly related to population and income distribution in Canada, with households in Ontario accounting for 41.8 per cent of all Internet shoppers, followed by British Columbia with around a quarter of all purchases. They note, however, that e-commerce is overwhelmingly a middle-class phenomenon, with regions of Canada with lower incomes or lower population densities having much lower rates of e-commerce sales activity.

Much of this discussion on the e-shopper has focused on the PC and the Internet as the medium of choice. For much of the 1990s, however, the development of television shopping was often mooted as the likely channel to dominate the e-commerce market. Television shopping channels were already common in the United States, and by the early 1990s had entered the UK market. Penetration of cable and satellite television was low in Europe compared with North America but the arrival of digital television (DTV) was seen as the catalyst for the growth of interactive television. Much of this optimism has failed to materialize. DTV

Table 9.2   Segmentation of Online Consumers in the UK

Group 1 Virtual Virgins

Of those online, this group is least likely to have bought online. Less than 2 per 1,000 will have made any form of online purchase last month. Their time online is half the national average and they are likely to have started using the Internet more recently than other people.
With the exception of chatting, this group do Internet activities less frequently than average. Because of their relative inexperience they are more likely to worry about security and delivery problems with buying online and to consider the process to be difficult.
People in this group are twice as likely as those in any other group to be female. The elderly and children are more commonly found in this type than any other.

Group 2 Chatters & Gamers

This group, predominantly young males, might spend as much time online as the most avid type of Internet user; however they tend not to be buyers. Only one in five has ever made an online purchase. They may consider shopping online to be difficult and their fear of delivery and security problems is above average.
These people are avid chatters and gamers who use news groups and download as frequently as the most active and experienced surfers. Nearly half are under 25. The schoolchildren in this type are more likely to connect from school/university than any other e-type, although connection from home is still the most frequent.

Group 3 dot.com Dabblers

As average Internet users, these people have mixed feelings regarding the pros and cons of online shopping. Around 40 per cent will have made some form of purchase online, and with the exception of chatting, their interests spread across all forms of Internet activity.
These people may see benefits of the Internet in convenience and speed of delivery. Alternatively a specialist product not available elsewhere may have introduced them to buying online. In any event their enthusiasm for e-commerce is not yet complete.

Group 4 Surfing Suits

Although they spend less time on the Internet than average, these people can be quite enthusiastic online purchasers. They are more likely than average to have bought books, software, hardware, holidays, groceries, insurance and tickets for events online.
Shopping online is seen to offer benefits such as range of product information, speed of ordering, price advantages, and an element of fun. They are less likely to fear e-commerce. They control their time on the Internet, and surfing, searching, e-mail and news groups tend to be preferred to chat, games and magazines.

Group 5 Wired Living

These are cosmopolitan young people and the most extensive Internet users, spending four and a half hours online each week. They are more experienced than most online and on average they have been using the Internet for three years. Over 70 per cent will have purchased over the Internet, covering between them the full gamut of products available for purchase. Over 60 per cent of these people are educated to degree level.
These people use the Web as part of their lifestyle. Preferred interests tend to be newsgroups, news and magazines, with only an average interest in games or chat.

Source: CACI, 2000

services have not proven as popular as expected and operators have made losses or have gone out of business (ON Digital in the UK).

Even if DTV was to become more popular in Europe, evidence from the United States suggests that the motivations for watching television are very different from PC usage. The latter is individualistic compared with the companionship associated with the television. Pace Microtechnology, one of the companies involved in making set-top boxes for existing analogue television sets, has undertaken research into consumer attitudes to digital TV services (Ody, 1998). Most potential consumers are interested in DTV because of the enhancement of traditional features (better picture quality, sound, more channel choice) rather than to use it for shopping purposes.

It is clear that DTV is still a long way off from challenging the Internet as the medium for home shopping, especially as cheap Internet access PCs are made available on the market. Reynolds (2002) indicates that convergence between the two technologies will take time because the two markets are sufficiently dissimilar. This is reflected in the early adopters of cable and satellite television, who tended to be from lower income socio-economic groups – a different market segment from the early adopters of the Internet.

Longitudinal surveys undertaken by various authors in the late 1990s have shown how the e-tailing market has matured in terms of both the customer base and the range of online offerings. In the United States the peak period of demand for Internet retailing is between Thanksgiving and Christmas. Lavin (2002) draws on consumer surveys undertaken by consultancy companies during Christmas 1998 and 1999 and her own primary research of retailers' Web sites during the same period. She comments that the profile of the Web shopper had changed, e-tailers had worked to meet rising consumer expectations and the 'first to market' advantage of early adopters had been eroded. The customers of 1998 were predominantly male, technologically proficient and relatively affluent. More significantly they were not mainstream shoppers and had low expectations for their online purchase experience. She equates this with the innovator and early adopter stages of the product adoption lifecycle. A year later, with a rapidly growing market, the profile of the online customer had changed to a more balanced gender and age with overall lower average incomes. These are more likely to be mainstream shoppers with higher expectations from their purchase experiences. This early majority segment raised the stakes for online providers. Considerable investment was made to upgrade sites, advertise on traditional media to attract customers, and in logistical infrastructure to ship products to customers' homes. Despite this, the 1999 Christmas period was notorious for failure to meet the Christmas deadline, partly due to consumers delaying purchase to the last minute but also to sheer volume of business in the network.

In the UK, Ellis-Chadwick, Doherty and Hart (2002) completed a longitudinal study of Internet adoption by UK multiple retailers from 1997 to 2000. Again, as in Levin's study, the primary research was largely based on reviewing retail Web sites over this four-year period to ascertain how Internet business models were being developed. They report a sixfold increase in the number of retailers offering online shopping to their customers. Companies have moved from offering purely informational services to a fully serviced transactional e-shop. In the case of the well-established retailers, they have been more creative in linking their sites to other companies with complementary products: for example, birthday.co.uk to Thorntons, suppliers of chocolates and Wax Lyrical, a specialist candle retailer.

These studies, and other more sector-specific research investigations, indicate that retailers are responding to this changing market environment. As the market matures consumers tend to behave in a similar fashion to dealing with traditional retail outlets. The basics of convenience, product range, customer service and price will always feature in a consumer's 'evoked set' of attributes. Above all, retailers have become brands and customer loyalty has been established through continually high levels of service. It is not surprising therefore that traditional retailers with strong brand equity can gain even more leverage through a sound Web strategy. They have the trust of the consumer to begin with, and the capital to invest in the necessary infrastructure. Many dot.com pure players needed to build a brand and tackle the formidable challenge of delivering to customers' homes. This is why it has taken Amazon.com so long to register a profit. Nevertheless, Amazon.com has strong brand presence, and research by Brynjolffsson and Smith (2000) indicates that the company can charge higher prices because of this brand equity, or what they term 'heterogeneity of trust'. In their survey of online pricing in specific markets, they showed that Amazon.com had a market share of around 80 per cent in books yet charged a 10 per cent premium over the least expensive book retailer researched.

All of this research shows that e-tailing has been most successful to date where a multi-channel 'click and bricks' approach is adopted. In this context, we are referring to non-food products, where traditional department stores and clothing specialists have considerable experience of dealing with the non-store shopper through their catalogues and 'low tech' selling techniques. These companies were well equipped to deal with home deliveries and a returns policy. Similarly the early e-tailing specialist pioneers with CDs, books, videos and computing equipment already had an infrastructure to deal with home-based orders. The grocery sector is much more complex, and home delivery is more associated with food service and added-value products. Nevertheless, the sector has attracted most attention in the literature, and we turn to a more detailed assessment of the market and the online issues pertaining to grocery in the next section.

THE GROCERY MARKET

Despite the fact that online grocery sales account for less than 1 per cent of retail sales in most country markets, this sector has attracted most attention from researchers and government bodies, including the DTI in the UK (DTI, 2001). Grocery shopping impacts on all consumers. We all have to eat! However, our populations are getting older so shopping is more of a chore; conversely, the younger, time-poor, affluent consumers may hate to waste time buying groceries. The relatively slow uptake of online grocery shopping in the United States can be attributed to the lack of online shopping availability, in that only about one-third of super-market operators offer some type of home shopping service.

Morganosky and Cude (2002) have undertaken one of the few studies on the behaviour of online grocery shoppers. Their research was based on a longitudinal study of consumers of Schnucks Markets, a St Louis-based chain of supermarkets operating in Illinois, Missouri and Indiana. The first two surveys in 1998 and 1999 asked Schnucks' online shoppers to complete a questionnaire online on the completion of their order. The final survey re-contacted respondents from the 1999 survey to track their shopping behaviours in 2001.

The results here did have some parallels with other surveys of non-food online shopping, most notably more sophisticated consumers who had moved on from being 'new' users to experienced online shoppers. This is further reflected in their willingness to buy most or all of their groceries online, and to improve their efficiency at completing the shopping tasks. Online grocery shoppers bought for the family. They were younger, female and better educated with higher incomes. The final survey showed that customer retention rates were good. The main reason for defections was the relocation to another part of the United States where the same online service was not available.

Although similar empirical research has not been carried out in the UK, trade sources indicate that the online consumer has become more experienced and is buying more online. The two main e-grocers in the UK, Tesco and Sainsbury, claim that their online customers spend more than their conventional customers. Tesco also explodes the myth that online customers would not buy fresh products because of the so-called 'touch and feel' factor. Indeed the opposite is true: of the top 10 selling lines, seven are fresh, with skinless chicken breasts at number one (Jones, 2001).

Tesco, however, is one of the few success stories in e-grocery. In Europe, grocery retailers are powerful 'bricks and mortar' companies and the approach to Internet retailing has been reactive rather than proactive. Most Internet operations have been small, and few pure players have entered the market to challenge the conventional supermarket chains.

The situation is different in the United States, where a more fragmented, regionally orientated grocery retail structure has encouraged new entrants into the market. In the late 1980s this came in the form of Warehouse Clubs and Wal-Mart Supercenters; by the 1990s dot.com players began to challenge the traditional supermarket operators. (Table 9.3 identifies the key players, along with Tesco for comparison.) Unfortunately these pure players have either gone into liquidation, scaled down their operations, or been taken over by conventional grocery businesses.

Why have pure players failed? Laseter *et al* (2000) identify four key challenges:

- limited online potential;
- high cost of delivery;
- selection–variety trade-offs;
- existing entrenched competition.

Table 9.3 The major existing and former e-grocers

	Tesco UK	**Webvan USA**	**Streamline USA**	**Peapod USA**
Background	The biggest supermarket chain in the UK	Started as a pure e-grocer in 1999	Started as a pure e-grocer in 1992	Started home delivery service before the Internet in 1989
Investments in e-grocer development	US $58 million	Approx US $ 1200 million	Approx US $80 million	Approx US $ 150 million
Main operational mode	Industrialized picking from the supermarket	Highly automated picking in distribution centre (DC)	Picking from the distribution centre, reception boxes, value adding services	Picking from both DC and stores
Current status	The biggest e-grocer in the world. Expanding its operations outside the UK. Partnering with Safeway and Groceryworks.	Operations ceased July 2001	Part of operations were sold to Peapod in September 2000. The rest of operations ceased in November 2000.	Bought by global grocery retailer Royal Ahold. Second biggest e-grocer in the world.

Source: Tanskanen, Yrjola and Holmstrom, 2002

Ring and Tigert (2001) came to similar conclusions when comparing the Internet offering with the conventional 'bricks and mortar' experience. They looked at what consumers would trade away from a store in terms of the place, product, service and value for money by shopping online. They also detailed the 'killer costs' of the pure play Internet grocers, notably the picking and delivery costs. The gist of the argument presented by these critics is that the basic Internet model is flawed.

Even if the potential is there, the consumer has to be lured away from existing behaviour with regard to store shopping. Convenience is invariably ranked as the key choice variable in both store patronage and Internet usage surveys. For store shoppers, convenience is about location and the interaction with staff and the store experience. Internet users tend to be trading off the time it takes to shop. However, as Wilson-Jeanselme (2001) has shown, the 58 per cent net gain in convenience benefit is often eroded by 'leakages' in the process of ordering to ultimate delivery. Furthermore, the next two key store choice variables in the United States tend to be price and assortment. With the exception of Webvan, pure players offered a limited number of stock keeping units (SKUs) compared with conventional supermarkets. Price may have been competitive with stores but delivery charges push prices up to the customer. In the highly competitive US grocery market, customers will switch stores for only a 3–4 per cent differential in prices across leading competitors. Ring and Tigert therefore pose the question, 'What percentage of households will pay substantially more for an inferior assortment (and perhaps quality) of groceries just for the convenience of having them delivered to their home?' (2001: 270).

Tanskanen *et al* (2002) argue that e-grocery companies failed because an electronic copy of a supermarket does not work. They claim that e-grocery should be a complementary channel rather than a substitute, and that companies should be investing in service innovations to give value to the customer. Building upon their research in Finland, they maintain that the 'clicks and bricks' model will lead to success for e-grocery. Most of the difficulties for pure players relate to building a business with its associated infrastructure. Conventional retailers have built trust with their suppliers and customers. The customer needs a credible alternative to self-service, and the Finnish researchers suggest that this has to be achieved at a local level, where routine purchases can be shifted effectively to e-grocery. To facilitate product selection, Web-based information technology can tailor the retail offer to the customer's needs. The virtual store can be more creative than the restrictions placed on the physical stocking of goods on shelves; however, manufacturers will need to provide 'pre-packaged' electronic product information for ordering on the Web.

THE LOGISTICAL CHALLENGES

Forecasts of the growth of online retail services are invariably demand-driven and assume that it will be possible to deliver orders to the home at a cost and service standard home shoppers will find acceptable. This is a bold assumption. Over the past decade many e-tail businesses have failed primarily because of an inability to provide cost-effective order fulfilment. Several market research studies have identified delivery problems as a major constraint on the growth of home shopping. Anderson Consulting (quoted in Metapack, 1999), for example, found that six of the 10 most frequently quoted problems with online shopping were related to fulfilment. As Verdict (2000) notes, 'Persuading customers to buy direct once is relatively simple. Keeping them coming back is far more difficult and is dependent on their satisfaction with all stages of the delivery experience.' A survey by Ernst and Young (2000) also revealed that high shipping costs were a major concern of potential online shoppers in the UK, the United States, France and Germany.

The greatest logistical challenges are faced by companies providing a grocery delivery service to the home. They must typically pick an order comprising 60–80 items across three temperature regimes from a total range of 10–25,000 products within 12–24 hours for delivery to customers within 1–2 hour time-slots. For example, Tesco is currently picking and delivering an average of 110,000 such orders every week. New logistical techniques have had to be devised to support e-grocery retailing on this scale.

Online shopping for non-food items has demanded less logistical innovation. Catalogue mail order companies have, after all, had long experience of delivering a broad range of merchandise to the home, while some major High Street retailers have traditionally made home delivery a key element in their service offering. Online shopping is, nevertheless, imposing new logistical requirements. First, it is substantially increasing the volume of goods that must be handled, creating the need for new distribution centres and larger vehicle fleets. Second, many online retailers are serving customers from different socio-economic backgrounds from the traditional mail order shopper. As they live in different neighbourhoods, the geographical pattern of home delivery is changing. Third, online shoppers typically have high logistical expectations, demanding rapid and reliable delivery at convenient times.

DEFINITION OF THE HOME DELIVERY CHANNEL

The home delivery channel terminates at the home or a nearby customer collection point. It is less clear where it begins. For the purposes of this review, the start of the home delivery channel will be defined as the 'order penetration point' (Christopher, 1992). This is the point at which the customer order, in this case transmitted from the home, activates the order fulfilment process. This physical process usually begins with the picking of goods within a stockholding point. Only when picked are the goods designated for a particular home shopper. Distribution downstream from this point is sometimes labelled J4U, 'just for you'.

With the move to mass customization, an increasing proportion of customer orders are penetrating the supply chain at the point of production. Consumers, for example, can configure a personal computer to their requirements online and relay the order over the Web straight to the assembly plant. Where this occurs the home delivery channel effectively starts at the factory.

Within multi-channel retail systems, this order penetration point is the point at which home deliveries diverge from the conventional retail supply chain which routes products to shops. For example, in the case of those supermarket chains that have diversified into home shopping, the order penetration point is either the shop or a local fulfilment (or 'pick') centre, where online orders are assembled. Both of these outlets draw supplies from a common source, the regional distribution centre. It makes sense, therefore, to regard the home delivery channel for grocery products as starting at the shop or the pick centre.

While the upper levels of the home delivery channels for grocery and non-food products are markedly different (Figure 9.1), the last link in the chain (the so called 'last mile') presents similar logistical problems for different types of online retailer. We will examine first the 'upstream' fulfilment process and then focus on the 'last mile problem'.

DISTRIBUTION OF ONLINE PURCHASES OF NON-FOOD ITEMS

The distribution of these items normally exhibits the following characteristics:

1. They are generally supplied directly to the home from the point of production or a central distribution centre. Each order comprises a small number of items (often just one) and the order picking is centralized at a national or regional level. A large proportion of the orders are channelled through the 'hub and spoke' networks of large parcel carriers or mail order companies. By carrying a loose assortment of orders, the vehicles operated by these companies typically have lower load factors than those achieved by vehicles moving solid pallet-loads of products through the traditional echelon-type distribution channels which supply conventional retail outlets.

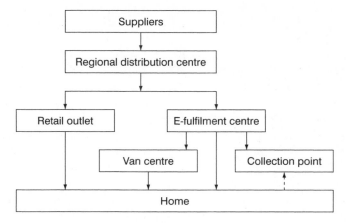

Figure 9.1a   Online Grocery Distribution

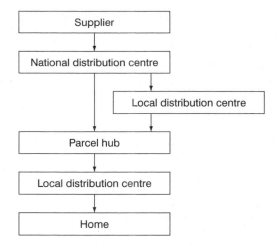

Figure 9.1b   Delivery of Online Order via Parcel Network

2. Within these J4U delivery networks, each order must be individually packaged at the central distribution point. This not only increases the volume of packaging in the supply chain: it also takes up more space on vehicles in both the forward and reverse channels.
3. Within home shopping systems, whether catalogue- or Internet-based, there is a large flow of returned product. Typically, around 30 per cent of non-food products delivered to the home are returned to e-tailers (in contrast to 6–10 per cent for 'bricks and mortar' retailers) (Nairn, 2003). This requires a major reverse logistics operations

comprising the retrieval, checking, repackaging and redistribution of returned merchandise.

Wide fluctuations in online demand for particular products, particularly newly released items, can cause the flow of freight through home delivery channels to surge. This was illustrated by the distribution of the fourth and fifth *Harry Potter* books through the Amazon.com networks to arrive on the doorsteps of tens of thousands of households on the day of publication. In the United States, for example, Fedex delivered 250,000 copies of the fifth book in the series for Amazon on its publication date, using its network of 130 overnight flights and 20,000 'home delivery contractors and Fedex express couriers'.

Concerns have been expressed that online retailing is likely to generate more transport and impose a heavier burden on the environment than store-based retailing (Hesse, 2002). Research by Matthews, Hendrickson and Soh (2001), however, suggests otherwise. They compared the externalities associated with the distribution of books through a conventional retail channel and from an online bookseller, and came to the conclusion that the latter was less environmentally damaging. According to their calculations, which included 'trucking, air freight, production, packaging and passenger trips', energy consumption, air pollution, greenhouse gas emissions and the quantity of hazardous waste were respectively 16 per cent, 36 per cent, 9 per cent and 23 per cent lower in the case of online retailing.

DISTRIBUTION OF ONLINE GROCERY SALES

In contrast to the average general merchandise order, which comprises from one to three separate items, the average online grocery order contains 60–100 items, many of which are perishable and need rapid picking and delivery. This requires localized order picking in either an existing shop or a dedicated fulfilment (or 'pick') centre. Over the past few years there has been much discussion of the relative merits of store-based or fulfilment centre picking.

The main advantage of store-based fulfilment is that it minimizes the amount of speculative investment in new logistical facilities for which future demand is uncertain. Webvan, for example, was planning to build a network of 26 new automated warehouses, at a cost of approximately US $35 million each, to provide e-grocery delivery across the United States. Fewer than half of these warehouses were set up before the company went bankrupt in 2001. As a 'pure player' in the e-grocery market, Webvan did not have an established chain of retail outlets and would have had to form an alliance with an existing retailer to adopt the store-based model. Four British supermarket chains (Sainsbury, Asda, Somerfield and Waitrose), as 'bricks and clicks' retailers, had the option of pursuing store-based or pick-centre fulfilment and opted initially for the latter. Tesco, by contrast, opted for the store-based model. Its experience is described below.

Basing home delivery operations at existing shops allows retailers to improve the utilization of their existing assets and resources. Retail property can be used more intensively and staff shared between the store and online operations. It is possible to pool retail inventory between conventional and online markets, improving the ratio of inventory to sales. This also gives online shoppers access to the full range of products available in a supermarket to which most of them will be accustomed.

Another major benefit of shop-based fulfilment is that it enables the retailer to achieve a rapid rate of geographical expansion, securing market share and winning customer loyalty much more quickly than competitors committed to the fulfilment centre model.

On the negative side, however, integrating conventional and online retailing operations in existing shops can impair the standard of service for both groups of customer. The online shopper is disadvantaged by not having access to a dedicated inventory. Although a particular product may be available on the shelf when the online order is placed, it is possible that by the time the picking operation gets underway conventional shoppers may have purchased all the available stock. Where these in-store customers encounter a stock-out they can decide themselves what alternative products to buy, if any. Online shoppers, on the other hand, rely on the retailer to make suitable substitutions. Substitution rates are reckoned to be significantly higher for store-based fulfilment systems than for e-grocers operating separate pick centres. For example Ocado, the only UK e-grocer to rely solely on a pick centre, claims that it can achieve substitution rates of less than 5 per cent, whereas customers using its store-based competitors sometimes experience substitution rates more than twice this level (McClellan, 2003). In comparing substitution rates, however, allowance must be made for difference in product range. Ocado's range of around 10,000 products is less than half that of the major supermarket chains engaged in online shopping.

Doubts have been expressed about the long-term sustainability of store-based fulfilment. As the volume of online sales expands, conflicts between conventional and online retailing are likely to intensify. At the 'front end' of the shop, aisles may become increasingly crowded with staff picking orders for online customers. In practice, however, much of the picking of high-selling lines is done in the back store-room. It is at the 'back end' that space pressures may become most acute. Over the past 20 years the trend has been for retailers to reduce the amount of back storage space in shops as in-store inventory levels have dropped and Quick Response replenishment become the norm. This now limits the capacity of existing retail outlets to support the online order fulfilment operation. New shops can, nevertheless, be purpose-built to integrate conventional retailing and online fulfilment. The Dutch retailer Ahold has coined the term 'wareroom' to describe a dedicated pick facility colocated with a conventional supermarket (Mees, 2000).

Most of the purpose-built fulfilment centres so far constructed are on separate sites. They offer a number of logistical advantages over store-based picking. As their inventory is dedicated to the online service, home shoppers can check product availability at the time of ordering and, if necessary, alter their shopping list. The order picking function should also be faster and more efficient in fulfilment centres, as they are specially designed for the multiple picking of online orders with high levels of mechanization. Significant teething problems with the early fulfilment centres set up in the UK, however, resulted in pick rates falling well below target levels.

To be cost-effective, dedicated pick centres must handle a large throughput. The threshold level of throughput required for viability also depends on the breadth of the product range. It is very costly to offer an extensive range in the early stages of an e-tailing operation when sales volumes are low. Offering a limited range can cut the cost of the operation but make it more difficult to lure consumers from conventional retailing. Another inventory-related problem which retailers using pick centres have encountered is the difficulty of disposing of excess stocks of short shelf-life product. When over-stocking occurs in a shop, consumer demand can be stimulated at short notice using price reductions or in-store merchandising techniques. It is more difficult using electronic media to clear excess inventory of fresh produce from fulfilment centres that consumers never visit.

Several studies have argued that store-based fulfilment is more appropriate in the early stages of a retailer's entry into the e-grocery market. It represents a low-risk strategy and allows new business to be won at a relatively low marginal cost. As the volume of online sales grows, however, the cost and service benefits of picking orders in a dedicated centre steadily increase until this becomes the more competitive option. Several break-even analyses have been conducted to estimate the threshold online sales volume at which the fulfilment centre model is likely to be superior. This volume is likely to vary from retailer to retailer depending on the size and layout of shops, the nature of the upstream distribution system, the product range and the customer base. It will also be highly sensitive to the allocation of retail overheads between the conventional and online shopping operations.

A further complicating factor is the geography of the retail market. The relative efficiency of the two types of fulfilment is likely to vary with the density of demand and level of local competition in different parts of the country. In a mature e-grocery market, dedicated pick centres may serve the conurbations, while store-based distribution remains the most cost-effective means of supplying the rural hinterlands. The US e-grocer Peapod has a policy of using store-based fulfilment when penetrating new local markets, working in collaboration with retail chains. Once volumes have reached an adequate level, as in Chicago and San Francisco, the company has invested in 'distribution centres'.

Experience in the UK suggests that most new entrants to the e-grocery market opted for the fulfilment model prematurely. Somerfield and Asda both set up pick centres and closed them down within a couple of years. Sainsbury was also originally wedded to the fulfilment centre concept, establishing two centres in London (Park Royal) and Manchester. It shut the Manchester depot in 2001 and has been expanding its online business primarily through store-based fulfilment. It is now generally acknowledged that at the present level of e-grocery sales in the UK, the store-based distribution model, pioneered by Tesco, is the most cost-effective. By supplying online orders from its existing shops Tesco has secured 60 per cent of the UK e-grocery market, achieved 95 per cent coverage of the UK retail market and established itself as the world's largest online retailer. Through an alliance with the US retail chain Safeway, it has successfully exported its system of store-based fulfilment to North America.

THE LAST MILE PROBLEM

In making the final delivery to the home, companies must strike an acceptable and profitable balance between customer convenience, distribution cost and security. Most customers would like deliveries to be made urgently at a precise time with 100 per cent reliability. This would minimize waiting time and the inconvenience of having to stay at home to receive the order. Few customers would be willing to pay the high cost of time-definite delivery, however.

The relationship between the width of home delivery 'windows' and transport costs has been modelled for the London area by Nockold (2001). Expanding the window from 180 minutes to 225 minutes and 360 minutes was found to cut transport costs by, respectively, 6–12 per cent and 17–24 per cent. Eliminating the time constraint completely yielded cost savings of up to a third. Similar research undertaken in Helsinki has indicated that transport cost savings of 40 per cent are possible where carriers can deliver at any time during the 24-hour day.

Such flexibility can usually only be achieved where a system of 'unattended delivery' is available. Figure 9.2 provides a classification of the main forms of unattended delivery (McKinnon and Tallam, 2003). A fundamental distinction exists between unsecured and secured delivery. Unsecured delivery, sometimes called 'doorstepping' in the UK, involves simply leaving the consignment outside the house, preferably in a concealed location. This eliminates the need for a return journey and can be convenient for customers, but obviously exposes the order to the risk of theft or damage.

When no one is at home, the delivery can be secured in four ways:

- Giving the delivery driver internal access to the home or an outbuilding.
- Placing the order at a home-based reception (or 'drop') box.
- Leaving it at a local collection point.
- Delivering the order to a local agency which stores it and delivers it when the customer is at home.

Home Access Systems

A prototype home access system has been trialled in the English Midlands. This system employed a telephone-linked electronic keypad to

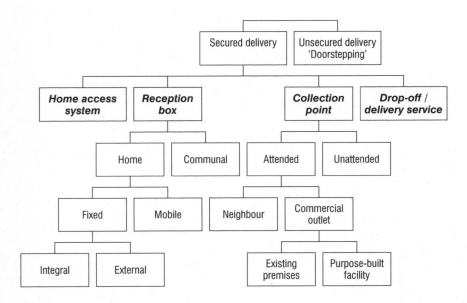

Figure 9.2 Classification of Unattended Delivery Systems

control the opening and shutting of the garage door. The keypads communicated with a central server, allowing the 'home access' agency to alter the pin codes after each delivery. When the driver closed the door, the keypad device issued another code number confirming that the delivery was made. At the same time a confirmation message was sent to the customer's mobile phone or e-mail address. It was found that this system could cut average drop times from 10 minutes to 4 minutes and, if coupled with a 5-hour time-window, achieved a productivity level (measured in drops per vehicle per week) 84 per cent higher than the typical attended delivery operation (Rowlands, 2001).

Home Reception Boxes

Several types of reception box have so far been developed:

- **Fixed, integral box:** these can either be built into the house at the time of its construction or 'retrofitted'. One system, installed in a few upmarket houses in the UK, comprises three chambers for ambient, chilled and frozen product and provides access directly into the kitchen.
- **Fixed, external box:** in the short/medium term, there is likely to be more rapid uptake of external boxes, which are much cheaper to install and do not require structural modification to the property. They typically have a keypad which is in communication with a service centre and can be activated by a single-use pin code issued to a delivery driver. Boxes vary in size and shape, and in some cases are either insulated or refrigerated to store products requiring temperature control.
- **Mobile reception box:** mobile reception boxes are filled by the supplier at their premises, delivered to the customer's home and secured temporarily to an outside wall. The main system of this type operating in the UK connects the box to an electronic device resembling an intercom (called the 'Homeport') by means of a steel cable. The supplier or carrier retrieves the box once it has been emptied and can use it to recover any returned items.
- **Communal reception boxes:** communal boxes are more suited to apartment blocks and generally comprise banks of lockers. One of the main systems employs luggage locker technology that has been extensively used in railway stations and airports around the world. These have been adapted to the role of reception box by establishing a communication link with a service centre which issues pin codes to delivery drivers and customers.

Collection Points

Having to travel to a collection point significantly reduces the convenience of home shopping and may only be acceptable to a small proportion of online shoppers. Market surveys suggest that for around two-thirds of home shoppers in the UK the most popular form of unattended delivery is leaving goods with neighbours (Verdict Research, 2000). Local shops, post offices, petrol stations and railway stations have also assumed the role of collection points. Communal reception boxes have been used in these locations to automate the collection process. With the customers' approval, collection points can be used either as the initial delivery location or as a secondary dropping-off point when there is no one at home.

Local Drop-off and Delivery

This represents an extension to the collection point service, where the company not only receives the order on the customer's behalf but also delivers it to his or her home at a convenient time. When the goods arrive, the customer is notified by e-mail, phone or mobile text message, and asked to specify a narrow time window within which the goods can be delivered.

To date, there has been very limited investment in home reception facilities. Many of the companies marketing innovative solutions to the last mile problem have gone out of business, while others have redirected their attention to the faster growing and more lucrative B2B market for the unattended delivery of shop orders, spare parts and laundry. One of the first companies to introduce reception boxes, the American e-grocer Streamline, installed them within customers' garages, essentially combining the home access system with the use of a box. The company failed to achieve long-term viability and ceased trading in 2000. The mobile reception box operator, Homeport, ran a trial in a district of London with the supermarket chain Sainsbury but this too did not prove commercially sustainable. Experience with reception boxes has been more encouraging in some other countries, such as Finland (Punakivi and Tanskanen, 2002). Investment in a fixed box at an individual home can only be justified at present where the customer makes regular use of an e-grocery service. The volume of non-food product being delivered to the home is still much too low to make such an investment worthwhile for the average household. For example, it has been estimated that in 1999 only around 17 packages were delivered to the average household in the UK (McKinnon and Tallam, 2003).

It is likely that, for the foreseeable future, communal reception boxes strategically located at public buildings, transport terminals and local shopping centres offer the best prospects of commercial viability. They appear to strike a reasonable balance between the conflicting demands of customer convenience, delivery efficiency and security. They can also integrate flows of B2C and B2B orders to achieve an adequate level of throughput.

CONCLUSIONS

Despite the collapse of the dot-com bubble, online retailing has been enjoying healthy growth in recent years, and this is predicted to continue. The future rate of growth will partly depend on the quality and efficiency of the supporting system of order fulfilment. After a shaky start, many e-tailers have established effective logistical systems and built up customer confidence in the delivery operation. This has been most easily achieved in the non-food sector, where well developed home delivery systems already existed and, in essence, only the ordering medium changed.

E-grocery logistics has presented more formidable challenges. In retrospect, the initial rush to build dedicated pick centres seems to appear reckless. Store-based fulfilment offers a surer path to market growth and profitability, though doubts remain about its longer-term sustainability if online grocery sales continue to grow at their current rate. The more successful 'bricks and clicks' retailers may eventually have to invest in new facilities to accommodate future growth. As consumers' commitment to home shopping strengthens they too are likely to start investing in home reception facilities, partly to liberate themselves from the need to stay in for deliveries. Online retailers may also promote a switch to unattended delivery by passing on some of the resulting transport cost savings in lower delivery charges. This trend could be further reinforced by local authorities keen to constrain the growth in van traffic in urban areas and have more deliveries made during the night on uncongested roads.

REFERENCES

Brynjolfsson, F and Smith, M (2000) Frictionless commerce? A comparison of internet and conventional retailers, *Management Science*, **46** (4), pp 563–85

CACI (2000) *Who's Buying Online?*, CACI Information Solutions, London

Christopher, M (1992) *Logistics and Supply Chain Management*, Financial Times/Pitman, London

Department of Trade and Industry (DTI) (2001) @ Your Home: New markets for customer service and delivery, Retail Logistics Task Force, Foresight, London

Ellis-Chadwick, F, Doherty, N and Hart, C (2002) Signs of change? A longitudinal study of Internet adoption in the UK retail sector, *Journal of Retailing and Consumer Services*, **9** (2), pp 71–80

Ernst and Young (2000) *Global Online Retailing*, Ernst and Young, New York

Ganesh, J (2004) Managing customer preferences in a multi-channel environment using Web services, *International Journal of Retail and Distribution Management*, **32**, forthcoming

Hesse, M (2002) Shipping news: the implications of electronic commerce for logistics and freight transport, *Resources Conservation and Recycling*, **36** (3), pp 211–40

Jones, D (2001) Tesco.com: delivering home shopping, *ECR Journal*, **1** (1), pp 37–43

Laseter, T, Houston, P, Ching, A, Byrne, S, Turner, M and Devendran, A (2000) The last mile to nowhere, *Strategy and Business*, 20, September, 40–48

Lavin, M (2002) Christmas on the Web: 1998 v 1999, *Journal of Retailing and Consumer Services*, **9** (2), pp 87–96

Mandeville, L (1995) *Prospects for Home Shopping in Europe*, FT Management Report, Pearson, London

Matthews, H, Hendrickson, C and Soh, D L (2001) Environmental and economic effects of e-commerce: a study of book publishing and retail logistics, *Transportation Research Record*, 1763, pp 6–12

McClellan, J (2003) Sweet smell of success, *Guardian*, 4 Sept

McKinnon, A C and Tallam, D (2003) Unattended delivery to the home: an assessment of the security implications, *International Journal of Retail and Distribution Management*, **31** (1), pp 30–41

Mees, M D (2000) The place of the food industry in the global e-commerce universe: Ahold's experience, paper presented to the CIES conference on Supply Chain for E-commerce and Home Delivery in the Food Industry, Berlin

Metapack (1999) *Be-ful-filled*, Metapack, London

Michalak, W and Jones, K (2003) Canadian e-commerce, *International Journal of Retail and Distribution Management*, **31** (10), pp 5–15

Morganosky, M A and Cude, B J (2002) Consumer demand for online food retailing: is it really a supply side issue?, *International Journal of Retail and Distribution Management*, **30** (10), pp 451–8

Nairn, G (2003) Not many happy returns, *Financial Times*, 5 Feb

Nockold, C (2001) Identifying the real costs of home delivery, *Logistics and Transport Focus*, **3** (10), pp 70–71

Ody, P (1998) Non-store retailing, chapter 4 in *The Future for UK Retailing*, ed J Fernie, FT Retail and Consumer, London

Punakivi, M and Tanskanen, K (2002) Increasing the cost efficiency of e-fulfilment using shared reception boxes, *International Journal or Retail and Distribution Management*, **30** (10), pp 498–507

Reynolds, J (2001) The new etail landscape: the view from the beach, *European Retail Digest*, **30**, pp 6–8

Reynolds, J (2002) E-tail marketing, chapter 15 in *Retail Marketing*, 2nd edn, ed P J McGoldrick, McGraw-Hill, London

Ring, L J and Tigert, D J (2001) Viewpoint: the decline and fall of Internet grocery retailers, *International Journal of Retail and Distribution Management*, **29** (6), pp 266–73

Rowlands, P (2001) Why access is the key, *elogistics*, 15, Nov/Dec

Tanskanen, K, Yrjola, M and Holmstrom, J (2002) The way to profitable Internet grocery retailing – 6 lessons learned, *International Journal of Retail and Distribution Management*, **30** (4), pp 169–78

Taylor, E (2002) Swiss online grocer LeShop thrives thanks to low costs, *Wall Street Journal*, 15 Feb

Verdict Research (2000) *Electronic Shopping, UK*, Verdict, London

Wilson-Jeanselme, M (2001) Grocery retailing on the Internet: the leaking bucket theory, *European Retail Digest*, **30**, pp 9–12

10

Transforming technologies: retail exchanges and RFID

Leigh Sparks and Beverly Wagner

Recent years have witnessed a transformation of the retail landscape (Dawson, 2000, 2001). The way in which retailers manage their supply chains has been altered fundamentally (Sparks, 1998; Fernie and Sparks, 1998). The nature and extent of these supply chains has also changed. Retailer activity has become more global in its scope. Logistics and other activities have to be managed over greater distances than ever before. The nature of retail competition itself has changed, with an increase in business range and concentration. From being a local activity, retailing for some companies has progressed through the national level, to an international and in certain cases a global scale.

As retailers grow and seek to enhance their activities and reduce costs, they search for the most appropriate management methods, tools and activities. For some, an almost virtual organization has evolved with outsourcing being its prime activity (as with Benetton and Tommy Hilfiger). Some elements of the business, for example, supply or production, can readily be out-sourced (as with Tesco's distribution centres), whereas some activities remain internal (such as Tesco's Clubcard data). In either case closer relations amongst a network of contractors become essential. The nature of these retailer relationships varies. Some are more collaborative or associative than transaction focused (Dawson and Shaw, 1990). In all cases, however, the need to control costs, yet provide requisite service on this scale, becomes a key focus of attention. An array of new concepts has therefore been introduced into the management of retail supply chains in an attempt to improve performance: for example Quick Response (QR) (Fernie, 1994; Fiorito, May and Straughn, 1995; Kincade, Vass and Cassill, 2001), Efficient Consumer Response (ECR) (Kurt Salmon Associates, 1993; McMichael, Mackay and Altmann, 2000) and Collaborative Planning, Forecasting and Replenishment (CPFR) (Angeles, 2000) have become common techniques. The benefits arising from these are sometimes questioned, however (Kotzab, 1999). To some extent, these are tools within a wider potential restructuring of supply chains.

This restructuring takes a number of forms. Some involve relationship changes, others physical infrastructure investment or disinvestment. Strategic issues need consideration, but then so do tactical practices. In essence, all aspects of supply chains are being reexamined and reconsidered. Some changes are small and specific, though with considerable implications: for example, GPS tracking systems in vehicles. Others are large and complex with many ramifications, such as the move to stockless distribution. One common aspect of many of the changes being considered and implemented is technology. Technology has been used in supply chains for a considerable time, normally to provide dimensions of control and information. There is no doubt that investment in information and other technologies can deliver huge benefits if applied to the right problems and if the organization is structured appropriately.

This chapter looks at two technologies that have emerged in recent years. Both have been claimed to have the potential to transform aspects of the retail supply chain. Neither is without its controversies and detractors, but then neither is also without its adherents. In the first case, retail exchanges or B2B marketplaces, there was much hype about their potential, perhaps associated with the dual issues of the dot.com boom and the thought of competing with Wal-Mart more equally. The practice has perhaps been less spectacular, although some exchanges remain in operation and report good business. The second technology (Radio Frequency Identification: RFID) is hardly off the pages currently, and again is being held out as a technology with a huge future in supply chains. The chapter aims, by considering these two technologies, to show the potential that technologies have for transforming supply chain operations, but also to raise questions about why the pace of change is slower than might be anticipated.

RETAIL EXCHANGES

Business-to-business (B2B) exchanges are essentially Web-enabled market spaces that bring together buyers and sellers (Lightfoot and Harris, 2003; Lu and Antony, 2003). They have been described as a 'killer application'

..ods, 1999) due to the potential they hold out to efficiently ..ge procurement activities in distribution channels. Through a variety of applications they can affect the power in a supply chain, enabling buyers and suppliers perhaps to leverage their position and to extend their reach. By utilizing common tools and standards, opportunities for efficiency and wider sourcing and new markets may also emerge.

There are a number of ways of cataloguing such exchanges. Lu and Antony (2003) divide them into:

- marketplaces based around a specific industry sector (vertical marketplace);
- marketplaces based around products and services (horizontal marketplace);
- marketplaces focused on functions.

Whatever the form, they work by providing space that allows matching and aggregation. Marketplaces contain a matching mechanism that brings together buyers and sellers and thus matches their needs and capabilities, perhaps in a dynamic pricing environment. They also contain an aggregation mechanism that brings together a large number of buyers and sellers in one place, aiming to reduce transaction costs and improve choice and market efficiency. The consortia marketplaces may be constructed from either horizontal or vertical approaches.

There is another way of looking at marketplaces however. Table 10.1 positions them along a continuum from public to private. The table also recognizes however that some marketplaces may be private and open to suppliers for only one firm. This internalizing process is a demonstration of the power that some firms have in the market, but also suggests that there are benefits over and above the price-driven approach suggested by Lu and Antony (2003).

In the retail industry, there have been a number of such exchanges developed. Perhaps unusually, one of the first (begun in 1991 and moved to the Internet in 1997), and still one of the most influential has been a private exchange, Wal-Mart's Retail Link. Probably due to the sheer power of Wal-Mart, this exchange has become the standard for its suppliers and has been identified as one of the advantages that Wal-Mart enjoys over its competitors:

> Retail Link provides information and an array of products that allows a supplier to impact all aspects of their business. By using the information available in Retail Link, suppliers can plan, execute and analyze their businesses – thus providing better service to our common customers. Retail Link is a website that is accessible to any area within your company. Wal-Mart requires all suppliers to participate in

Table 10.1 Comparison of Public, Consortia and Private Exchanges

	Public e-markets	Consortia exchanges	Private exchange
Ownership	By third party	Jointly by 2 + industry incumbents	By one company
Access	Public	Equity holders and selected trading partners	Invitation only
Examples of functionality	Procurement through online catalogues, auctions	Procurement through online catalogues, auctions. Recent expansion into inventory management.	Collaborative value chain processes. Interaction in real time.
Main source of value	Price savings from aggregation, discovery	Price savings from standardization, discovery	Savings in value chain process, total cost of ownership
Business processes	Standardized Non-proprietary	Typically standardized, non-proprietary	Customized, proprietary
Relationship with trading partners	One-off, sporadic	Typically one-off, sporadic	Long-term, committed
Examples	Fastparts.com, Medibuy	Covisint, Transora	Dell Computers, Wal-Mart

Source: Hoffman, Keedy and Roberts, 2002

> Retail Link because of the benefits it provides. Should you become a supplier with Wal-Mart, you will be provided with the requirements for accessing Retail Link. (www.walmartstores.com/wmstore/wmstores/Mainsupplier.jsp, accessed 1 Dec 2003)

Based on a data warehouse of over 100 TB (Terabytes), through Retail Link, Wal-Mart provides to its suppliers an array of information on how their products are sold in Wal-Mart stores. Each evening, over 170 million rows are added to the sales table, representing line items on a customer receipt. By 4:00 am every morning, over 4,000 suppliers can receive information on their sales in every Wal-Mart store across the globe for the day before. Depending on their financial arrangements with Wal-Mart, some suppliers can get market basket detail that shows not only how many of their own products were sold, but also what other products were purchased by the consumer at the same time. Additionally, each Retail

Link supplier has access to up to two years of historical sales data on its products in the Wal-Mart chain. Access to this information allows for better collaborative forecasting and replenishment, which increases sales and margins for all involved. Some suppliers take this even further and work with Wal-Mart to create co-managed inventory, where the supplier takes over much of the assortment and planning functions to help improve sales (Wal-Mart, 1999).

Retail Link provides massive advantages for Wal-Mart as it allows real-time, visible analysis of performance by lines of business, individual products, suppliers and stores. Suppliers are organized through common standards and share common tools for the analysis of current and historical data, which in turn helps estimates of future activity and performance. Such benefits have encouraged other leading retailers such as Tesco to develop their own information exchanges.

Wal-Mart gained a lead on many of the other leading retailers by its early investment in Retail Link. One of the responses to this development has been the development of consortia retail exchanges. Of these, two main retail ones have been developed.

Global NetXchange (GNX) was initiated in February 2000 by Carrefour and Sears Roebuck, and now has more than 30 leading companies as customers including Kroger, Metro, Coles Myer, PPR and Sainsbury (see www.gnx.com).

WorldWide Retail Exchange (WWRE) was set up in March 2000, by an initial consortium of 17 leading retailers. Amongst its current 64-plus members are Ahold, Auchan, Best Buy, Casino, Delhaize, Gap, JC Penney, Jusco, Kingfisher, Kmart, Marks and Spencer, Safeway (UK and US), Target, Tesco, Dixons, Dansk, Edeka, Dairy Farm and El Corte Ingles (see www.wwre.com).

GlobalNetXchange claims to be a globally integrated retail supply chain network, leveraging the Internet to seamlessly connect trading partners across extended retail supply chains. This open network changes the way retailers collaborate with their global supply chain partners to satisfy demand, quickly and profitably. Table 10.2 suggests how this is achieved. The links with techniques such as CPFR are clear. In addition however, the exchange supports a range of auctions and complex bid/quote processes. With supplier and retailer catalogues online, searching, sourcing and spot purchasing are made easier. In the third quarter of 2003, GNX conducted nearly 3,200 auctions worth US $1.6 billion.

Examples of activities include (www.gnx.com):

- Pinault-Printemps-Redoute changing its apparel buying process through online negotiations with GNX. By enabling simultaneous negotiations with multiple suppliers, improving the quality and

Table 10.2   GNX Methods of Integration

Collaborative demand forecasting: retailers and suppliers can improve forecast accuracy by enabling collaborative demand planning processes. Trading partners can share their production and demand forecasts via demand planning tools. These will deliver automatic consolidation of forecasts, comparison of demand and production forecasts, and identify exceptional conditions. Exceptions can be reviewed by the entire supply chain, and the appropriate adjustments to both production and demand forecasts made instantaneously.

Collaborative supply planning: trading partners can reduce inventory and improve cycle times by sharing production schedules and proactively resolving problems. This sharing of information allows manufacturers to compare production and capacity schedules and identify unusual conditions. Exceptions can be reviewed and schedules can be adjusted appropriately in order to create synchronized supply plans.

Global inventory visibility: suppliers and other trading partners are able to share information about current inventory levels in order to rapidly fulfil urgent needs for critical purchases. Inventory levels may be published by product and location when the need arises; trading partners can then search these locations to determine where inventory is available.

Collaborative order processing: members can improve customer service across a 'virtual supply chain' by instituting collaborative order processing. Trading partners can request an availability check for a product or service. This request can then be forwarded automatically to the identified supplier. GlobalNetXchange provides the trading partner with accurate availability date and source of supply.

Source: www.globalnetxchange.com/

consistency of information from vendors and reducing extra steps, paperwork and travel, procurement cycle times and costs were reduced (costs by 10 per cent), buyer productivity was raised and purchase prices were optimized.
- Metro linked with Procter & Gamble using the GNX Web-based CPFR tool, to enable them to jointly manage the promotions planning process, share real-time information and gain visibility into supply chain processes. At the pilot stage forecast accuracy was improved and 46 per cent more stock-keeping units (SKUs) could fit into the range. Warehouse inventory levels fell by two weeks with high on-shelf availability. The collaborative process itself was less labour and time intensive.
- Sainsbury aimed to use GNX to streamline its new product development and lifecycle management process for retailer brand products. Sainsbury estimate that development times for entire new product lines was reduced by about 33 per cent. In addition paperwork was

reduced, inefficiencies and errors were eliminated and due diligence was more proactively managed.

The WWRE was established to give participating retailers and manufacturers the opportunity to simplify, rationalize and automate supply chain processes, thereby eliminating inefficiencies in the supply chain (see www.wwre.com). The WWRE enables Web-based transactions among retailers and suppliers operating in the food, general merchandise, textile/home and drugstore sectors. WWRE sees exchanges as revolutionizing trading relations in a number of ways. First, it creates open systems in which firms can establish short or long-term relations with one or more partners. Second, buyers and suppliers who previously had trouble reaching each other can be connected. Suppliers can gain access to more buyers. Buyers can participate easily and view items from multiple suppliers. Third, the electronic interface will lower transaction costs for both buyer and seller. Finally, this transparency is likely to drive down prices by rapidly developing and implementing new e-business models and advanced technologies. Costs across product development, e-procurement and supply chain processes are reduced through WWRE activities. Value is generated through three layers (WWRE, 2003):

- application-based value such as e-procurement, negotiations, efficiency gains by simplifying, eliminating and automating existing business processes;
- service-based value such as sourcing and logistics services, service gains by improving existing business processes in an efficient and innovative way;
- collaborative-based value such as VICS CPFR, innovation gains by new facilities provision for collaborative commerce.

Table 10.3 summarizes some of the solutions and services offered by WWRE. GNX provides similar solutions using slightly different descriptions (Table 10.2). GNX and WWRE seem to be focusing on process change within their members' organizations, encouraging them to take the collaborative exchange concept on board and use the exchange applications to drive change management (*Retail Week*, 22 Mar 2002). However, to a considerable extent these 'new' solutions do resemble the four tenets of ECR: efficient assortment, efficient store replenishment, efficient store promotion and efficient product introduction.

Are we therefore seeing old wine in new bottles? Eng Yong and Spickett-Jones (2002) reported that current Internet exchanges are more suitable for commodity-based products and services, and that key issues concerning collaborative planning, forecasting and replenishment have

Table 10.3 Summary of Solutions and Services Offered by WWRE

Solution/ service	Function
CPFR	Collaborative Planning develops mutually agreed forecasts based on the best data available to both parties. Results have been improved trading relationships and streamline processes.
World trade logistics	WTL address trade compliance, logistics costs estimation and analysis. Designed to streamline and automate global supply chain trade logistics operations in one centralized location
Surplus Goods Exchange	The SGE offers an efficient, low-cost and neutral end-to-end online trading process that integrates all aspects of freight logistics, financial settlement and dispute resolution
WISP	Worldwide Indirect Sourcing and Procurement (WISP)
Design and planning management	Supporting collaborative new product development
WWRE university	Offers online course registration, career development tools, training materials

Source: www.wwre.com

been impeded by the short-term focus of transaction-based activities in e-marketplaces. The main reasons why ECR and CPFR were inhibited were that the fundamental close relationship, essential for co-operative behaviour between buyer and supplier, did not exist (Kotzab, 1999; Perry and Sohal, 2000; Angeles, 2000).

Retail exchanges therefore bring into question the universal trade-off between richness and reach. Richness means the quality of information, defined by the user, such as accuracy, bandwidth, currency, customization, interactivity, relevance and security. Reach means the number of people who participate in the sharing of that information. Until recently it has been impossible to share simultaneously richness and reach (Evans and Wurster, 2000). The Internet has changed this, and retail exchanges aim to exploit the opportunities presented in terms of both richness (greater collaboration) and reach (opening up new markets for both large and small suppliers). However, this goal will remain uncertain until common standards are available that will enable everybody to communicate with everyone else at virtually zero cost. It is this, according to Evans and Wurster, that constitutes the 'sea change'. When proprietary EDI systems can be superseded by industry-wide extranets and everyone can exchange rich information without the constraints of reach, the channel choices for marketers, supply chains and the boundaries of organizations will be thrown into question.

Retailers are large enough to force radical changes along the supply channel. But this can only be effective if all parties in that channel are developing at the same pace: that is, the supply channel is only as strong as its weakest link. Some suppliers may not have the structures, systems and procedures to support radical supply chain change. Traditionally, supply chain management has been sub-optimized because parties in the channel are not able to articulate the architecture of their supply chain. It remains doubtful if retailers have really thought through the implications of retail exchanges in the longer term for themselves and the consequences on their supply channel partners. Retail exchanges may not be the 'killer application' yet, but gains may be accrued along the way as retailers and others begin to realize what the possibilities are. Change is not as radical as was once envisaged, but then perhaps it never is? This leaves us with a number of questions about retail exchanges (see Sparks and Wagner, 2003).

1   Will the Exchanges Simply Reflect the Traditional Marketplace?

The ways in which relationships in retailing and supply chains changed in the 1990s and the move away from transactional approaches is well documented. Any description of major retail supply chains has now to consider relationships and partnering as a key focus. It is also clear that as these changes have progressed, so the depth and nature of the relationships have also changed. But what do retail exchanges do to these relations? Although exchanges are in the context of electronic marketplaces there are some personal elements to them, particularly with regard to the establishment, but they are essentially impersonal, transactional-based operations. To a great extent, retail exchanges could be perceived as a retrograde step back to the previous method of operations, albeit that the scale and scope of the transactions differ.

2   How Will the Exchange Affect Co-operation Between Trading Partners?

Exchanges not only enable relationships to form and to continue, but also offer a ready ground for testing prices, quantities and specifications. The fact that exchanges may be easy to use, and could become the business norm, might expose business relationships to broader scrutiny. What is not yet apparent is the true extent to which buyers or suppliers are willing to use such exchanges compared with traditional business practices. The fact that the consortium exchanges are controlled by a group of competitors adds further to the complexities surrounding business relations in retail supply. There is a danger of falling foul of competition law.

3 How Can Businesses Participate in the Exchange to Create Value for Themselves and Prevent it Shifting to Competitors?

Exchanges have the potential to be exclusive clubs. Exchanges also however have the potential to alter existing relationship practices. The *raison d'être* for exchanges is one of price reduction from scale efficiencies, so smaller local firms may find it tough to break in. The impact of exchanges is therefore likely to accelerate tendencies towards concentration. This will occur at the buyer and the supplier level, but is also likely to impact on those physically and virtually handling the transactions. Will they become simply mechanisms to enable the big to get even bigger, or is this an ideal platform for large-scale industry-wide supply chain process improvements?

RADIO FREQUENCY IDENTIFICATION (RFID)

The last few years have been filled with claims about another potentially transforming technology. Radio Frequency Identification (RFID) has become the 'hot topic' in supply chains and retailing. As one of its proponents states:

> RFID has the potential to become one of retail's truly rare transforming technologies ... the business case is compelling ... RFID has the ability to reduce labour costs, simplify business procedures, improve inventory control, productivity and turnover, increase sales, reduce shrinkage, and improve customer satisfaction.
>
> (LakeWest Group, 2002: 1–2)

This of course is not a new technology, and neither are the claims about its impact wholly novel, though they do tend to hyperbole (for instance, '20–20 visibility in the supply chain and 100 per cent availability is just around the corner', *Retail Week*, 14 Nov 2003, p 25). Transponders have been around for decades. The difference now is the change in their cost, size and capability.

An RFID system typically contains a tag or label embedded with a single chip computer and an antenna, and a reader (much like a wireless LAN radio) that communicates with the tag (see www.rfidjournal.com for a glossary of terms). This basic system structure however contains a number of alternative choices for implementation. For example tags can be passive or active. Passive tags pick up energy from the reader to operate and communicate with the reader. In essence they are simply 'read'. They have no power source and are short read-range, but are cheap and probably last longer. Active tags have an embedded power source that provides for a greater range but reduces tag life and raises costs. Active tags can store a variety of data and can be read and written to. With readers being fixed position or hand-held/movable, tags able to transmit in a field rather than one direction and various choices of frequency depending on the range required or the product involved, the scope for flexible systems is apparent.

Tags can be applied at a variety of levels. In the supply chain, they could be applied to every single item produced, as well as to every carton, box, crate or pallet in which the product might be handled. Non-stock items can be tagged as easily as stock items. The tag could be visibly attached to a product (possibly detachable later) or hidden invisibly or even woven into the fabric, for example a sweater or even a bank note. In comparison with bar-codes, tags can be read around corners and through materials. This means that a pallet of products or a trolley of groceries can be simultaneously scanned/read.

There are also choices to be made in terms of data storage on the tag. Tags can be read-only, thus containing a unique identifier only. Alternatively tags can contain read and write capabilities allowing additional information to be held or added to each time they are read. A tag for example can be programmed to hold all information about a product as well as the distribution points it passed before it reached the customer. Some systems allow data to be stored on the tag in a portable dynamic database. Others allow data to be edited, added to or locked, which can be valuable in different circumstances. As might be expected given such different possibilities, one of the big issues in RFID has been the agreeing of standards for data. Other questions that need to be resolved include the choice of frequency and the ability to read chips from different countries or even companies.

Table 10.4 provides a way of thinking about RFID functions. It suggests that some of the activities within RFID are basically the replacement of current activities. For example, the RFID tag can act essentially as a 'super bar-code'. Advantages derive from this area of application through the ability to things better. However, RFID also offers the potential to be able to do new things. For example it will be possible to have remote and unattended activities to a greater extent than currently. It will also be possible to have temperature and other regimes checked by reading RFID tags. The ability to do both new things and existing things more efficiently is clearly an attraction to proponents of the technology.

A number of areas of benefit are therefore claimed to be available through the introduction of RFID. These include (LakeWest Group, 2002):

- Reduced out-of-stocks and improved shelf management. Real-time product movement information can be captured using RFID and so replenishment will be more efficient, in-store product misplacement will be identified and inventory movement at warehouse and store will be more effective.
- Reduced shrinkage/fraud. RFID provides embedded tracking capabilities which mean that inappropriate product movement will be more readily identified.
- Improved productivity and streamlined processes. The abilities of RFID in terms of remote or unattended scanning, plus the speed at which this is achieved (for say a mixed pallet of goods) means that there is the potential to reduce labour costs. Time and accuracy benefits are generated.

Table 10.4   RFID Approaches

Function	Activity	Value
Super bar-code	Permits faster and multiple reads of labels without opening containers. Accurate tracking via unique identifier.	Faster scanning (productivity). Accurate tracking (reduce shrinkage). Real-time stock location (higher availability, increased sales). ePODs (reduced disputes).
Carry additional information (read/ write only)	R/W tags may include sell-by date etc. Added information on each tag may pose a security risk.	Permits some high-speed checking locally (quantity per pallet etc). Decentralized information (to be balanced against security risk).
Perform new tasks (active tags only)	Maintain records of events (eg when opened, temperature regime). Locate products by tags associated with beacon.	E-seals when filling containers, provide accurate shipping manifest for customs (secure shipping lanes). Telematics related benefits.

Source: adapted from www.ilt2003.co.uk/g/logos/MurrayBrabender_files/frame.htm (accessed 10 Nov 2003)

- Enhanced point-of-sale checkout efficiency – these time and accuracy benefits apply equally to the store checkout.

The benefits of RFID are therefore fairly clear. RFID provides the ability to have total visibility at the item level throughout the supply chain and to achieve this visibility with more speed, greater accuracy and fewer people than were ever thought possible. This has obviously attracted considerable attention, and RFID is being proposed for many areas of the supply chain and the retail store (NCR, 2003). Retailers have begun to explore the possibilities of the technology through various trials (see for instance LakeWest Group and MeadWestvaco Intelligent Systems, 2003; various issues of www.rfidjournal.com). For example:

- Benetton announced its intention to embed RFID tags into all of the garments in one of its lines to track items arriving at the back of store.
- Prada tagged all of its merchandise in its New York Epicenter store so store staff could access a database on all stock items available without having to check the back-room. RFID tags have also been embedded in its customer loyalty cards, allowing dynamic accessorizing in the changing room among other personal features.
- Tesco has used RFID technology and a security camera to detect motion on razor blades in store in a smart shelf scheme run with Gillette. It has also announced that it will in 2004 put RFID tags on cases of non-food items at its distribution centers and track them through to stores.
- Wal-Mart is asking its top 100 suppliers to put RFID tags carrying Electronic Product Codes on pallets and cases by the start of 2005. Wal-Mart is contacting the suppliers ahead of this, but will probably not issue a compliance order in 2004, moving to that over time. Wal-Mart receives roughly 1 billion cases per year from its top 100 suppliers. The company will not be tracking every single case from the top 100 suppliers by 1 January 2005, but that is the eventual aim. The current goal is to track all pallets and cases. By announcing this statement, Wal-Mart is pushing the pace on RFID implementation (as it did on exchanges).

More detailed information on two of the experiments and trials is presented in the boxes on pages 201 and 202. These provide summaries of the experiments that Marks and Spencer and Sainsbury have been carrying out. They raise some of the potential benefits and issues in RFID implementation and point to some of the potential problems. All these experiments and testing show that there is a belief and willingness to see RFID implemented in the supply chain, but that it may not be as simple or straightforward as first envisaged. There are a number of ways of thinking about the problems of implementation with RFID (Table 10.5).

Marks and Spencer Pilots RFID

Marks and Spencer has been looking at RFID for some time. It has had an experimental scheme in food distribution that is now ready to roll out. Marks and Spencer has also however recently trialled RFID tracking tags in clothes at one of its UK stores.

The small-scale (one store, four week) pilot is basically a technology test aimed at stock accuracy, so as to lower safety stock and warehouse/store contact with the merchandise. Inaccuracies from incorrect delivery, damage and other merchandise movement compound to create a large problem at store level. As a result forecasts are driven by deduced not real stock. Manual stock counts are needed to remedy this, at some cost. Ideally the goal would be to keep a minimum of stock, maintained on a real-time basis. But stock is held in store and at the warehouse due to mistrust of forecast information. Suppliers also hold safety stock. Reducing the stock held and the need for handling and counting would be a considerable benefit.

The tags are contained within throwaway paper labels called intelligent labels attached to, but not embedded in, a selection of men's suits, shirts and ties. The passive tags hold the number unique to each garment. The information associated with this number is held on Marks and Spencer's secure database and relates only to that product or garment's details: for example, the size, style and colour. The intelligent label is attached to the garment alongside the pricing label and is designed to be cut off and thrown away after purchase. For items such as shirts, which are pre-packed, the tag is stuck onto the transparent shirt bag.

Two scanners are used for the tags. A portal installed at the distribution centre and the loading bay of the store allows rails of hanging garments and trolleys containing packaged garments, to be pushed through and read at speed. A mobile scanner in a shopping trolley that has a hand-held reader will scan several garments at the same time out on the shop floor. This is pioneering, but hardly a satisfactory long-term solution, given its size, and Marks and Spencer have expressed some frustration at the lack of readiness of technology in this area.

Given high-profile media interest in consumer privacy issues, Marks and Spencer contacted one of the leading consumer advocacy groups before the trial (CASPIAN – see www.nocards.com) to discuss privacy implications. It is understood that it took some of the concerns into account. The pilot focuses on only the store operational benefits of RFID and not on any potential links to consumers.

Marks and Spencer emphasize that many of the figures for potential savings appear to be highly speculative, and that the costs and benefits have yet to be fully understood. There may also be differential aims and costs/benefits depending on product group. Marks and Spencer believe that the business case for tagging food items is based more around efficiency and speed of handling with some degree of accuracy (hence tray-level tagging), whereas the clothing business case is primarily built around accuracy (hence item-level tagging) with some efficiency benefits. In the long run the company may benefit from its ability to run RFID within a closed-loop environment, given its retailer-brand policy. Implementation issues may therefore be somewhat reduced.

Sources: adapted from material at www.amrresearch.com, www.spychips.com/, www.silicon.com (accessed 1 Dec 2003), Ft.com (accessed 25 Nov 2003) and *Retail Week,* 14 Nov 2003, p 26.

The Value of RFID for the Retailer: The Sainsbury's Case

Sainsbury's RFID trial was predicated on a basis of an information-enriched supply chain. The trial focused initially on tracking chilled goods with one supplier, a single depot and a single store, before it was widened to other goods in the line going to the store. The RFID tags were applied to recyclable plastic crates. The tags were programmed with:

- the description and quality of the product in the crate;
- the use-by dates of these products;
- the crate's own ID number.

Programming was achieved at the end of the production line. Goods were then read at the depot's goods receipt area and on delivery to the store.

Benefits achievable from a full-scale implementation were estimated to be £8.5 million per annum based mainly on retail store replenishment productivity, reduction of stock loss and on removal of checking stock and codes. Payback for the system was estimated to be between two to three years. These benefits were estimated without any supplier participation, which could be considerable if item stock-outs are minimized.

Source: adapted from Karkkainen, 2003: 532–4.

Table 10.5 Problems in RFID Implementation

Area	Problem	Description
Technology	Size and data storage	Functionality comes at a cost in terms of money and size. Smaller tags with increased data capacity at a lower cost are needed.
	Scanning accuracy	When several items are read closely in conjunction, problems of interference arise. Tags can be faulty at production causing misreads. Readers may be insufficiently accurate.
	Infrastructure costs	Readers are not yet cheap enough and will undoubtedly also develop in capabilities, causing upgrade issues
Costs	Cost vs functionality	The current cost to manufacture even the basic tags may be prohibitive. When functionality is additional then costs rise.
Standardization	Product identification	All points along the distribution channel need to recognize that standardization is the key to the technology. Without standardization a global system will not work. Some steps have been made in this direction.
	Manufacture and equipment standards	Standardization among manufacturers to avoid bespoke systems is also needed
Others	Consumer privacy	Considerable adverse reaction to the trials has been generated (see www.spychips.com), with consumer concern about personal data tracking and privacy intrusion at the forefront.
	Operations and maintenance	If tags are to be reused then data management becomes an even bigger issue
	Intelligent use of data	The data collected have major impacts on people and processes. RFID is not simply a replacement technology and thus a creative vision of new processes and the skills of the people involved is needed.

Source: adapted from LakeWest Group (2002), various issues of www.rfidjournal.com

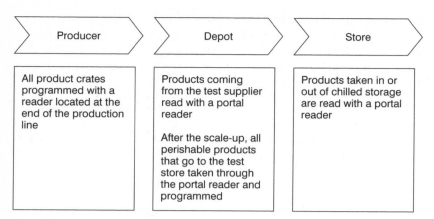

Figure 10.1 Sainsbury's RFID Trial

The table suggests that there are a number of dimensions to the problem of implementation. While RFID has been used in some business sectors for some time, the extension to the retail supply chain presents new problems. These new problems are due to the scale of the retail supply chain (one Woolworths' distribution centre for example has over 100,000 dollies and cages) and the environmental characteristics under which the systems will have to operate. As such there are always going to be technological problems as the technology is used in new situations and new generations of technology are developed. Given the scope of the possible RFID implementation in the retail supply chain, there are also always going to be issues of costs. While the cost of basic tags has fallen, their sheer ubiquity of use in a retailer demands a huge volume. Costs therefore have to be minimal. At the same time, as this is a supply chain issue, there is also concern over the cost of implementation and compliance. To what extent can the costs and benefits of the technology be shared by retailers, suppliers and logistics services providers?

Quite a lot of the problems posed in Table 10.5 can be put down to the timing of technology adoption. In any innovation there are obviously leaders and laggards. In this case, as the claims for RFID are so broad, there are leaders and laggards in aspects of implementation ranging from the type of tag to the standards to be used, components of the supply chain to be tested and so on. Some of the issues may be termed teething troubles; other issues may force a fundamental rethink about the whole transforming nature of the technology. Despite the bold claims of its proponents, and a widespread belief it is a question of when, not if, a totally transparent global supply chain at the item level still seems some way off. More likely are small-scale closed-loop developments focused on particular supply chains or problem areas.

Given the critical nature of Wal-Mart's mandate to its top 100 suppliers (noted above) it is worth considering further the latest news about this situation (www.amrresearch.com: accessed 1 Dec 2003). From a mid-November meeting between Wal-Mart and these suppliers, they report that:

- Wal-Mart did not recommend any specific solutions, vendors, or provide an implementation guide.
- Operational changes saw the project constrained to Texas, pallet not carton level reading required and other changes to protocols and data requirements.
- Data requirements seem to be pushing up the likely final specifications for the tag (and therefore the cost).
- Some specific technology, implementation and deployment problems remain.
- Suppliers need urgently to understand what all this will mean for their production processes and costs.

In short, there still seems a long way to go, despite a deadline of only 13 months. Perhaps the Wal-Mart example shows the substantial difficulties in implementation for retailers and suppliers. The list in Table 10.5 may be far from complete. Even for a relatively limited application in the retail supply chain, there still seems much to do to implement RFID in a cost-effective and useful manner. This may be an issue of time rather than technology, but this is by no means certain.

Two particular problems deserve further consideration. First, and probably unexpectedly, there has been a considerable and voluble consumer backlash against the technology on the grounds of privacy invasion. Tags can be placed in individual items and can continue to work after a consumer has purchased the product. Individual items can be associated with individual consumers and a very detailed picture of purchase and behaviour can be drawn up. Consumer advocates have been vocal in their criticism (see www.spychips.com) and as a result, many of the trials identified earlier (such as Prada and Benetton) have been halted. While RFID may have begun as a supply chain initiative, the potential for consumer identification is clear, whether done deliberately or accidentally. Any allegation of use of hidden RFID tags to spy on consumers provokes bad publicity for retailers, whatever the real situation.

Second, while a lot of thought has been given to the technology itself, not much seems to have been devoted to the handling of the data the systems could generate and the use of this data. Rewriting the supply chain using RFID is a change management project writ large. As such there is need for much greater concern over how the data are to be stored and analysed, and how their use will need to focus on aspects of process and people change. The implications are considerable.

The technology itself is advancing rapidly and needs therefore to be monitored carefully. Capital costs are not going to be cheap however, despite the fall in prices in tags. People, processes and technology will be affected by any implementation, particularly if the data from the systems can be applied appropriately. Given that a total supply chain solution is some way off, it is likely that retailers are going to have to run several types of systems for some time, adding further to the cost issues (AT Kearney, 2003).

CONCLUSIONS

The claim that a technology will transform a business is too easily made. There have been many false dawns in retailing and retail supply systems. The two technologies considered here, retail exchanges and RFID, are the latest in a long line of such potential transformations. Yet, in the end, companies still have to move boxes from a point of production to some point of consumption. The focus has to be on doing this in the most effective and efficient way. Here, the technologies do have things to offer. By focusing on the detailed applications (new product development and tagging merchandise-ready units for example) so costs can be driven out of the system, control can be improved and the detailed operations of the supply chain can be enhanced. Is this a transformation? Probably not. But is it important to retailers? Definitely.

REFERENCES

Angeles, R (2000) Revisiting the role of the Internet-EDI in the Current Electronic Scene, *Logistics Information Management*, **13** (1), pp 45–57

AT Kearney (2003) *Meeting the Retail RFID Mandate*, November [Online] www.atkearney.com/shared_res/pdf/Retail_RFID_S.pdf (accessed 1 Dec 2003)

Dawson, J A (2000) Retailing at century end: competing in volatile markets, *Industrial Marketing Management*, **29**, pp 37–44

Dawson, J A (2001) Is there a new commerce in Europe? *International Review of Retail and Distribution Management*, **11**, pp 287–99

Dawson, J A and Shaw, S (1990) The changing character of retailer-supplier relationships, in *Retail Distribution Management*, ed J Fernie, Kogan Page, London

Eng Yong, T and Spickett-Jones, G (2002) *An Investigation of the Concept of E-Marketplace in Supply Chain Management*, British Academy of Management Conference, London

Evans, P and Wurster, T S (2000) *Blown to Bits: How the new economics of information transforms strategy*, Harvard Business School Press, Boston, MA

Fernie, J (1994) Quick Response: an international perspective, *International Journal of Physical Distribution and Logistics Management*, **24** (6), 38–46

Fernie, J and Sparks, L (eds) (1998) *Logistics and Retail Management*, Kogan Page, London

Fiorito, S, May, E and Straughn, K (1995) Quick response in retailing: components and implementation, *International Journal of Retail and Distribution Management*, **23** (5), pp 12–21

Hoffman, W, Keedy, J and Roberts, K (2002) The unexpected return of B2B, *McKinsey Quarterly*, 3 [Online] http://www.mckinseyquarterly.com/article_page.asp?ar=1210&L2=24&L3=47 (accessed 1 Dec 2003)

Karkkainen, M (2003) Increasing efficiency in the supply chain for short shelf life goods using RFID tagging, *International Journal of Retail and Distribution Management*, **31** (10), pp 529–36

Kincade, D H, Vass, D and Cassill, N L (2001) Implementation of technology and relationships to supply chain performance: apparel manufacturers' perspectives, *International Review of Retail, Distribution and Consumer Research*, **11**, pp 301–27

Kotzab, H (1999) Improving supply chain performance by efficient consumer response? A critical comparison of existing ECR approaches, *Journal of Business and Industrial Marketing*, **14** (5/6), pp 364–67

Kurt Salmon Associates (1993) *Economic Consumer Response: Enhancing customer value in the grocery industry*, Kurt Salmon Associates, Washington, DC

LakeWest Group (2002) *RFID: Retail's new transforming technology*, June [Online] http://www.lakewest.com/PDFdocs/RFID per cent20Retails per cent20New per cent20Transforming per cent20Technology_June per cent202002.PDF (accessed 1 Dec 2003)

LakeWest Group and MeadWestvaco Intelligent Systems (2003) *RFID in Retail: The future is now*, June [Online] http://www.lakewest.com/PDFdocs/RFID per cent20In per cent20Retail per cent20The per cent20Future per cent20Is per cent20Now_June per cent202003.pdf (accessed 1 Dec 2003)

Lightfoot, W and Harris, J R (2003) The effect of the Internet in industrial channels: an industry example, *Industrial Management and Data Systems*, **103** (2), pp 78–84

Lu, D and Antony, J (2003) Implications of B2B marketplaces to supply chain development, *TQM Magazine*, **15** (3), pp 173–79

McMichael, H, Mackay, D and Altmann, G (2000) Quick Response in the Australian TCF industry: a case study of supplier response, *International Journal of Physical Distribution and Logistics Management*, **30** (7/8), pp 611–26

NCR Corporation (2003) *50 Ideas for Revolutionizing the Store through RFID* [Online] www.ncr.com/repository/articles/pdf/sa_RFID_whitepaper.pdf (accessed 1 Dec 2003)

Perry, M and Sohal, A S (2000) Quick Response practices and technologies in developing supply chains, *International Journal of Physical Distribution and Logistics*, **30** (7/8), pp 627–39

Scully, A and Woods, W (1999) *B2B Exchanges: The killer application in the business-to-business internet revolution*, ISI Publications

Sparks, L (1998). The retail logistics transformation, in *Logistics and Retail Management*, ed J Fernie and L Sparks, pp 1–22, Kogan Page, London

Sparks, L and Wagner, B (2003) Retail exchanges: a research agenda, *Supply Chain Management*, **8** (1), pp 17–25

Wal-Mart (1999) The role of standards in the growth of global electronic commerce, prepared statement by Wal-Mart Stores, Inc before the Subcommittee on Science, Technology and Space of the Committee on Commerce, Science and Transportation, United States Senate, Washington, 28 Oct 1999 [Online] www.senate.gov/commerce/hearings/1028hab.pdf (accessed 1 Dec 2003)

WWRE (2003) WWRE Overview Presentation [Online] /www.world-wideretailexchange.org/cs/en/press_room/exec_speeches.htm (accessed 1 Dec 2003)

11

Enterprise resource planning (ERP) systems: issues in implementation

Mark West and Leigh Sparks

INTRODUCTION

Drucker (1962) described the supply chains of businesses as the one area where managerial results of great magnitude could be achieved. Companies have subsequently strived to meet this challenge and to obtain value from their supply chains. The retail sector is often a leader in this process, and there are many examples where retailers in managing specific market sectors, such as Tesco with food, Zara with fashion, have managed to shorten, improve and obtain much value from their supply chains. However, there are many other retailers who, through their own complexity or lack of capability, fail to move forward with the supply chain transformation process. Why can some retailers take such great strides and others continue to have problems in supply chain management? Perhaps it derives from the need to fuse together three elements:

- an effective operational infrastructure (processes),
- and a focused and expert workforce (people),
- linked by creative and innovative business enablers (technology).

Recognizing the need to enhance supply chains is one thing. Implementing appropriate solutions to achieve results is another. This chapter describes and measures the change process undertaken by a retailer when it chose to replace its myriad of computer systems with an end-to-end Enterprise Resource Planning (ERP) system. The retailer in question remains anonymous, in order to focus attention on the issues involved. Some elements have also been adjusted to emphasize issues. Once it has been decided to implement a supply chain solution, what problems and setbacks can be expected and how might they be managed?

The chapter contains four sections. First, we consider ERP and the reasons retailers choose to implement such solutions. Second, we provide the main case study and the situation the retailer found itself in at initial ERP implementation. Third, an analysis of the revised second ERP implementation is presented. Finally some lessons are drawn.

ERP: A BACKGROUND

Enterprise systems have three properties (Mabert, Soni and Venkataramanan, 2001):

- ERP systems are multifunctional in scope, tracking a range of activities such as financial results, procurement, sales, manufacturing and human resources.
- They are integrated in nature, meaning that when data are entered into one of the functions, information in all related functions is also changed immediately.
- They are modular in structure and usable in any combination of modules. A firm can implement all the modules or a subset of them, as well as connect to other support systems, including 'bolt-ons'.

There are two main reasons that businesses abandoned their 'legacy' (data processing) systems in favour of the new 'enterprise' approach (Davenport, 1998). First, businesses wish to overcome the fragmentation of information stored throughout a variety of computer systems. Integration is seen as beneficial in this as in other aspects of supply chains. Second, the cost associated with the ongoing maintenance of multiple systems is high, and often represents an enormous drain on a company's finances (for example, the holding of duplicate data sets in two or more systems, and additional computer hardware to cope with data processing of numerous computer applications). In addition a more pressing imperative for change during the late 1990s (and one that is relevant to this case study) was that of the 'Year 2000' compliance threat, where companies replaced their various different systems with one stable 'Year 2000' compliant ERP system (James and Wolf, 2000).

The caveat to the enterprise approach is that it requires businesses to recognize that existing processes, and subsequently employees' roles, may need to be changed to fall in line with the 'Industry Best Practice' approach that the total ERP integrated concept promotes. The utilization of 'Industry Best Practices' and the exploitation of new technology as an enabler, make up a process of re-engineering or effectively 'starting over' by 're-creating a company, based upon current technology and what I know today' (Hammer and Champy, 1994). The imposition of IT only upon existing systems and processes is a limited solution. Existing systems will have been based upon past rules of competition, strategies and competencies, which may no longer apply.

It is clear that an enterprise system imposes its own logic on a company strategy, culture and organization (Davenport, 1998). For example, the very benefits the enterprise system provides, such as universal information access and flatter, more flexible organization structures can paradoxically take control of the organization and move it away from the very thing that it was set up to be: to a command and control culture working through the adherence of standard practices and procedures. Enterprise solutions are organization-challenging. Businesses therefore should not underestimate the effect an ERP implementation can have on the way a business is managed and organized:

> Going live with ERP means making the transition from a traditional organization to an integrated one and to a process-based mode of operation.
> This transition was of unparalleled extent and complexity for all companies, but was often treated only as a software installation until disruption occurred to business processes after implementation.
> An ERP system is a Trojan Horse. It will bring discipline, cross-functionality and change to your corporation whether you are ready for it or not.

> (Hammer, quoted in Bassirian, 2000)

The importance of ERP and systems integration to the supply chain processes was highlighted by Holmes (1995), who stated that 66 per cent of the surveyed companies were actively engaged in this process to enable different functional units to work more effectively and efficiently together:

> The leading edge companies have taken the individual pieces of the supply chain and made continuous improvement types of thing happen. Now they are approaching the next quantum step, which is, after achieving some success in fixing your transportation, your warehousing and so on, to plug it all together and make it work.

Christopher (1998) argues that the gap between the theory and reality of making this quantum leap is more difficult than it first seems. His views parallel those of Davenport and Hammer above, who have both voiced concerns over the complexity involved with making business transformation happen. This is a continued topic of development for the software houses that provided the initial ERP systems of the 1990s. Bywater (2001) stated that today's emphasis for technology development is 'Cross-Business Collaboration', which promotes open systems and shared data as its mantra. Just as internal company IT integration was the focus for the 1990s, Web-based solutions are the extension to the enterprise estate for the coming years. Essentially the focus is 'business network redesign', involving the redesign of existing processes and linkages between different organizations. Redesign implies a step beyond simple transaction and inventory management between organizations, and moves into the realms of process linkage and knowledge leverage in the creation of new added value.

Supply chain management has been positioned as the integration and transformation of supply chain activities. The emphasis in supply chain management has switched from functional activity to interactivity across the supply chain and within organizations. The implementation of systems to allow this to happen is however not necessarily straightforward. As this initial introduction to ERP has suggested, the introduction of such systems has possibly profound repercussions for existing processes and people. Implementation has therefore to be carefully managed, and it has to be recognized by organizations that it can be threatening to current supply chain (and other) processes.

A RETAIL CASE STUDY

Background

The case study described here is derived from events at an important established retailer. Some aspects have been adapted to raise specific issues, and the case is developed from the interpretation of events by the authors. It is presented so as to draw lessons from the experiences and to raise issues about implementation of enterprise systems. The case does not set out to suggest that this retailer 'got it right or wrong' but rather to point to the implications of decisions to change system approaches in retailing and retail supply. If anything the case recognizes (and sympathizes with) the problems retailers are confronted with in implementation of change.

During the mid-1990s, like so many other retailers, this retailer undertook a strategic review of all its information technology systems to judge their potential readiness for operation beyond 'Year 2000'. With no guarantees for ensuring compliance, the findings of the review suggested the replacement of the current myriad of systems applications with an enterprise solution. In line with the thinking of Walters and Rands (1999), the existing EPOS system was the first to be replaced, while discussions continued with regard to using an enterprise solution to support the finance, merchandise, store operations and distribution functions of the business.

The organizational structure of the business at the time reflected a 'functional' or 'silo' format, where individual business leaders were encouraged to manage and operate their respective business units or departments as separate businesses. Distribution was one such business. This of course contrasts with the enterprise approach, which encourages businesses to operate centrally by cutting horizontally across these vertical silos and apportioning responsibility on an end-to-end basis.

By replacing a multitude of systems with one consolidated enterprise system, the retailer believed it could consolidate and streamline its current working practices through the adoption of 'Industry Best Practices'. These would assist it to become more efficient and ultimately more responsive to its customers' needs (with the right stock, right place, right time). Other commercial benefits targeted were the reduction of costs associated with running multiple system operating platforms, the eradication of manual keying processes for vendor purchase ordering, and the automation of stock replenishment between the retailer's shops, its warehouses and vendors.

System Selection Process and Project Team Establishment

The approach to the system selection process centred upon a 'single vendor' supplier of ERP technology as opposed to a mixture of 'best of breeds' applications. This decision reflected the business's desire to move away from the multiple applications it was currently running and the costs associated with them. A number of software providers were identified, and a team of key senior managers and directors, headed by the Information Technology Systems Director, initiated the selection process.

The selection team concluded that the system chosen met the criteria required by the business. These criteria are recognizable through several key distinguishable concepts (Bancroft, Seip and Sprengel, 1998):

- One single database for all corporate data, without any redundancy.
- Software functionality configurable to different customers' needs.
- Best practice and standardized business processes.
- Online system with no batch interfaces.

The approach to the implementation took the form of a project team, jointly led by the retailer and its implementation partner in the form of an Executive Steering Group. Mabert *et al* (2001) note that a success factor for implementing ERP solutions is a cross-functional implementation team headed by a senior management leader fully dedicated to the ERP project and often colocated to improve communications. The project team was made up of operational experts representing the key business functions of information technology, merchandising, finance, distribution and shop floor operations. The need to actively involve individuals within this project team was paramount.

Business Process Review

The first task for the project team was to document the 'as is' business processes of the company. This follows the approach of Hammer and Champy (1994), who state that just as companies have organization charts, they also have process maps that give a picture of how work flows through the company. A process map also creates a vocabulary to help people discuss re-engineering.

The project team was organized into specialized subgroups representing the hierarchical 'vertical' management structure of the business rather than the 'horizontal' end-to-end business processes. For example the distribution group only focused on documenting the internal processes carried out within the distribution centre (DC) rather than the end-to-end process that would include demand creation (sales team) and vendor fulfilment (no team assigned). This approach seemed to maintain current separateness in the process.

The next step in the project should have been to revisit the 'as is' processes with the organizational heads to create 'to be' processes. Mabert *et al* (2001) define the importance of this by reference to a 'play book':

> Teams should spend more time up front on defining in great detail exactly how the implementation should be carried out. This includes what modules and process options should be implemented and how the senior management priorities would be incorporated in the implementation process. Such a strategy allows the creation of a 'play book', which then becomes the implementation 'bible'.

However, this exercise was not carried out. The Steering Group had instructed the project team to configure the ERP system to the existing business processes. The impact of this decision upon the project was grossly underestimated at the time, with management believing that changing a few system configurations would be better than changing the way the business operated. At this point both the ERP service provider and the consulting partners stressed the interdependency of the ERP system with 'Industry Best Practices', but were rebuked by a strong retailer management team that referred back to one of the prime unique selling points, namely that ERP 'software functionality is configurable to different customers' needs'. Marion (2000) says to 'forget about vendor promises of easy customization and flexibility' and lists 'fine-tuning ERP packages to exactly match your business' as hazard number three on his list of 12 hazards to be avoided when implementing an ERP solution (see Table 11.1 for all 12, which will be discussed later in this chapter).

The reaction of the retailer to the potential of change illustrated the denial stage of the change process identified by Adams, Hayes and Hopson (1976) and described by Davies (1992): 'people deny the situation and act as if nothing has changed'. This unwillingness to engage change became the mantra of the business. The organizational climate within the project team plummeted into 'anger' and 'depression' stages (Davies, 1992), as the team realized that the change imperative paradigm had collapsed. This in itself brought the project team into conflict with both the management of the company and the wider business community, as it was recognized nothing in the business would change. It became a case of 'just getting the system in, warts and all' as one senior retail executive stated at the time. In essence ERP was being used to update existing business practices, which were based on functional activities designed under very different circumstances.

The Project Implementation

While warnings went unheeded, the retailer did follow advice given concerning roll-out and the merit of 'phased' as opposed to 'big bang'. An aggressive roll-out schedule was undertaken, however. As Marion (2000) states:

> The typical ERP approach was to switch the entire company to the new system over a weekend. Doing everything at once looked like a faster approach than a phased roll out by product or geography. That was then, this is now. Today, only masochists take this approach.

Pre-Implementation System Training

The training requirement for the business represented almost a thousand individuals, who needed to be trained not only on the pure ERP system functionality but on the new technologies (NT) of Windows and Web browsers. The under-estimation and subsequent under-budgeting of training needs was a continuing theme and determining factor for the implementation (see also Mabert *et al*, 2001 and Marion, 2000).

The investment in training was significant but still lower than the industry guidelines (10 per cent). The effectiveness of the training can be examined from both a training and a user perspective. The former concluded that the training programme was effective based upon the number, type of courses trained over the period and the cost involved. Interestingly an analysis of feedback sheets from each course suggested that the training courses tended to centre on the operation of NT, rather than drilling down into the bones of the ERP system. In essence the training courses were prescriptive in their nature, focusing on the operation of standard route paths and transaction types. In hindsight it is evident that this approach (while necessary due to the sheer number of employees requiring training), was to cause the organization problems in the post-implementation phase of the project, where employees grappled to understand how the whole 'enterprise' fitted together and consequently the importance of their job roles.

Grappling with Post-Implementation

During post-implementation it was felt that the new system did not provide the level of management reporting that the legacy system had done in the past, and which was urgently needed to run the business effectively. This is another hazard identified by Marion (2000). The lack of reporting became the focus for the project. The system was increasingly customized to satisfactorily support the perceived business need. This customization of the core ERP code to support users' reporting and to avoid changing processes, combined with a lack of understanding of how an 'enterprise' system works, created apathy and lack of interest among employees as they began to feel failed by the system and the company. Information was hard to access, resulting in shipments of new merchandise being delayed and vendors not being paid on time, all of which bred a culture of blame between warring factions or 'silos' such as buying, distribution and finance.

It was a case of each part of the business trying to address its own problems rather than collectively pulling together to solve the root cause of issues rather than the symptoms. For example the fact that merchandise was getting stuck at the distribution centre awaiting processing, because it did not appear on the purchase order, was a symptom. The cause of the problem was vendor/buying disciplines regarding supplying what was ordered. As a result the responsibilities placed upon individuals grew, as did the stress and strain to which they were subjected. The apathy and lack of interest spread from the employees to the top of the company, and the project lost executive sponsorship. Process owners complained that too many decisions had been taken without their involvement. What resulted was a melee of re-work and delays to the aggressive implementation plan.

A Time for Change

The retailer therefore undertook a strategic review of the implementation project. As a result a new steering group was formed. What followed was a voyage of discovery that unearthed the cold fact that as much as 40 per cent of the core ERP system had been customized. This meant that not only was it impossible for the retailer to accept system upgrades from its ERP supplier, but the majority of recorded 'open' issues centred upon this customized code. Over the next year occurred a period of uncertainty and change as the retailer battled to understand and then plan to put right the mistakes made during the initial implementation.

Despite this effort and the lessons learnt from benchmarking with other retailers, many of the 12 hazards to implementing an ERP system identified by Marion (2000) were encountered, and remained in effect due to the configuration of the existing system. Table 11.1 compares the beginning of the initial ERP implementation and the point at which it was finally recognized that no further progress could be made with the current version of the ERP system. At the start of initial implementation nine of the 12 hazards were present. Even some time later little had improved, and by the end of the initial implementation the situation, while changed, was not really much further forward.

The Way Forward

After much deliberation a further project was started to implement a newer version of ERP through the adoption of 'Industry Best Practice'. The project commenced immediately with a set of meetings involving the business user community and aimed at formulating an 'Operational Business Process Blue-Print' to overlay against the ERP provider's industry standard templates. Subsequently, a further set of meetings was held to revisit, confirm and find solutions to processes that did not match the industry templates. This new adoption and approach is analysed below.

Table 11.1   Marion's 12 Obstacles to be Overcome when Implementing
an ERP System: Initial Implementation

	Start of initial implementation	Finish of initial implementation
1 Underestimating the importance of change management	Present	Present
2 Picking software before deciding on business process	Present	Present
3 Fine-tuning ERP packages to exactly your business	Present	Present
4 Under-budgeting for training.	Present	Present
5 Embracing a 'Big Bang' (whole company) approach.	Absent	Absent
6 Giving short shrift to vendor selection	Present	Absent
7 Keeping legacy systems alive	Present	Present
8 Fragmenting development by department or location	Absent	Present
9 Allowing apathy (or 'not-my-job disinterest') at the top	Present	Absent
10 Relying on your new ERP system for conventional management reports	Present	Present
11 Trusting 'open systems' promises from the ERP interfaces	Absent	Absent
12 Assuming ERP is a project with a finite timetable.	Present	Present

Second Revised Implementation: Analysis of Effects

The initial implementation had clearly collapsed. The revised second
implementation took notice of the reasons this collapse had occurred, and
planned appropriately. The details of this revision can be assessed in a
number of ways. Here, they are considered in terms of the effects on
supply chain practice, enterprise approach hazards and in terms of organizational culture.

Evidence for the adoption of 'Supply Chain Best Practices'

From functions to processes: The first evidence of the organization moving
towards best practice was demonstrated by discussions surrounding the
organization structure of the business. This represents the legal and
trading framework under which the retailer trades. The first decision
made was to reduce the existing company coding structure. This

not only reflected the true nature of the businesses as legal entities but eradicated the need for the manual posting of account journals, as the ERP system performs this task automatically. Immediately, 'a better way of doing work' was identified. This provided an immediate message to the business that demonstrated the company's commitment to the project. The business was being seen to change towards a more process-focused model.

Evidence of the retailer adopting changes to its organization chart were also observed, with new job descriptions being created. This is demonstrated clearly by the retailer's move away from the existing departmental structure of the organization, which had one buyer assigned to one or multiple departments, to a buyer having overall responsibility for a particular product grouping or category. The scope and size of some of these groupings required the business to embrace a new role of 'merchandiser', to support the buyer. This reflects an industry approach that sees the need for generalists with broad-based management skills to assist and support product specialists.

The organization of the new structure and the processes and procedures needed to underpin it were extracted through the series of meetings that involved a cross-section of employees from all the core business disciplines. This demonstrated a dramatic contrast with the approach initially undertaken by the retailer ('management knows best').

From profits to performance: The retailer used traditional and conventional fiscal measurements such as profitability and gross margin. Therefore the mention of Key Performance Indicators (KPIs) as a method for judging the efficiency of the business had always been greeted with a certain amount of cynicism. However, what became evident from the second implementation meetings was a genuine interest in both these qualitative and quantitative measurement mechanisms. For example, one question was about the 'meaning' of the time and cost involved to process inbound stock from point of receipt at the distribution centre to delivery on the shop floor. While there were many answers to this question in the business, and some subjective comments deriving from negativity amongst the current organizational functions involved in the process, the most common answer centred on 'what gets measured, gets managed'. It was also agreed that the effectiveness of the manager responsible for the process determined the quality and cost of the service. The introduction of the KPI principle and the interest stimulated from it during the initial meetings proliferated across the organization. By the second set of meetings a prepared audience wanted to embrace the methodology into the new business model.

From products to customers: The KPI debate continually evolved through stages of discussion which led to the importance of having the right product in the right place at the right time. Arguably, this could be construed as the first attempt to recognize the significance of customers to the business and the need to have the right goods on display, and not what happened to have been bought and stored in the warehouse. This point was emphasized by reference to the mountain of redundant and obsolete stock held by the retailer. The ERP provider gave a presentation on 'Product lifecycle management' and showed the assembled group how a proposed segmentation of the product base would work. The segmentation of supply chains is recognized by industry experts, who have encouraged vendors to co-manage or even manage and control their stock levels for a retailer's business.

From inventory to information: The continued focus on inventory turned discussion to the use of information to manage the processes of product lifecycle, agility and leanness (Naylor, Naim and Berry, 1997; Mason-Jones, Naylor and Towill, 2000). Through sharing and using information effectively a fair amount of intermediate inventory could be eliminated. This is a realization that is just seeping through into the retail elements of the business. The benefits of such an approach were supported at one of the meetings by a buyer: 'Effective use of information and replenishment has enabled me to grow my sales by 15 per cent and reduce my age stock position by 50 per cent over a period of three months.'

This is evidence, albeit limited, that the pre-existing 'functional silos' within the retailer, and particularly those of merchants and distribution, were being dismantled. In the process a joint approach to solving problems was being built. The advantages of using systems to forecast, plan and replenish stock over the traditional method of 'gut feel' will continue this development.

From transactions to relationships: The extension of this approach to using information up and down the supply chain was discussed in the meetings with a view to collaborating with vendors at a future date. This building of relationships with vendors is something that many retailers are very keen upon, particularly the sharing of information. Supporting interviews with industry benchmarks at this time reported:

A lot of suppliers came to us and said, 'Very difficult to get hold of your buyers during the season, we don't know what's selling out. We come into the store and see you have sold out of a particular item. If only you had told us we could have supplied more or provided an alternative.

Now they know that we have the information but that it requires the buyer or merchandiser to trawl the data and then place an order with the vendor. Hence, you can imagine if the supplier had access to this information themselves, they would be able to do the replenishment or substitutions themselves.

Another retailer commented that it is time to take the sharing of information with vendors to another level:

> For the last 10 years, US retailers such as Federated and Nordstrom who are clearly in competition with each other have used the same information sharing system called QRS. The system holds all the details of the vendor's product catalogue and each retailer has their own access to the data for the purpose of downloading it to place a purchase order. Product pricing will still be part of the initial buyer negotiations, but to all intents and purposes this is driven by volume discounts and hence the ability for vendors to be open about cost price.
>
> So basically, what I'm suggesting is alliancing for purchasing. It is I believe something that has been developed by the supermarket chains in Europe and not something the high street retailers have yet followed. Hence an opportunity for department stores in the UK, as we all share basically the same vendor base and it is an opportunity to leapfrog forward and jointly reduce our administration costs.
>
> All this being said, what defeats me is why other retailers don't think they should be doing this and continue with 'It sounds great; just let me know when it's working.'

Evidence for the Adoption of an Enterprise Approach

This second implementation is clearly different from the initial implementation. Table 11.2 again uses Marion's (2000) obstacles or hazards to ERP implementation. In this table the 'finish' line is the second implementation and the end of the first implementation is reported as 'mid-term'. The table highlights the very different degree of avoidance of problems in the revised implementation. While not complete, in the main the implementation has avoided the obvious hazards. In essence an enterprise approach has been introduced.

Evidence for a Change in the 'Cultural Paradigm'

The physical evidence presented so far for the second implementation has suggested that the retailer is changing. However, there has been a suggestion that the communication surrounding the project was weak. It is this reliance on people buying into change that is now examined. Figures 11.1 and 11.2 summarize the culture when it was recognized that no further progress could be made with the initial implementation of the ERP system (Figure 11.1) and the culture to which the current change programme (second implementation) aspires (Figure 11.2). These figures underpin the discussion below.

Table 11.2 Marion's Twelve Obstacles to be Overcome when Implementing an ERP System: Revised Implementation

	Start of Initial Implementation	Mid-term (End of Initial Implementation)	Finish (Second Revised Implementation)
1 Underestimating the importance of change management	Present	Present	Absent
2 Picking software before deciding on business process	Present	Present	Absent
3. Fine tuning ERP packages to exactly your business	Present	Present	Absent
4 Under budgeting for training	Present	Present	Present
5. Embracing a 'Big Bang' (whole company) approach	Absent	Absent	Absent
6. Giving short shrift to vendor selection	Present	Absent	Absent
7. Keeping legacy systems alive	Present	Present	Present
8. Fragmenting development by department or location	Absent	Present	Absent
9. Allowing apathy (or 'not-my-job disinterest') at the top	Present	Absent	Absent
10. Relying on your new ERP system for conventional management reports	Present	Present	Absent
11. Trusting 'Open Systems' promises from the ERP interfaces	Absent	Absent	Absent
12. Assuming ERP is a project with a finite timetable	Present	Present	Absent

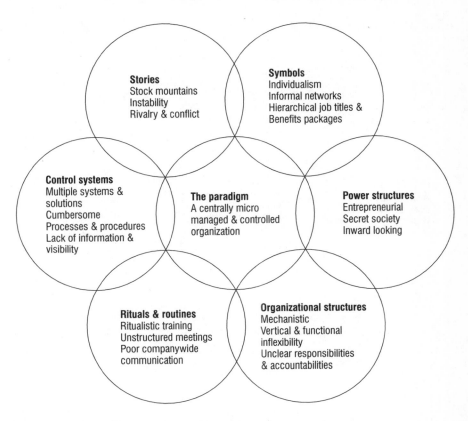

Figure 11.1 Culture at End of Initial Implementation

Evidence of Dynamic Pattern Formation

The organization structure of any retailer on ERP implementation is subject to a major transformation, and with it a shift in the power base of the organization as job roles and responsibilities change. The emotions attached to changes of this nature manifested themselves in this retailer, with one executive saying, 'Turkeys don't vote for Christmas!' Change can be extremely threatening.

As a result individuals within the organization aligned themselves with other like-minded folks and three predictable groups formed: those in favour, those against and those unsure. Hence, a political battle ensued. Resisters and change champions continued to win and influence both those who were unsure and each other with their respective views. It is this battleground Streatfield (2001) describes as a 'Fitness Landscape'. It is important to have a strong person at the helm who will drive through the

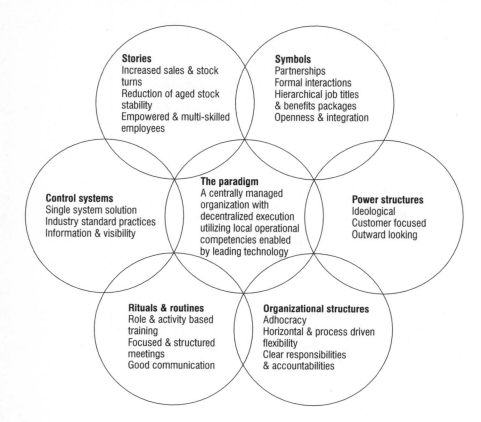

Figure 11.2 Culture Aspired to by Retailer

changes that are needed. It is the behaviour of this individual towards the opposing groups that will show what he or she will and will not tolerate, which in turn influences how change will be managed.

Strong management is needed to stem the flow of individuals regressing back to their comfort zone as the tasks of change become more difficult. It is this that caused the most alarm in the initial implementation. Line managers looked for excuses in case the implementation did not go well. Initially a focus was the lack of training and involvement of the business user community in the design process. Eventually top-line support was withdrawn. However, in the revised implementation these excuses could not be used, due to the process set-up. In essence the winner of the political battle determines the success of this revised implementation.

Evidence of self-organization and emergence: The emergence of three clear groups of opinion suggests that there is no evidence of an overall determinant for change. Instead informal networks developed from the meetings, where the stronger, more confident individuals who took control of these meetings to support or contest the vision grouped together and by so doing formed the 'Fitness Landscape'. As a result the weaker, less confident individuals were easy prey for the strong, and were influenced and recruited to join each of the particular groups. In many cases it is so much easier to follow than to lead.

It was therefore important for the retailer to ensure that there was no misunderstanding of what the company was or was not proposing. The 'Change Management Team' undertook this clarification role, and as well as being responsible for communication maintained a 'temperature check' on the readiness of the organization to accept the proposed changes. The strength of company-wide communication improved, with very focused and structured meetings that were able to extract opinion. However, it must be said that this was predominately from the support areas of the business. The change barometer itself showed that the buying and selling departments have been less vocal and appeared to be more apprehensive about the proposed changes.

Evidence of the qualities of interaction or relating: ERP systems were described by Davenport (1998) as 'imposing their own logic on an organization's culture'. This was not something this retailer consciously accepted when the decision to purchase a system was made. However, what is evident from the case study is that the retailer and its employees have a clear opinion of what this system will or will not bring to the organization and themselves. It is therefore safe to assume that the traditional organizational culture of the company is under threat. This is evidenced by the quality of the conversations and rhetoric between the two main groups (those for and those against) within the company. As individuals communicate they go over the past, and by doing so they will either create themselves a new future in which they play a part, or dwell in the past and therefore see no future for themselves. Those conversations are what the company is, what it was, and what it is becoming.

The open debates at the meetings and the subsequent emergence of specific groups assisted the retailer to recognize that there is sometimes a subconscious undertone to the organization, which does not always work to the direction set by the company. Now visible, it is naive to think that these differences will all be overcome before the new business model is finally implemented. In many aspects it would not be a good thing if they were, as constructive criticism is positive. However, exposure of the differences was a step forward.

Evidence of anxiety: With the political battle came tension and anxiety across the organization structure as the various factions battled with each other to maintain or change the operating landscape of the company.

Through this process the business benefited from the creativity anxiety and tension bring. For example during the meetings, lively debate prompted by passion and commitment to the subject created imaginative solutions to difficult and often political issues. The level to which this is negative or positive to the individual is dependent on whether the person has control over the situation about which he or she is anxious. Again during the meetings some individuals could be seen to be physically 'destroyed' at the end of the sessions if they believed they had lost their battle. However if they felt they had been successful, despite their physical state they showed elation. This clear division was demonstrated further when an offer of drinks at a local hostelry was made by one of the champions for change. The invitation was needless to say only accepted by the change champions.

Evidence of conversation: The restlessness of the organization during this period has continued, with many stories demonstrating rivalry and conflict. For example, the issue of overstocks has been used by the change champions to demonstrate the inadequacies of the current myriad of systems in keeping accurate stock files. Rightly, the resisters counter with the argument that it is people who manage systems and just changing the system will not guarantee accuracy. The expression of opinions has been, and continues to be, critical to the change process being undertaken. Interestingly, as this example shows, there is not a significant difference between the views of the two main groups. It is argued that it is more a case of each wanting the same thing, but in its own way. One individual said, 'It is not just a case of doing this for the company, but to protect our own future.'

Returning to Figures 11.1 and 11.2, we can again reiterate the progress that has been made. Figure 11.1 summarizes the cultural situation at the end of the initial implementation. The figure suggests that the retailer was subject to considerable cultural resistance and reaction. Figure 11.2 develops the position desired, and the aim of the revised second implementation. The contrast is considerable, but progress towards these 'ideal' objectives has been made. Similarly, Figure 11.3 depicts the balance between the three interdependent elements of processes, people and technology. It does this by showing the balance at the time the retailer initially implemented the ERP solution, the 'ideal' suggested by Conspectus (Bryant, 2002) and the position at the current stage of the second revised implementation.

The 'ideal' scenario has equidistant dependent elements. This was not achieved in the first implementation. In initial implementation both the 'People' and 'Process' elements were overshadowed by the 'Technology'. The project was technology rather than business driven. Conversely, 'today's' example clearly demonstrates a closer comparison to the ideal.

a) Retailer during initial implementation

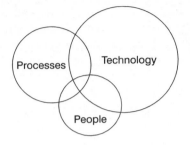

b) Conspectus (Bryant, 2002) ideal

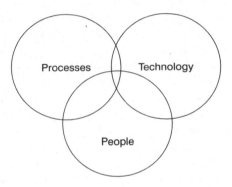

c) Retailer during revised second implementation

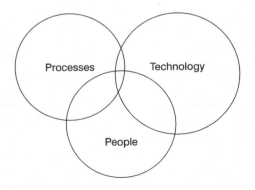

Figure 11.3 Past, Ideal and Present Project Balances

The evidence presented here supports this. It demonstrates the commitment to change, both through the adoption of 'Industry Best Practices' and the manner in which the company has encouraged its employees to take part in this process. The retailer is now as far away from the 'past' as it was from the 'ideal' at the beginning. This is a considerable achievement.

CONCLUSIONS

This case study has been prepared to consider issues of implementation in Enterprise Resource Planning systems. At one level it seems hardly to be about supply chain management, but that approach was deliberate. The case is designed to consider the interactions between technology, processes and people. These interactions are present in change implementation programmes in the supply chain and in other aspects of businesses. In the supply chain however they may have special resonance. A number of general conclusions may be drawn from the case study.

First, it is clear that the process of implementation is not an easy one in supply chains or in other aspects of businesses. Implementing change involves upsetting or changing the existing situation, and that causes stresses and strains in the organization. Given the difficulties of implementation, it is therefore strange to see so little time and effort devoted to the subject in management texts and in operational discussions. This case is not an isolated one. Implementation deserves more attention.

Second, the reasons implementation is not easy are relatively clear. If implementation is the combination of technology, processes and people, then often businesses do not have the correct balance amongst these elements. The existing processes are known within the business, and while they may not be perfect, they are familiar. The fear of the unknown in terms of processes is therefore real. Likewise, people fear change in many cases because they are unsure of the personal implications for them. There is therefore resistance. Only if the balance amongst the elements is appropriate will the resistance be reduced.

Third, implementation is not easy in supply chains. The existing business has to continue to deliver the product through the supply chain. Change implementation has to be managed so as to allow the existing business to continue without interruption. In change processes involving supply chains, there is considerable evidence that this is more difficult than it seems, and many retailers have had problems in this regard. In addition, supply chains deal in the end with inventory and stock, or if not these then with product. Product is the visible component of supply chains to many in retailing. As such, product problems such as over-stocking or under-delivery tend to be all too visible in the supply chain. It therefore becomes easy to 'point the finger' and to blame others for problems. Supply chain managers will retort that these are the symptoms of the problems and not the problems themselves. Disciplines in the supply chain are now often second nature, but it may be the case that similar disciplines are resisted elsewhere in the business.

Fourth, there is clearly a cultural dimension to supply chain change management. All the issues outlined above have to be thought through and worked through with the process managers and the employees throughout the business. Simply adding technology and expecting substantial change does not work. Implementation is often under-considered, but the dimensions of that implementation also need extensive thought.

Finally, it has to be pointed out that this case study has been essentially (though not totally) about change within a retail organization. This has involved all aspects of the organization, including the supply chain. Supply chain management however is increasingly about managing relationships amongst businesses, in addition to internal sections of the company itself. It is important to emphasize that the considerations raised here will also apply when supply chain management is implemented in the end-to-end supply chain. The potential for problems is considerable and due consideration of the implementation issues is required.

REFERENCES

Adams, J, Hayes, J and Hopson, B (1976) *Transition, Understanding and Managing Personal Change*, London, Martin Robertson

Bancroft, N, Seip, H and Sprengel, A (1998) *Implementing SAP R/3: How to introduce a large system into a large organisation*, Manning Publications, Greenwich, CT

Bassirian, H (2000) Expert warns of ERP perils, *Computer Weekly*, p 8

Bryant, J (Conspectus) (2002) *Supply Chain Management Systems*, Prime Marketing

Bywater (2001) *Technology Enabled Business Transformation*, Bywater plc

Christopher, M (1998) *Logistics and Supply Chain Management Strategies for Reducing Cost and Improving Service*, London, Financial Times, pp 4,18, 27

Davenport, T H (1998) Putting the enterprise into the enterprise system, *Harvard Business Review*, Jul–Aug, pp 121–31

Davies, G (1992) *20 Training Workshops for Improving Management Performance*, Gower, Aldershot

Drucker, P (1962) The economy's dark continent, *Fortune*, April, pp 265–70

Hammer, M and Champy, J (1994) *Reengineering the Corporation: A manifesto for business revolution*, Nicholas Brealey, London

Holmes, G (1995) *Supply Chain Management*, Economist Intelligence Unit, London

James, D, and Wolf, M L (2000) A second wind for ERP, *McKinsey Quarterly*, Spring

Johnson, G and Scholes, K (1999) *Exploring Corporate Strategy*, 5th edn, Prentice Hall, Harlow, p 63

Mabert, V A, Soni, A and Venkataramanan, M A (2001) Enterprise Resource Planning: common myths versus evolving reality, *Business Horizons*, **44** (3), 69–76

Marion, L (2000) Mastering ERP's 'Dirty Dozen': how to identify and overcome ERP's 'Top 12' obstacles, *ERP News*

Mason-Jones, R, Naylor B and Towill, D R (2000) Lean, agile or leagile? Matching your supply chain to the marketplace, *International Journal of Production Research*, **38** (17), pp 4061–70

Naylor, J B, Naim, M M and Berry, D (1997) Leagility: integrating the lean and agile manufacturing paradigm in the total supply chain, MASTS working paper no 47, republished in *International Journal of Production Economics*, **62**, pp 107–18

Streatfield, P J (2001) *The Paradox of Control in Organizations*, Routledge, London

Walters, D and Rands, C A (1999) Computers in Retailing, *International Journal of Physical Distribution and Logistics Management*, **29** (7/8), pp 465–76

Afterword

John Fernie and Leigh Sparks

As we indicated in the preface, this book is the third in a series of insights into current practice and trends in retail logistics. The first volume, *Retail Distribution Management*, edited by John Fernie, gave an indication of the key issues of the late 1980s. The title of the book gave a clue to the challenges facing logistics management at that time. Attention focused on distribution management and how to improve efficiency in getting goods to retail outlets. This was the era of centralization and the strategic decision whether to contract out or retain in-house the financing and management of logistical infrastructure.

The second book, *Logistics and Retail Management*, by the current editors, updated the earlier version, although notable changes in managing the supply chain were evident and the volume was essentially brand new. The earlier text had charted the beginnings of retail control of the FMCG supply chain. This was reinforced by initiatives such as quick response and efficient consumer response which promulgated greater collaboration between supply chain partners in order that costs and benefits of reducing lead times could be clearly identified, taking cost out of the system for mutual benefit. Relationship change was at the forefront of such collaboration. Incremental improvements in the logistics network were also evident. In the grocery sector, consolidation centres were built to improve vehicle utilization as retailers demanded more frequent deliveries of smaller quantities of product. Composite distribution became a feature of logistical support to retailers with large superstores/hypermarkets, in that mixed loads of ambient chilled, fresh and frozen products could be stored and distributed to store more efficiently. In the clothing sector, much attention centred on the issue of domestic versus offshore sourcing and how retailers could implement Quick Response (QR) initiatives to reduce lead times.

In that edition we did not make any speculative forecasts for the future of retail logistics. We pointed to some likely trends into the new millennium. These were predominantly associated with the British government's concern over traffic congestion and the need for improvement in transport efficiency to reduce the environmental impact of Just-In-Time (JIT) supply chains. Additionally, this volume was written at a time when the dot.com hype was at its peak, with forecasts of even 15–25 percent of retail sales being attributed to online sales by the early 2000s. If such sales were to be realized, we expressed further environmental concerns pertaining to the rise in van traffic through residential neighbourhoods.

This volume therefore essentially completes a trilogy. What are the challenges now for logistics management in the future? With the exception of e-tail logistics, there is a feeling of déja vu about the concerns expressed by senior logistics managers on the key issues to be addressed. Invariably product availability or the 'last 50 yards' issue with regard to on-shelf availability is of prime concern. It is somewhat alarming that on-shelf availability for some of our major grocery retailers is no better than it was 30 to 40 years ago for many key value items (KVIs). In short, if it is not there, it cannot be sold. In the 1960s and 1970s customers could easily go to the nearest store to pick up a manufacturer's brand unavailable at their preferred store. In the days of car-oriented supermarkets it would seem that store switching is less likely than in days when a greater number of outlets and companies prevailed. Continual non-availability of key items can be a major factor in diminishing store loyalty.

It is not surprising, therefore, that much of the focus of CPFR initiatives is not only on promotional items but also on KVIs to enhance on-shelf availability. Availability in store is not just a grocery sector problem; it is relevant and acknowledged by all retailers, especially those in highly competitive markets, for example clothing. In order to sell in store, replenishment times need to be reduced so that the overall supply chain is more flexible to meet changing consumer demands.

In many ways this is a re-run of issues originally raised in the 1970s and 1980s. Indeed, Sainsbury's recent poor profit performance was partly blamed on the restructuring of its logistical network; comments that applied to Asda in the late 1980s! The main difference now is that retailers have a range of tools that allows for massive supply chain savings to be realized. The problem is that the infrastructure changes required and the systems enhancement needed by companies involve massive capital investment at a time when competition is fierce and achieving sales growth is difficult. All of these supply chain initiatives, many emanating from forums expounding the benefits of QR, ECR and CPFR, are also resource hungry in terms of management time, and have considerable implications for the relationships amongst people, processes and technology. In retailing, competitive advantage is invariably achieved on the successful implementation of such initiatives, available to all but only realized by companies with the quality of management to achieve results.

Supply chain management has been a high-profile issue in the trade press in late 2003. For example, the UK trade magazine *Retail Week* has highlighted major supply chain changes being enacted by Sainsbury, Boots, Marks and Spencer, House of Fraser and Matalan to improve product availability and reduce costs. The first three companies in this list were innovators in distributive management in the 1960s and 1970s. They were the first to centralize their distribution and build RDCs. In *Retail Distribution Management*, it was noted that a 1–2 per cent of Sainsbury's net profit margin could be attributed to efficiency in retail distribution. However, 30 to 40 years later, other retailers have caught up and, in the case of innovative companies such as Tesco, have surpassed them in terms of supply chain efficiency.

Part of Sainsbury's response to competition from Tesco and Wal-Mart's entry to the UK has been to upgrade its ageing distribution network. It is well on the way to creating nine 'fulfilment factories' by 2005 that will handle 10,000 ambient, chilled and produce lines. These large warehouses (650,000 square feet) will cost about £70 million each and will supply more than 150 supermarkets and up to 150 smaller format stores.

Tesco has been particularly innovative in seeking new solutions to improve on-shelf availability, and reduce stockholding levels in the supply chain. This was not always the case. It was the shock of stock-outs in the late 1970s from a direct store delivery operation that highlighted the importance to the company of supply chain management and drove recognition that the supply chain was an integral part of overall company strategy. In the 1980s Tesco was in the forefront in creating composite distribution centres. In the 1990s Tesco implemented ECR and CPFR initiatives to further improve supply chain efficiency. In the late 1990s much of Tesco's management philosophy has been linked to the concept of 'lean thinking'.

Tesco maps the value stream as orders go back up the supply chain and products go downstream to identify areas where duplication occurs and multiple handling of product occurs, excessive stock levels arise and there is poor truck utilization. These analyses through mapping product and information flows are ongoing.

One initiative that has created a high degree of controversy in the early 2000s has been the advent of factory gate pricing. Both Tesco and

Sainsbury have been the prime instigators of this initiative in the wake of their review of supply chain practices. Although backhauling and consolidation of loads was a feature of the previous decades, this was organized on a fairly ad hoc manner, with a series of bilateral transport contracts between logistics service providers (LSPs) and retailers and manufacturers. Now, and in the future, the larger grocery retailers will be sourcing products 'ex-works', thereby managing the entire transport operation from factory to consumer.

The concept of factory gate pricing is not just being applied to the grocery sector. Similar principles are being adopted in non-food, and especially the fashion sector. Non-food by its very nature has a longer and more complex supply chain than grocery products. The first step by most retailers was to source offshore or to apply QR principles to give domestic suppliers lead-time advantages. Offshore sourcing may reduce costs, but in non-food, 90 per cent of product is moved by sea, incurring long lead times and possible high markdowns due to the mismatching of supply with local demand.

A recent trend which is likely to be maintained is that the Middle East and eastern Europe will continue to be popular for sourcing some fashion garments because of their relative proximity to an enlarged EU, compared with sourcing from the Pacific Rim. As Marks and Spencer has acknowledged, however, the quest for low-cost sourcing is only one solution to competing in highly competitive pricing markets.

Availability is more relevant to fashion than it is in food. Hence, concepts from the food sector are being applied in non-food. Instead of FOB the retailer is also seeking to source ex-works, liaising with LSPs to consolidate loads and prepare floor-ready merchandise to minimize handling at the downstream part of the supply chain. Other developments in fashion have seen time-based competition become more critical, with retailers such as Zara emerging and competing successfully in part on supply chain speed and excellence. Time will remain fundamental to such sectors.

The management of product flow throughout the supply chain has been of critical importance. It has been the advances in information systems over the last two decades that have acted as enablers facilitating supply chain efficiency. Bar-codes, EDI, ERP systems and Internet-based exchanges have all reduced the administrative costs of communication amongst supply chain partners. The next potential major technological breakthrough that will have a significant impact upon supply chain costs is RFID technology.

Potential benefits to retailers are claimed to be immense. Shrinkage costs retailers between 1 and 2 per cent of sales per year. Out-of-stock, as discussed above, is a key challenge for logistics managers. RFID could lead to the effective tracking of goods from factory to home. Issues of cost and concerns over consumer privacy threaten the implementation of RFID, but it may be the case also that proponents have minimized some of the management and data use implications.

It is probable that the technology will be rolled out in stages, focusing on obvious issues and bottlenecks in supply chains. Initially the focus will be on tracking pallets, dollies and bins as they move from picking to the backroom of the store. This will give cost savings in labour through greater automation of tracking and more visibility. Shrinkage and stock-holding levels should be reduced. As the costs of tags reduce and if fears over consumer privacy are addressed, RFID tags will be used at the item level and implemented at store level. For retailers seeking to maximize on-shelf availability, this should give ongoing up-to-date information on sales and in-store inventory, with consequent supply chain effects.

Earlier in the chapter we identified e-tail logistics as one area where activity is considerable, though perhaps not yet at the level anticipated by most commentators. Major changes may still occur therefore. These will occur once the e-tailing sector achieves greater stability. In the last few years a shakeout of the dot.com sector has occurred. In the non-food sector a well-established delivery system is now in place and this system is being refined to accommodate the multi-channel strategy which is being adopted by most successful retailers. Traditional catalogue retailing incurred a high rate of 'returns' through the logistical network. This is being reinforced by online retailing, where around one-third of non-food products delivered to the home are returned. The reverse logistics task of retrieval, re-packaging and returning or rerouting merchandise is complex enough from home to warehouse, but Web-shoppers are also returning merchandise to their nearest store. 'Bricks and clicks' may increase customer spend and enhance loyalty but it also adds to costs. The need to invest in systems and infrastructure to accom-modate such changes is leading to the formation of alliances amongst retailers to share these costs and build upon their relative expertise in supply chain functions.

E-grocery logistics has posed more formidable challenges. The initial 'hype' associated with the dot.com boom led to much investment in dedi-cated picking centres. In retrospect this was a flawed strategy based on unrealistic demand projections. Store-based fulfilment offered a more risk-averse approach to e-grocery. Demand was met from existing assets and the e-grocer could refine its systems and customer service as it gained experience of the market. Nevertheless there are questions about the long-term sustainability of such a model if online grocery sales continue to grow at current rates. The sharing of the same inventory between store and online shopper could ultimately lead to poor customer service levels for both sets of shoppers. Thus there may come a time in the near future when investment in 'stand-alone' picking centres will be necessary in specific geographical markets.

Regardless of the fulfilment model used, the 'last mile' problem is far from being resolved. Customers prefer narrow time slots for attended delivery; retailers prefer to utilize their transport assets around the clock. Ideally, the unattended delivery option is best for most parties as customers are not constrained by delivery times, retailers can reduce their transport costs and local authorities can reduce van congestion with 24-hour deliveries. But will customers invest in home reception facilities or be willing to pick up groceries in communal reception boxes? Initial reactions to such proposals have been lukewarm to say the least, leaving key problems to be overcome.

So what are the challenges? Existing supply chains will be affected by changes in retailers, consumers and the environment, and technologies will be applied to meet specific operational issues. Some companies may transform their supply systems through the relationships they build with key suppliers, logistics services providers and even other retailers. New ways of meeting changing consumer demands will be the focus of much effort, though the cost bases remain uncertain. Retailers will be concerned to ensure they obtain the right balance between lean and agile approaches to their supply systems in order to meet the challenges of spatial reach and rapid reaction. Whatever the broad outcomes, leading retailers will be those with quality management able to apply change in supply, to drive effectiveness and efficiency within an appropriately balanced concern for people, processes and technology. Others will fail to meet these difficult challenges. As ever, it will be exciting and interesting.

Index

Page numbers in *italics* indicate figures or tables